Pinch of Nom

MEAL PREP

Pinch OF Nom

MEAL PREP

**PREP-AHEAD +
QUICK ASSEMBLY
SLIMMING MEALS**

BLUEBIRD

CONTENTS

INTRODUCTION
8

MAKE AHEAD
40

BATCH COOK
86

ON THE GO
122

FREEZE AND GO
168

MULTI SERVE
190

STORE CUPBOARD
240

NUTRITIONAL INFO
276

INDEX
280

ACKNOWLEDGEMENTS
286

MAKE AHEAD 40

BREAKFAST

Breakfast Burritos

Breakfast Loaded Potatoes

MEALS

Masala Spiced Chicken Burger with Mango Chutney Yoghurt

Sausage, Fennel and Chilli Pasta

'Nduja Chicken Orzo

Hot Honey Halloumi Flatbreads

Honey and Lime Glazed Salmon with Herby Grains

Romesco-Style Chicken Salad

Creamy Chicken and Mushroom Tagliatelle

Thai-Style Chicken Meatballs

Sticky Garlic and Chilli Tofu

Roasted Beetroot, Lentil and Feta Salad with Creamy Balsamic Vinaigrette

Herby Courgette Fritters and Tzatziki

Mediterranean-Style Gnocchi Traybake

LIGHT BITES *and* SWEET TREATS

Root Vegetable Stacks

Ploughman's Sausage Rolls

Chocolate Orange Mousse

Mojito Trifle

BATCH COOK 86

BREAKFAST

Sausage and Egg Breakfast Slice

Banana Buckwheat Pancakes

MEALS

Korma-Style Cauliflower with Coriander Rice

Spicy Chicken Chowder

Greek-Style Shepherd's Pie with Feta Mash

Roasted Cauliflower and Sesame Soup

Chicken, Broccoli and Mushroom Gratin

Greek-Style Chicken with Butter Beans

Beef, Beetroot and Barley Stew

Sweet Potato Gnocchi with Broccoli and Ricotta

Caramelized Onion Mac and Cheese

Chicken Pot Pie

SWEET TREATS

Rhubarb and Custard Arctic Roll

Banana Crunch Ice Cream

ON THE GO 122

BREAKFAST

Apple Crumble Breakfast Pots

Chocolate Overnight Oats

Smoky Breakfast Sandwich

Banana Chia Breakfast Bowl

Breakfast Cookies

Banoffee Overnight Weetabix Pots

Butternut Squash Muffins

Cottage Cheese Bagels

MEALS

Cowboy Caviar

Chicken Shawarma Skewers

Chicken and Chorizo Quesadillas

Noodle Pots

Harissa Aubergine and Halloumi Salad

Maple-Roasted Carrots with Whipped Feta and Giant Couscous

Courgette, Lemon and Ricotta Tart

New York Deli Wrap

Butternut Squash, Carrot and Coconut Soup

LIGHT BITES *and* SWEET TREATS

Cheese and Bean Pinwheels

Blueberry Crumble Squares

Triple Berry Bakes

Banana Crumble Muffins

Chocolate Custard Swirls

FREEZE AND GO 168

MEALS

Citrus Chicken Stew
Spicy Chickpea Soup
Mexican-Style Rice Soup
Shredded Turkey Rolls
Five-Spice Beef with Plums
Teriyaki-Style Chicken Drumsticks
Gammon and Pineapple Chilli
Boston Beans

MULTI SERVE 190

MEALS

Crunchy Asian-Style Salad
Peanut and Lime Salmon Salad
Sweet Chilli Chicken Noodle Salad
Nutty Mushroom Stuffing Potato Hash
Stuffed Butternut Squash
Veggie Wellington
Shredded Beef in Red Wine
Meat and Potato Pie
Beef and Red Wine Lasagne
Roast Chicken with Lemon Gravy
Sweet and Sour Chicken Curry
Chicken Pesto Pasta Bake
Chipotle Chicken Traybake
Chipotle Chicken Enchiladas
Creamy Chipotle Chicken
Sausage, Mushroom and Apple Casserole
Sausage, Mushroom and Apple Hotpot
Sausage, Mushroom and Apple Cobbler
Sicilian-Style Bruschetta
Sicilian-Style Meatballs
Sicilian-Style Spaghetti

STORE CUPBOARD 240

BREAKFAST

Pineapple Upside Down Pancake Traybake
Gingerbread Porridge

MEALS

Corned Beef and Pickle Pie
Mushy Pea Nuggets with Curry Sauce
Creamy Ham and Pea Rice
Ham Foo Yung-Style Eggs
Tuna Puttanesca Pasta
Tuna Kedgeree
Chinese-Style Curried Noodles
Korean-Style Butter Beans

LIGHT BITES *and* SWEET TREATS

Pea Falafel with Garlic Tahini Sauce
Chai-Spiced Scones
Jam Butty Pudding
Cherries Jubilee Waffles
Peach Custard Cake
Cherry Bakewell Cookies
Orange and Cranberry Biscotti

HELLO

Prep, cook and relax! Welcome to Pinch of Nom's first ever meal-prep guide, packed with 100 recipes for making mealtimes a breeze.

This book will help you become a meal-prepping pro. We know how tricky it can be juggling healthy cooking with busy schedules, fussy eaters, lack of kitchen space and that endless question... 'What's for dinner?' Meal prepping is a great way to stay on top of your healthy-living goals.

This is more than just a cookbook. Inside, you'll find simple, clever recipes that all save on time, energy and cupboard space, with ideas for batch-cooking, freezer-friendly meals and quick dinners that can be scaled up or down depending on what you need. When life gets busy and there's a lot on your plate, it's all too easy to skip cooking or reach for the snacks that don't actually make you feel good. We've also included two meal plans (see pages 34–35) to give you inspiration and get you started. With a plan in place and meals ready to go, it's much easier to stay on track, feel in control and, most importantly: enjoy what you eat!

Are you...

- **short on energy?**
- **struggling to please the whole family?**
- **finding it hard to find delicious prep-ahead recipes?**
- **unsure where to start with planning?**

Whatever you need, we've got your back! Get ready to find cooking fun again.

WHY MEAL PREP?

We've all been there: You've done the food shop, your cupboards are stacked and you're imagining calm evenings where dinner is on the table in no time at all. And then ... life happens! Work runs late, errands get in the way, the laundry's piling up and your perfect meal plan suddenly vanishes into thin air. That's exactly why we put this cookbook together. We're on a mission to make mealtimes healthier and tastier, and hopefully a lot less stressful, too!

These recipes aren't about spending hours in the kitchen or needing a freezer the size of a garage. They're smart, simple ways to cook that save you time AND energy. You might make something once and enjoy it twice (check out our multi-serve recipes

Caramelized Onion Mac and Cheese (see page 112)

on pages 192–239), prep a few ingredients ahead of time, or use the same staples in different dishes so nothing goes to waste. We want to give you the power to make practical choices that fit around your life, instead of taking it over.

From breakfasts that put a smile on your face – like our Gingerbread Porridge on page 244 – to midweek dinners that properly fill you up (flick to our Sausage, Mushroom and Apple Casserole on page 228 and our Caramelized Onion Mac and Cheese on page 112), you'll find something here for every occasion and household. You didn't think we'd forgotten the sweet treats, did you? You'll love our nostalgic Pineapple Upside Down Pancake Traybake on page 242, or if chocolate's your weakness... our Chocolate Orange Mousse on page 82 is well worth a try. No fancy gadgets, no complicated skills, no need for loads of hours to spare. Just simple, tasty recipes that actually work in real life.

We hope this book helps you feel confident in the kitchen and encourages you to try a few new flavours along the way! Most of all, we hope it helps you spend less time stressing and more time enjoying the meals you've made. Whether it's a quick supper after work or something a little bit special at the weekend, we're determined to make cooking manageable, fun, and most importantly ... delicious!

Thank you SO much for being part of our Pinch of Nom family. We absolutely love seeing what you create and celebrating your kitchen wins with you, however big or small. Here's to happier mealtimes every single day of the week!

Kay x Kate

WHAT IS MEAL PREP?

The aim is to make your week in the kitchen run a little smoother. A bit of planning, a bit of chopping, and a bit of clever thinking upfront means less faffing later on and more time to actually enjoy your meals. We're not expecting you to spend hours in front of the oven or make picture-perfect meals.

It's all about being practical, making your life easier and still eating well in the process. There are lots of ways to meal prep, and in this book, we've split them into six handy types to suit every lifestyle.

MAKE AHEAD

Individual meals you can cook in advance and pop straight in the fridge or freezer. Some are ready to eat, and others just need a quick finish later.

BATCH COOK

Recipes that make multiple portions at once. Eat some now, store some for later. Perfect for busy families or leftovers that actually get eaten.

ON-THE-GO

Portable meals for workdays, commutes or those hectic mornings when toast just isn't enough. These also work for picnics and family days out.

FREEZE AND GO

Pop all the ingredients into a freezer-safe bag or container, freeze and cook later. Or, if you're hungry now, just follow the tips to cook straight away.

MULTI SERVE

Big base recipes that can be used in loads of ways across the week. Make once, eat three times, stretch much further.

STORE CUPBOARD

Quick, convenient, and low-cost recipes using ingredients you probably already have.

Noodle Pots (see page 146)

HOW TO MEAL PREP?

Ready to become a meal prepping pro? Start with a plan: check your cupboards, fridge and freezer, then decide what meals suit your week. Make a shopping list and stick to it! No wandering the aisles and buying ALL the things.

GET-AHEAD POWER HOUR

When it comes to the prep itself, try a 'power hour', a focused session where you chop, portion and cook as much as you can. Here are two power hour ideas using a selection of our favourite recipes.

Power Hour 1

Chocolate Overnight Oats (page 126)
Pop the oats, cocoa powder, yoghurt, honey and toppings into a jar or container and keep in the fridge for up to 5 days.

Spicy Chickpea Soup (page 172)
Prep all the ingredients in a bag and freeze. When you're ready, just cook it on the hob or in your slow cooker and you've got an easy lunch that'll warm you up without any hassle.

Banana Crumble Muffins (page 164)
Mix, bake and store in an airtight container for up to 4 days, or freeze for up to 3 months. Perfect for a sweet treat on busy days.

Shredded Beef in Red Wine (page 208)
Prep and cook on the hob, in the oven or in your slow cooker. This keeps in the fridge for 3–4 days, or it can be frozen. This is a Multi-Serve recipe so it can be served in 3 ways!

Power Hour 2

Triple Berry Bakes (page 162)
Prep the ingredients, bake and store in the fridge for up to 4 days. Or you can freeze for later breakfasts.

Noodle Pots (page 146)
Prep and assemble, then store in the fridge for 3–4 days for a quick lunch that's ready when you are.

Chocolate Custard Swirls (page 166)
Prep, bake and store in an airtight container for up to 4 days and you've got yourself a cheeky sweet treat fix for minimal effort.

Roast Chicken with Lemon Gravy (page 216)
Prep, cook, and store in the fridge for up to 3 days, or freeze. Ring the changes and serve it as Chicken Pesto Pasta Bake or Sweet and Sour Chicken Curry.

MIX-AND-MATCH PREPPING

A little prep goes a long way! Here are some tips for getting your grains, carbs, veg, proteins and extras ready so mealtimes feel effortless.

GRAINS *and* CARBS

Grains are brilliant for meal prep because they're filling, versatile and keep well.

Rice, pasta, quinoa, couscous and orzo can all be cooked in advance and stored in airtight containers in the fridge for up to 3–4 days. Once cooled, portion them out so they're easy to grab when you need them. Cooked grains can also be frozen in portions if you want to keep them for longer.

Bake a few **jacket potatoes or sweet potatoes** at a time and store them in the fridge for up to 3 days. They can be reheated in your microwave or air fryer, and then topped with whatever you fancy.

If you like **wraps and flatbreads**, keep a pack in the cupboard or freezer so you've always got something quick to build a meal around.

VEGGIES

Veg can take the most time to prep, so getting ahead here makes all the difference.

Harder vegetables like carrots, peppers, onions, broccoli and courgettes can be washed, chopped and stored in containers in the fridge for 3–4 days. This makes them easy to throw straight into stir-fries, traybakes or pasta dishes. If you're worried about your carrots going brown, pop them in an airtight container of water and give the water a change every few days. They'll stay fresh and crunchy for longer.
Leafy greens like spinach or lettuce are best washed, dried well and stored with a piece of kitchen roll in a container to absorb moisture. This helps them stay fresh for longer.

Roasted vegetables are another simple but life-changing trick. Broccoli and Brussels sprouts get beautifully crispy in the oven and are great tossed into salads, stirred into pasta or added to grain bowls. Butternut squash and sweet potato caramelize wonderfully and taste amazing in soups, wraps and curries. Peppers, onions and cherry tomatoes roast to perfection and are brilliant in omelettes, sandwiches and pasta sauces. You can also try cauliflower, carrots, courgettes, parsnips ... the list goes on!

When it comes to the roasting itself, it's super simple. Just pop them in the oven on a tray, with a coating of low-calorie cooking spray and your preferred seasoning. Some might take a little longer than others, but it's easy to check online for timings, and we'll always guide you through exactly how to roast the veg in our recipes.

Frozen vegetables are also great to have on hand. Things like peas, sweetcorn, chopped onions and mixed veg can all save time and reduce waste.

PROTEINS

Having a protein ready to go gives you a strong base point for a lot of meals.

You can batch cook **chicken breast, turkey mince, lean beef and tofu** and store them in the fridge for up to 3 days, or freeze them in portions. They're great for adding to wraps, salads and pasta or rice dishes.

Plant-based proteins like lentils, chickpeas, and beans are fantastic for meal prep too. If you're using dried lentils, cook a batch and keep them in the fridge for 3–4 days. You can also drain, rinse and store tinned beans and chickpeas in a sealed container ready to use.

Boiled eggs keep in the fridge for up to a week and make for a fab on-the-go snack or a simple addition to salads and lunches.

SAUCES, DRESSINGS *and* EXTRAS

A good sauce can completely transform a meal, so prepping a few simple ones in advance can be a real time saver.

Tomato-based sauces (like our Sicilian-Style Tomato Sauce on page 234), curry bases (our korma curry base on page 92 and Massaman Curry Base on page 66), and **pasta sauce**s (try our pesto pasta sauce on page 220) are ideal for batch-cooking. You can keep them in the fridge for 3–4 days, or freeze them in portions. Freezing them flat in freezer bags makes them easy to stack and quick to defrost.

Little touches make meals feel finished without creating extra work later on. You can prep extras like **chopped herbs, grated cheese and sliced spring onions**. Parsley, coriander, basil and the like can be kept fresh in a little container in the fridge or wrapped in a damp kitchen towel. This helps them last longer, ready to be sprinkled over your meals. If your herbs are store-bought, you should usually be able to find storage instructions on the packets, too.

HOW TO MIX AND MATCH

Here are some ideas to get started with mix-and-match meals using recipes in the book and other elements you have prepped ahead.

DOUBLE UP ON SALMON

It could be as simple as cooking two extra salmon fillets from the Peanut and Lime Salmon Salad on page 195 and pairing them with some steamed veggies, a few new potatoes, a squeeze of lemon and a drizzle of zingy lime and chilli dressing.

TWO SALADS, ONE DRESSING

Get extra mileage on the Roasted Beetroot, Lentil and Feta Salad with Creamy Balsamic Vinaigrette recipe on page 70 by making double the dressing and tossing it with some cooked halloumi cubes, salad leaves and your favourite cooked grains for a speedy but nutritious lunch.

VERSATILE ROASTED VEG

Another dish with double the dinner potential is our Mediterranean-Style Gnocchi Traybake on page 74. Take the roasted vegetables, add to cooked pasta and stir through some low-fat cream cheese for a creamy Mediterranean pasta moment.

FROM SOUP TO STEW

Reimagine the Spicy Chickpea Soup on page 172 with some cooked chicken breast, and serve it over couscous or rice for another flavour-packed meal that comes together in no time at all.

MORE MASH

For a shortcut to cosy comfort, make double the mashed potato topping from the Greek-Style Shepherd's Pie on page 98 and serve it with your favourite sausages, roasted onions and a good splash of gravy.

Peanut and Lime Salmon Salad *(see page 195)*

MAKE YOUR MEALS GO THE EXTRA MILE

Once you learn how to properly store, freeze and reheat your leftovers, you'll waste less food. And everything will taste just as delicious the next day!

MAKE SPACE

It's a good idea to check you've got space in your fridge or freezer before you start cooking. You don't want leftovers going to waste!

DIVIDE INTO PORTIONS

Store leftovers in individual-sized servings – your food will cool, freeze and defrost loads quicker when you portion it out. Plus, it makes it so much easier when you want to grab leftovers for a one-person lunch or dinner!

USE AIRTIGHT CONTAINERS *and* BAGS

Storing food correctly is the key to keeping leftovers fresh for longer. Whether you use containers or bags, make sure they seal properly to avoid 'freezer burn' (uninvited air damaging your food). Containers that are also microwave-safe are the best investment, as there's no need to buy separate Tupperware for the sake of reheating.

USE REFRIGERATED FOODS WITHIN 2–3 DAYS

Lots of our Meal Prep recipes will taste even better after 24 hours in the fridge, when all the flavours have had more time to develop. You'll just need to keep an eye on how long you store cooked food in the fridge, using leftovers within 2–3 days to avoid the risk of food poisoning. We have given guidance on any recipes you can keep in the fridge for a little longer, otherwise make sure you freeze leftovers as soon as possible after cooking and cooling.

PUT A LABEL ON IT

You can freeze food for 3–6 months, so it's important to add a freezer-proof label that includes the date on which the meal was cooked. If you're stocking-up the freezer for busy days, it's a good idea to also add the name of the recipe, and organise your freezer drawer so that older portions are easy to grab and use up first. Depending on the recipe, some food can be stored beyond 6 months and still be safe to eat, although it might start to lose flavour.

DEFROST THOROUGHLY

Please take care not to reheat food until it has defrosted thoroughly in the fridge or microwave.

STANDARD FREEZING AND REHEATING GUIDELINES

For most recipes, you'll be able to follow our standard freezing and reheating guidelines below (we'll let you know if a recipe requires more specific instructions):

- Allow food to cool and then freeze as soon as it is cold enough.
- Place in a container or bag that is suitable for freezing.
- Add a label telling you the name of the recipe and the date you're freezing it.

The general consensus is that you can keep food frozen for around 6 months, although after 3 it'll start to lose its flavour.

You should reheat and eat defrosted food within 24 hours. Please don't reheat frozen food until it has defrosted thoroughly in a fridge or microwave. NHS guidelines (correct at the time of writing) state that you should reheat food until it reaches 75°C/167°F and holds that temperature for 2 minutes. Always make sure it's piping hot throughout (you should stir while reheating to ensure this).

If you're ever unsure about freezing and reheating a recipe safely, we'd strongly advise referring to the official NHS guidelines.

STORING RICE

Meal Prep dishes that contain rice are safe to freeze and reheat, but only if they're stored in the right way. Cool the food as quickly as possible (ideally within 1 hour) by putting it in a wide, shallow container. The longer rice is left at room temperature, the greater the risk that it could grow harmful bacteria. Keep cooked rice or rice dishes in the fridge no longer than 1 day before reheating, or you can freeze and defrost thoroughly in the fridge before reheating. Always make sure you reheat rice until it is piping hot, and never reheat it more than once.

Korma-Style Cauliflower with Coriander Rice *(see page 92)*

THE FOOD

As a classically trained chef, Kate has always loved recreating dishes and putting an original spin on classic recipes. This is how the very first Pinch of Nom recipes came to be, and it's this passion that means we can continue to bring fresh new flavours to you today. Kate and her small team of trusted recipe developers love nothing more than getting into the kitchen and experimenting with ingredients until some Pinch of Nom magic is created!

It's always been our mission as a recipe team to make it easy to cook healthy, homemade food, and this book is no exception. We've dedicated a lot of time to experimenting, taste-testing and coming up with new and inventive ways to turn everyday ingredients into make-ahead meals that tick boxes for deliciousness and convenience in equal measure. This includes reimagining classic favourites, like our Boston Beans on page 188, and creating entirely new recipes (our Korean-Style Butter Beans on page 260 are truly something special). We've taken things one step at a time to make meal prep fun and flexible and still full of flavour. It's been fun figuring things out, and we hope you'll enjoy cooking up all our creations yourself!

Meal prepping is all about saving time and pennies; we've kept everything as stripped back as possible, and we've relied on fuss-free ingredients that you can use across multiple dishes. From time to time, you might find a less common ingredient that adds something really special to a dish, but we'll always try to make sure you get to use it again somewhere else.

If you've followed Pinch of Nom since day one, you'll know that it's hugely important to us that absolutely anyone can pick up our books and give cooking a go. All of the recipes we've picked suit any level of cooking skill, so even if you've never tried batch cooking or meal prep before, you'll have no trouble with our slimming-friendly breakfasts, lunches, dinners, sides and desserts.

We've made sure there's something for everyone. Fancy a lighter option for breakfast? We've got you. Need something filling for lunch? Sorted. Want a show-stopper for dinner that can double as leftovers? Absolutely. And the sweet stuff... oh, the sweet stuff is here too! You'll have plenty to keep cravings at bay while still smashing your goals.

As always, our vegetarian and vegan dishes are flagged with easily noticeable badges. You'll also spot that we've dropped in hints and tips for getting the most from your ingredients, so we're always there to help.

The aim is simple: mealtimes should feel manageable, stress-free, and exciting! With this book, you can finally feel organised, creative, and in control – and we can't wait for you to get stuck in!

RECIPE TAGS

EVERYDAY LIGHT

These recipes can be used freely throughout the week. All the meals, including accompaniments, are under 400 calories. Or, in the case of sweet treats, under 200 calories. Of course, if you're counting calories, you still need to keep an eye on the values, but these recipes should help you stay under your allowance.

WEEKLY INDULGENCE

These recipes are still low in calories at between 400 and 500, or 200–300 for sweet treats, but should be saved for once or twice a week. Mix them into your Everyday Light recipes for variety.

SPECIAL OCCASION

These recipes are often lower in calories than their full-fat counterparts, but we like to save them for a special occasion. This tag indicates any main meals that are over 500 calories, or over 300 for sweet treats.

Greek-Style Chicken with Butter Beans *(see page 104)*

All of the calculations and dietary indicators are for guidance only and are not to be taken as complete fact without checking ingredients and product labelling yourself.

RECIPE ICONS

VEGGIE · VEGAN · FREEZE ME · BATCH COOK · DAIRY FREE · GLUTEN FREE · LOW CARB · HIGH PROTEIN · BASE RECIPE

HIGH PROTEIN

These recipes are packed with extra protein, with at least 20% of the calories in each serving coming from a source of protein. The benefit of this is that they keep you fuller for longer, give you an extra burst of energy, and help you hit your fitness goals!

GLUTEN-FREE RECIPES

We have marked gluten-free recipes with an icon. All these recipes are either free of gluten or we have suggested gluten-free ingredient swaps of common ingredients, such as stock cubes and Worcestershire sauce. Please check labelling to ensure the product you buy is gluten-free.

FREEZABLE RECIPES

Look out for the Freeze Me icon to indicate freezer-friendly dishes. The icon applies to the main dish only, not the suggested accompaniments.

BATCH COOK

These are recipes designed to be made ahead and frozen. They'll guarantee you always have a tasty homemade dish ready to defrost and enjoy.

BASE RECIPES

The Multi Serve chapter makes use of versatile base recipes that are the starting point for several dishes. These save time and keep variety and flavour on the table.

KCAL *and* CARB VALUES

All of our recipes have been worked out as complete meals, using standardised portion sizes for any accompaniments, as advised by the British Nutrition Foundation. Carb values are included for those who need to measure their intake.

KEY INGREDIENTS

PROTEIN

Lean meats are a great source of protein, providing essential nutrients and keeping you feeling full between meals. In all cases where meat is used in this book, we'd recommend using the leanest possible cuts and trimming off all visible fat. In many of our recipes you'll find that you can switch the type of protein for whatever meat you prefer. This especially applies to any mince recipes; turkey, beef or pork mince are easily interchangeable – just be mindful that you may need to adjust cooking times to suit if applicable! Fish is also a great source of protein, and it's naturally low in fat. Fish provides nutrients that the body struggles to produce naturally, making it perfect for lots of our super-slimming recipes. And don't forget, vegetarian protein options can always be used instead of meat in all of the recipes in this book.

HERBS *and* SPICES

We love a bit of spice! One of the best ways to keep your food interesting when changing ingredients for lower fat/sugar/calorie versions is to season it well with herbs and spices. Mixed spice blends, either shop-bought or homemade, are great for adding flavour in a pinch. Don't be shy with spices – not all of them burn your mouth off! We've added a spice-level icon to the recipes in this book, so you know what to expect. The beauty of cooking dishes yourself is you can adjust the heat to your liking – add more or less chilli to suit. Always taste your food before adding extra spicing; add spices, vinegars, mustard and hot sauces gradually, to taste.

STOCKS, SAUCE *and* THICKENERS

When you remove fat from a dish, flavours can dwindle. Adding spices is one way to boost flavours, but often the level of acidity in a recipe is much more important. When it comes to balancing and boosting flavours in our dishes, we love to use vinegar, soy sauce, fish sauce, Worcestershire sauce or Henderson's Relish. One of Pinch of Nom's essential ingredients is the humble stock cube or stock pot; they add instant flavour and they're so versatile. We use various flavoured stock cubes and pots throughout this book, but there's always an option if you can't get your hands on the exact ones we've used. It's worth noting that sauces, stock cubes and pots are often high in salt, so you may want to swap for reduced-salt versions.

Reduced-sugar ketchup isn't just great for topping chips, it also adds a rich depth of flavour to soups, stews and pasta sauces. We've also popped in a few recipes for our own low-calorie sauces and dips, like our hot honey in our Honey and Lime Glazed Salmon with Herby Grains on page 58, and our Hot Honey Halloumi Flatbreads on page 56.

From breakfasts to fakeaways and midweek dinners, we often use either syrup or honey to give dishes a touch of sweetness, without drying them out (be sure to bookmark page 68 for our delicious Sticky Garlic and Chilli Tofu!).

We're often asked for tips on how to thicken soups, sauces and gravies. In the pre-slimming days, we wouldn't have thought twice about using a few tablespoons of flour to thicken liquids. Nowadays, we're always on the lookout for lower-calorie and gluten-free options. Letting liquids reduce is a good way of thickening sauces without adding anything extra. As the moisture evaporates, the flavours get more concentrated too, so the end result will taste even better.

REDUCED-FAT DAIRY

Substituting high-fat dairy products with clever alternatives can make a dish instantly lower in calories. We often use reduced-fat cream cheese or spreadable cheese instead of full-fat versions, and reduced-fat cottage cheese is another handy option. You'll find it featured in recipes like Cottage Cheese Bagels on page 139, along with our Breakfast Burritos on page 42. In both of these dishes, it helps to keep things lighter without compromising on flavour or that all-important creaminess.

TINS

Don't be afraid to bulk-buy tinned essentials! Beans, tomatoes and sweetcorn all come in handy time and time again, and tinned fish is a real kitchen superstar too. Using tinned ingredients can really help to keep costs down, and you'll never know the difference. We've used tinned tuna in recipes like Tuna Puttanesca Pasta on page 254 and Tuna Kedgeree on page 257. Both simple yet tasty dishes that do well to show you just how useful tins can be!

FROZEN FRUIT *and* VEG

Frozen fruit and veg make great filler ingredients and are perfect low-cost alternatives anywhere that fresh ingredients aren't always necessary. Most of the time they're already peeled and chopped too, so they save time as well as money; you can just throw them in alongside your other ingredients.

PULSES, RICE *and* BEANS

High in both protein and fibre, keeping a few tins of beans and pulses in the cupboard is never going to do any harm! Rice is a fantastic filler and a great accompaniment to so many Pinch of Nom recipes.

BREAD, WRAPS *and* PASTRY

A great source of fibre, wholemeal bread is filling and versatile too. Wholemeal rolls, panko breadcrumbs, sourdough, wraps... we've used them all this time around! We often go for gluten-free breads as they tend to contain fewer calories and less sugar, so they're an easy swap when you want to shave off a few calories.

POTATOES

Potatoes are proper lifesavers when it comes to meal prep. Bake a few jackets, roast some chunks, or mash them up at the start of the week, and you can have lunch, dinner, or a quick side ready in a flash. We're obsessed with the Sweet Potato Gnocchi with Broccoli and Ricotta on page 110, and the Nutty Mushroom Stuffing Potato Hash on page 198 is proof that a few spuds and a bit of prep can go a long way! Chopped, sliced, mashed or filled, the humble potato will always have a place in our kitchen.

EGGS

Eggs are protein-rich, tasty and versatile! A simple egg can be used in so many different ways. From baking and binding ingredients together, to having a starring role in our Sausage and Egg Breakfast Slice on page 88, you'll never go wrong if you have a box of eggs in the house.

LOW-CALORIE COOKING SPRAY

One of the best ways to cut down on cooking with oils and fats is to use a low-calorie cooking spray. A spritz of this will make little difference to the end result of your food, but it can make a huge difference to the calories consumed. Make sure to spray your food directly and toss it to coat evenly, rather than spraying onto the pan, so you don't damage the non-stick coating on your pans or apliance.

Courgette, Lemon and Ricotta Tart *(see page 192)*

SWEETENER

There are so many sweeteners out there, it can be tricky to know which is the best substitute for regular sugar. Sweeteners vary in sweetness and swapping them weight-for-weight with regular sugar can give you different results. In our recipes we use granulated sweetener, not powdered sweetener, as it has larger 'crystals'. This can be used weight-for-weight anywhere that you're replacing sugar.

DRIED PASTA *and* NOODLES

We wouldn't want to live without pasta or noodles! They're not too pricey to stock up on, and they'll keep nicely in the store cupboard until you're ready to transform them into fakeaway favourites and midweek classics, like our Sausage, Fennel and Chilli Pasta on page 50.

MICROWAVEABLE RICE

Microwavable rice is a real time-saver, making it a useful staple to have in your kitchen cupboard! It's a filling and fuss-free base for many of the meals in this book, including the Mexican-Style Rice Soup on page 176 and the Korma-Style Cauliflower with Coriander Rice on page 92. We've also used it in our Sweet and Sour Chicken Curry on page 219. Popping it in the microwave means perfectly cooked grains every time without the stress of standing over a saucepan.

TOFU

Tofu is a brilliant ingredient for vegetarians and vegans, or for anyone looking to add a bit of extra protein to their meals. It has a lovely texture and soaks up flavours beautifully in recipes like our Crunchy Asian-Style Salad on page 192, and Sticky Garlic and Chilli Tofu on page 68. Cubed, sliced, marinated... you name it... tofu is a simple ticket to satisfying and protein-rich meals that are super tasty!

SELF-RAISING FLOUR, BAKING POWDER *and* ROLLED OATS

Whether you're an expert or a beginner baker, make sure you've got self-raising flour on hand. It's essential for giving cakes, muffins, and other baked goodies their perfect fluffiness. Sift flour together with baking powder to create treats like our Banana Crumble Muffins on page 164. Rolled oats are brilliant to keep in the cupboard too. Packed with filling fibre, they're perfect for energising breakfasts like our Triple Berry Bakes on page 162, or for adding texture and sweetness to snacks and desserts.

DRIED FRUIT, NUTS AND SEEDS

Nuts, seeds, and dried fruit are all amazing ingredients to keep in your kitchen, adding crunch, flavour, and even a protein boost to both sweet and savoury dishes. You'll spot them in our Nutty Mushroom Stuffing Potato Hash on page 198, with a tasty mix of toasted walnuts and chestnuts, and in our Orange and Cranberry Biscotti on page 274. They also feature in some of our favourite recipes, like Banoffee Overnight Weetabix Pots on page 134, Banana Crunch Ice Cream on page 120, and Blueberry Crumble Squares on page 160. All perfect examples of how these ingredients can elevate your everyday baking and cooking!

TINNED FRUIT

Tinned fruit makes whipping up sweet treats quick and simple! It's already prepped and ready to go, saving you time on peeling, chopping, and prepping fresh fruit. Even better, it's a smart way of adding natural sweetness and juicy flavour to your desserts while saving on calories. It's a lifesaver for recipes like our Peach Custard Cake on page 270, and our Pineapple Upside Down Pancake Traybake on page 242 – two nostalgic dishes that'll take you back to the best parts of school dinners!

FROZEN FRUIT

Just like tinned fruit, frozen fruit is a total lifesaver for meal prepping. Having a stash in the freezer means you can always throw something together without worrying about it going off. No more scrabbling to see if those blueberries in the bottom of the fridge are still edible, just grab what you need and go. Use it to whip up our Triple Berry Bakes on page 162, or our Chocolate Overnight Oats on page 126.

OUR FAVOURITE KIT

KITCHEN BASICS

NON-STICK PANS

When you're meal prepping, a good pan is your best friend. Whether you're cooking a quick sauce, softening veggies, or giving a bit of colour to a batch of protein, the right pan makes everything easier. Non-stick pans are brilliant because they mean less oil, less sticking, and less stress. Keep them happy by washing gently with soapy water, and you'll get years of reliable service. We always suggest having a good set of saucepans, plus a small and large frying pan. They really make prepping ahead so much simpler.

KITCHEN KNIVES *and* KNIFE SHARPENER

Every kitchen needs a good set of knives. If you can, splurge on some good quality, super-sharp knives – blunt knives have a habit of bouncing off ingredients, which can make them more dangerous than sharper ones. You'll need to mind your fingers with super-sharp knives too, but you'll be glad you invested when you've got knives that glide through veg, saving you so much time and effort. Keep them nice and sharp so you can carry on slicing and dicing like a pro.

CHOPPING BOARDS

As well as protecting your surfaces, a good set of chopping boards is key to a safe and hygienic kitchen. We'd recommend a full set of colour-coordinated boards, with separate ones for veg, meat, fish and dairy. They make it so much easier to keep your ingredients separate, and most sets are simple to clean and tuck away once you've finished cooking.

HOB

We often use the hob for sautéing sauces, softening veggies, or cooking other bits that can't be prepped ahead in the fridge or freezer. If your hob is ceramic or a hot plate, some dishes might take a little longer to cook, but everything works just the same.

FOOD PROCESSOR, BLENDER, STICK BLENDER *and* ELECTRIC WHISK

These are essential pieces of kit for a lot of Pinch of Nom recipes. We like to make sauces from scratch, so a decent blender or food processor is a lifesaver. A stick blender can be used on most occasions if you're looking for something cheaper or more compact. It's well worth the investment for the flavour of all those homemade sauces. An electric whisk is nice to have when you need to whip up a scrummy sweet treat in a hurry.

MIXING BOWLS

A couple of mixing bowls will come in handy time and time again. We'd suggest getting at least two; a smaller one and a large one will see you through most kinds of recipes. Smaller bowls give you more control when you're whisking ingredients and larger bowls mean more room to mix it up.

PASTRY CUTTERS *and* COOLING RACK

All of your baked goodies will cool down quicker on a rack. While it can be tough to resist, resting time is essential to prevent a soggy bottom. A good quality pastry cutter will effortlessly slice readymade sheets into the ideal size and shape too.

MEASURING SPOONS

Want to make sure you never get muddled between a tsp and tbsp? Pinch of Nom has absolutely, definitely never made this mistake. Honest. But these days we're never without a trusty set of measuring spoons, which help make sure it's not a tablespoon of chilli when it should have been a teaspoon. Just make sure you use a butter knife to level off the spoon – you'll be surprised how much extra you add when the spoonful is heaped.

HEATPROOF JUG

A measuring jug is essential for measuring out wet ingredients. We recommend getting a heatproof version that you can stick in the microwave when needed.

FINE GRATER

Using a fine grater is one of those surprising revelations. You won't believe the difference between grating cheese with a fine grater versus a standard grater. 45g of cheese, for example, can easily cover an oven dish when using a fine grater. You can also use it for citrus zest, garlic and ginger – it helps a little go a long, long way.

GARLIC CRUSHER

You'll never miss the faff of finely chopping garlic once you've invested in a garlic crusher. Relatively cheap to pick up, you won't go back after you've squeezed that first clove into a perfect paste. It'll save you so much time and it helps your garlic spread evenly throughout the dish.

WOODEN OR METAL SKEWERS

Threading meat, fish or vegetables onto skewers is a great way to lock in flavour and keep everything juicy. You can turn them as they cook for even cooking, and make sure every bit of your meat is coated in marinade. Don't forget to soak wooden skewers in water first so they won't catch or burn while cooking on the hob or under the grill.

TUPPERWARE AND PLASTIC TUBS

Meal prep and airtight food containers go hand in hand. Choose containers that are freezer, microwave, and oven-safe so they can handle everything from batch cooking to leftovers. For a greener option, go for glass storage containers – just be sure to double-check they're freezer-safe.

GLASS JARS WITH TOPS

Glass jars with tops are such a handy bit of kit for prepping, storing, and serving all kinds of recipes. They're fab for keeping breakfasts fresh, like our Chocolate Overnight Oats on page 126, and you can even use individual jars to portion snacks or salads. They're also brilliant for showing off layered desserts or meals, so everything looks as good as it tastes.

WAFFLE MAKER

Our waffle maker only stars in one recipe in this book, but it's worth it! We've used ours for the Cherries Jubilee Waffles on page 268, where it helps create those crisp, golden pockets just waiting to be filled with juicy cherries and syrup. If that gets you hooked, you'll find even more waffle recipes on our website (pinchofnom.com), so you can wake up to a fluffy, feel-good breakfast whenever you fancy.

MUFFIN TIN

A muffin tin is a kitchen classic. Ideal for portioning and getting that lovely even bake, it's a must-have for any baker. We've used ours for our Banana Crumble Muffins on page 164, helping them rise beautifully and hold their crumbly topping in place. Even beyond muffins, a good tin is handy for mini quiches, frittatas, and little desserts – a real all-rounder in the kitchen!

Note on plastic: *We have made a conscious effort to reduce the amount of non-reusable plastic such as cling film when making our recipes. There are great alternatives to cling film now available, such as silicone stretch lids, beeswax food covers, fabric food covers and biodegradable food and freezer bags.*

MEAL PLAN 1

Everyday Light

MEAL PLAN 2

Family

WEEKLY MEAL PLANS

We know there are weeks when you need someone else to do the planning for you. So here are two sample meal plans for inspiration. Meal plan one, for 2 people, focusses on the delicious and filling Everyday Light recipes from the book. Meal plan two, for 4 people, is designed for families, and features only breakfast and main meal ideas from across the book and recipe categories. These two plans are intended as kick-off plans to show you how the recipes work for different situations. Feel free to swap any out and adapt as it suits you.

EVERYDAY LIGHT MEAL PLAN

Serves 2

SUNDAY 'POWER HOUR' PREP	**Breakfast Cookies** (page 132): Prep and bake these, then store them in an airtight container. They make 12 cookies, providing a quick breakfast or snack for during the week (they keep for 4 days). **Banoffee Overnight Weetabix Pots** (page 134): Prep and refrigerate in individual airtight containers (they keep for 4 days). **Mexican-Style Rice Soup** (page 176): Prep ingredients and pop the bag into the freezer. **Crunchy Asian-Style Salad** (Base, page 192): Prep the noodle and vegetable base. This stores perfectly in the fridge for 4–5 days.		
	BREAKFAST	**LUNCH**	**DINNER**
MONDAY WORK FROM HOME DAY 1	**Banoffee Overnight Weetabix Pots** ***Monday Night Prep**: Bake a double batch of the Sweet Chilli Chicken (page 196). Stir together the chilli dressing. Chill in separate containers.*	**AT HOME: Crunchy Asian-Style Salad** (page 192): Use one third of your prepped salad base and top it with the crispy baked tofu and sriracha-lime dressing (30 minutes in oven).	**Creamy Chicken and Mushroom Tagliatelle** (page 64): This comes together in just 25 minutes. It serves 4, so you can box up the remaining two portions for packed lunch on Wednesday.
TUESDAY OFFICE DAY 1	**Breakfast Cookies**: Grab a couple of these on your way out of the door. ***Tuesday Night Prep**: Take out your Mexican-Style Rice Soup dump bag from the freezer and leave to defrost in the fridge.*	**PACKED: Sweet Chilli Chicken Noodle Salad** (page 196): Pack up half of the remaining prepped Asian-style salad base and top it with half of the cooked chicken and chilli dressing.	**Chinese-Style Curried Noodles** (page 258): This uses store-cupboard staples and frozen stir-fry vegetables. It serves 4, providing lunch for later in the week.

	BREAKFAST	LUNCH	DINNER
WEDNESDAY OFFICE DAY 2	**Banoffee Overnight Weetabix Pots** ***Prep***: *Add the defrosted Mexican-Style Soup dump bag to the slow cooker (optional).*	**PACKED: Creamy Chicken and Mushroom Tagliatelle** Reheats easily in the microwave.	**Mexican-Style Rice Soup** (page 76): If you've cooked this in the slow cooker, it will be ready! If not, cook it on the hob. Freeze the leftover 4 portions.
THURSDAY OFFICE DAY 3	**Breakfast Cookies** ***Thursday Night Prep***: *Apple Crumble Breakfast Pots (page 124).*	**PACKED: Sweet Chilli Chicken Noodle Salad** (page 196): Top the remaining prepped Asian-style salad base with the remaining sliced cooked chicken and chilli dressing.	**Masala Spiced Chicken Burger with Mango Chutney Yoghurt** (page 46): Ready in 30 minutes. Refrigerate the remaining 2 burgers and the separate pot of the yoghurt.
FRIDAY WORK FROM HOME DAY 2	**Apple Crumble Breakfast Pots** Prepped the night before. It serves 4, leaving two portions for Saturday.	**AT HOME: Chinese-Style Curried Noodles** (leftovers): Reheat in the microwave or a saucepan with a splash of water.	**Greek-Style Chicken with Butter Beans** (page 104): This cooks in about 30 minutes. Serves 4, and freezes well so 2 portions can be saved for another weekday evening.
SATURDAY WEEKEND LONGER COOK	**Apple Crumble Breakfast Pots** (leftovers) or make the **Banana Buckwheat Pancakes** (page 90) for a Saturday brunch.	**Masala Spiced Chicken Burger with Mango Chutney Yoghurt**: Simply reheat the burgers in the oven.	**Sweet Potato Gnocchi with Broccoli and Ricotta** (see page 110): This serves 4, leaving leftovers for Sunday.
SUNDAY WEEKEND LONGER COOK	**Cherries Jubilee Waffles** (page 268): You can freeze any leftovers for a quick midweek breakfast.	**Chipotle Chicken Traybake** (page 222): As this is a base recipe it can be used to make two other meals for the week ahead.	**Sweet Potato Gnocchi with Broccoli and Ricotta** (leftovers) Delicious reheated in the microwave.
MEALS TO TAKE OVER INTO NEXT WEEK:	4 x portions of the **Chicken Traybake** – see serving suggestions in the Multi-Serve chapter on pages 224–227. 4 x portions of **Mexican-Style Rice Soup** – in the freezer. 2 x portions of **Greek-Style Chicken and Butter Beans** – in the freezer. 2 x portions of **Cherries Jubilee Waffles** – in the freezer.		

FAMILY MEAL PLAN

Serves 4

SUNDAY 'POWER HOUR' PREP	**Butternut Squash Muffins** (page 136): This makes 12 muffins, perfect for snacks during the week. Once cooled, keep them in an airtight container for up to 5 days. **Gammon and Pineapple Chilli** (page 186): Prep ingredients and pop the bag into the freezer. **Shredded Turkey Rolls** (page 178): Prep ingredients and pop the bag into the freezer. **Sausage and Egg Breakfast Slice** (page 88): This makes 8 egg slices, providing a quick breakfast for during the week. Wrap individually and keep in the fridge for up to 4 days.	
	BREAKFAST	**DINNER**
MONDAY	**Sausage and Egg Breakfast Slice**: Prepped in your power hour. Grab 4 slices of your pre-baked slice and reheat in the microwave until piping hot.	**Greek-Style Chicken with Butter Beans** (page 104): Ready in less than 45 minutes, this is an easy way to start the week.
TUESDAY	**Sausage and Egg Breakfast Slice**: Prepped in your power hour. Reheat the remaining 4 slices.	**Corned Beef and Pickle Pie** (page 246): A quick pie using a blitzed bread-and-cheese crust (15 mins prep, 35 mins bake). Enjoy the remaining 2 portions for lunches.
	***Tuesday Night Prep**: Take the Shredded Turkey Rolls (page 178) bag out of the freezer to defrost in the fridge overnight. Prep your Chocolate Overnight Oats (page 126).*	
WEDNESDAY	**Chocolate Overnight Oats** ***Prep**: Add the defrosted Turkey Rolls dump bag to the slow cooker (optional).*	**Shredded Turkey Rolls** (page 178): If you've cooked this in your slow cooker, it will be ready to roll! If not, it's prepped and ready to cook in the oven. Assemble 4 rolls and save the rest of the meat for Friday.
	***Wednesday Night Prep**: Take the Gammon and Pineapple Chilli bag out of the freezer to defrost overnight.* ***BONUS Snack Prep** (optional): Blueberry Crumble Squares (page 160): These take just 10 minutes prep and bake for 30 minutes. The recipe makes 16 squares and will keep for up to 4 days in an airtight container or can be popped into the freezer to enjoy another day.*	

	BREAKFAST	DINNER
THURSDAY	**Gingerbread Porridge** (see page 244): Ready in under 10 minutes. ***Prep**: Add the defrosted Gammon and Pineapple Chilli dump bag to the slow cooker (optional).*	**Gammon and Pineapple Chilli** If you've cooked this in your slow cooker, it will be ready to roll! If not, it's prepped and ready to cook on the hob. Freezes well so 2 portions can be saved for another day.
	***Thursday Night Prep**: Apple Crumble Breakfast Pots (page 124)*	
FRIDAY	**Apple Crumble Breakfast Pots**	**Shredded Turkey Rolls** Reheat your leftover shredded turkey in the microwave for 4 minutes, then assemble fresh rolls and bake.
SATURDAY **WEEKEND LONGER COOK**	**Pineapple Upside Down Pancake Traybake** (page 242): Serves 8, so save 4 portions for an easy Sunday morning breakfast.	**Caramelized Onion Mac and Cheese** (page 112): Enjoy slowly caramelizing the onions on the hob and baking this beautiful pasta dish for 1 hour 10 minutes. Leaves 2 portions for easy freezing.
SUNDAY **WEEKEND LONGER COOK**	**Pineapple Upside Down Pancake Traybake**: Enjoy reheated leftovers.	**Roast Chicken with Lemon Gravy** (page 216): Takes 15 minutes to prep and 2 hours to cook. Serve 4 portions tonight, leaving 4 ready to transform into dinners for early next week.
MEALS TO TAKE OVER INTO NEXT WEEK:	2 x portions of the **Roast Gammon and Pineapple Chilli** in the freezer. 2 x portions of the **Caramelized Onion Mac and Cheese** in the freezer. 4 x portions of the **Roast Chicken** – see serving suggestions in the Multi-Serve chapter on page 216.	

MAKE AHEAD

FREEZE ME

BATCH COOK

DAIRY FREE

USE DF CHEESES

GLUTEN FREE

USE GF TORTILLAS

HIGH PROTEIN

BREAKFAST BURRITOS

15 MINS 45 MINS MAKES 8

PER SERVING:
367 KCAL /38G CARBS

SPECIAL EQUIPMENT
Air fryer (optional)

low-calorie cooking spray
1 medium potato, no need to peel, cut into 1cm (½in) dice
1 red onion, peeled and diced
1 pepper, deseeded and diced (any colour)
250g 2%-fat minced turkey
1 tsp garlic granules
1 tsp smoked paprika
1 large flat mushroom, diced
80g spinach leaves, roughly chopped
8 medium eggs
150g reduced-fat cottage cheese
salt and freshly ground black pepper, to taste
8 wheat and white tortilla wraps, approx. 60g per wrap
80g reduced-fat Cheddar cheese, finely grated

TIPS

Use the remaining cottage cheese to make a batch of our Smoky Breakfast Sandwich on page 128.

To reheat your frozen burritos, allow them to defrost. Unwrap the defrosted sandwich, place on a paper towel and microwave for 2 minutes, or until piping hot. You can also crisp up in the air fryer if you wish. Air-fry at 180°C for 10 minutes, or until the tortilla wrap is crisp. Alternatively, crisp in a frying pan for a few minutes on each side.

Skip the drive-through and sail straight into a protein-packed morning with these easy-peasy Breakfast Burritos. They're packed with all the good stuff and keep you fuller for longer, making them perfect for those grab-and-go starts. We love making a batch, popping them in the freezer, and then reheating whenever we need a quick and cosy breakfast that sees you through to lunchtime.

Everyday Light

Preheat the oven to 220°C (fan 200°C/gas mark 7) and spray a baking tray with low-calorie cooking spray.

Add the diced potato to the tray along with the onion and roast in the oven for 10 minutes.

Remove the tray from the oven and add the pepper and minced turkey to the tray. Sprinkle over the garlic and paprika and roast in the oven for a further 10 minutes.

Remove the tray from the oven. Break up any large pieces of the minced turkey, then add the diced mushroom and spinach. Return to the oven for 5 minutes, or until the spinach has wilted a little.

Meanwhile, add the eggs and cottage cheese to a food processor and blitz until smooth. Season to taste with salt and pepper. Pour the egg mixture into the baking tray and mix lightly. Roughly flatten, then return to the oven for a final 10–15 minutes until the eggs are set.

Remove from the oven, cut into eight slices and leave the eggs to cool slightly in the tray so it is easier to handle. Microwave the tortilla wraps for 30 seconds so they are pliable, then divide the grated cheese between the wraps and add a slice of the egg to each wrap. Fold the left and right sides of the wrap over the egg filling, then fold over the bottom and top of the wraps to fully enclose. Place seam side down on a work surface.

If serving right away, bake in the oven at 220°C (fan 200°C/gas mark 7) for 15–20 minutes or air-fry at 180°C for 10 minutes until the tortilla wraps are crisp and lightly golden. If prepping ahead, wrap in non-stick baking paper and foil or cling film and store in the fridge for up to 4 days or the freezer in an airtight container for up to 3 months (see Tips).

VEGGIE

USE VEGGIE BACON SUBSTITUTE

FREEZE ME

BATCH COOK

DAIRY FREE

USE DF CREAM CHEESE AND CHEESE

GLUTEN FREE

HIGH PROTEIN

BREAKFAST LOADED POTATOES

15 MINS 30 MINS SERVES 4

PER SERVING:
330 KCAL /35G CARBS

- 2 baking potatoes, approx. 350g per potato
- 1 tsp garlic granules
- 10g fresh chives, finely chopped
- 50g reduced-fat cream cheese
- salt and freshly ground black pepper, to taste
- low-calorie cooking spray
- 4 eggs, beaten
- 3 cooked smoked bacon medallions, diced
- 40g reduced-fat Cheddar cheese, finely grated
- 1 spring onion, trimmed and finely sliced, to serve

TIPS

Alternatively, you can cook these potatoes in the air fryer, if you prefer. Air-fry at 180°C for 5–10 minutes until the cheese is bubbling and turning golden brown round the edges.

You can also freeze the cooked potatoes, reserving the cheese for when you're reheating. Top with cheese and reheat in the microwave for 3–4 minutes until piping hot.

Who doesn't love a jacket spud? We've taken everyone's favourite classic comfort dish and given it a proper morning makeover with these Breakfast Loaded Potatoes. Think fluffy centres mixed with scrambled egg, crispy bacon and chives, all piled back into their potato jackets and topped with golden melty cheese... yes please! Prep them ahead, pop them in the fridge and reheat whenever you need a warm, hearty breakfast that feels indulgent but is still brilliantly simple.

Everyday Light

Pierce the potatoes and cook for 5 minutes each in the microwave until soft. Leave until cool enough to handle.

Cut the potatoes in half and scoop out the centres into a large bowl. Add the garlic granules, chives, cream cheese and season to taste with salt and pepper. Mash until smooth. Leave the potato shells to one side.

Spray a frying pan with low-calorie cooking spray and set over a medium heat. Pour in the eggs and season to taste. Stir, lifting and folding the egg over itself until the eggs are just softly set. Remove from the heat and leave to stand for a minute to finish cooking. Preheat the oven to 220°C (fan 200°C/gas mark 7) .

Add the eggs and cooked bacon to the potato mixture and mix to combine.

Spoon the potato mixture into the potato shells. Place the potatoes on a large baking tray and sprinkle over the grated cheese. (You can freeze the cooked potatoes at this point, see Tips.)

Bake in the oven for 15–20 minutes until the filling is just turning golden brown and the potato skins are just crisping. Sprinkle over the spring onion and serve. The cooked potatoes will keep in the fridge for up to 3 days.

Reheat in the microwave for 3–4 minutes until piping hot.

FREEZE ME
BURGERS ONLY

BATCH COOK

DAIRY FREE
USE DF YOGHURT

GLUTEN FREE
USE GF BURGER BUNS

HIGH PROTEIN

MASALA SPICED CHICKEN BURGER *with* MANGO CHUTNEY YOGHURT

15 MINS + 1 HR PICKLING | 10 MINS | SERVES 4

PER SERVING:
397 KCAL /41G CARBS

SPECIAL EQUIPMENT
200ml mason jar or container

- 500g 5% fat minced chicken
- 2 garlic cloves, peeled and crushed
- 2cm (¾in) piece of root ginger, peeled and grated
- 1 tbsp garam masala
- 2 tsp ground turmeric
- 1 tsp chilli powder
- salt and freshly ground black pepper, to taste
- 1 tsp chopped fresh coriander
- low-calorie cooking spray
- 2 tbsp mango chutney
- 100g fat-free Greek yoghurt
- 4 burger buns, approx. 60g each
- 25g lettuce leaves

FOR THE PICKLED RED ONIONS

- 120ml white wine vinegar
- 1 tbsp white granulated sugar
- 2 tsp salt
- 1 tbsp black peppercorns
- 1 red onion, peeled and finely sliced

Can't decide between curry night and burger night? Good news… you don't have to! These juicy chicken burgers are infused with aromatic Indian spices for a complex flavour that's different to your typical beef burger. We've added a sweet mango chutney yoghurt and some tangy pickled red onions for even more zinginess. Make these when you need to brighten up your midweek.

Everyday Light

Place the minced chicken in a large bowl and add the crushed garlic, ginger, garam masala, turmeric and chilli powder. Add a good pinch of salt and pepper along with the chopped coriander and use your hands to combine all the ingredients together.

Divide the mix into four portions. Spray your hands with a little low-calorie cooking spray and shape each portion into a burger patty about 1cm (½in) thick. Set aside. You can freeze the burgers at this stage by putting non-stick baking paper between the burger patties so they don't stick together, placing them in a freezer-proof container and freezing for up to 1 month (see Tips).

Place the mango chutney and yoghurt in a medium bowl along with a pinch of salt and pepper. Mix well to combine and set aside.

To make the pickled red onions, add the vinegar and 120ml water to a saucepan and set over a medium heat. Add the sugar, salt and peppercorns and stir until the brine is warm and the sugar and salt have dissolved. Remove from the heat and leave to cool slightly.

Add the sliced onion to a clean mason jar or container and pour over the brine. Place the lid on, give the jar a shake to ensure the onion is coated in the brine and chill in the fridge for at least 1 hour, or until the red onions turn pink.

Spray a frying pan with low-calorie cooking spray and set over a medium heat. Place the burger patties in the pan and cook for 4–5 minutes until they become golden brown and have a nice crust.

Flip the burgers over and cook for a further 4–5 minutes until both sides are golden, crisp and cooked all the way through. Remove from the pan and set aside.

Cut the burger buns in half and place in the same frying pan, insides down, for 1 minute to toast.

To assemble the burgers, spread a spoonful of the mango chutney yoghurt on each side of the toasted bun. Place lettuce leaves on top of the bun and add the spiced chicken burger on top of that. Add a few of the marinated pickled onions and finish with the top of the bun.

The burgers will keep in the fridge for up to 3 days and the pickled onions will keep in the fridge for up to 2 weeks. Reheat the burgers in an oven preheated to 200°C (fan 180°C/gas mark 6) for 5–10 minutes until piping hot in the middle.

TIPS

These burgers are best cooked in a frying pan but can be cooked in the air fryer at 180°C for 8–10 minutes, if preferred.

If you've frozen the burgers, leave them in the fridge to fully defrost, then cook as per the recipe guidelines.

VEGGIE

USE VEGETARIAN SAUSAGES AND HARD CHEESE

BATCH COOK

DAIRY FREE

USE DF CHEESE AND CRÈME FRAÎCHE

GLUTEN FREE

USE GF PASTA

HIGH PROTEIN

SAUSAGE, FENNEL *and* CHILLI PASTA

10 MINS **25 MINS** **SERVES 4**

PER SERVING:
496 KCAL / 61G CARBS

SPECIAL EQUIPMENT
Pestle and mortar or mini food processor

400g reduced-fat pork sausages
low-calorie cooking spray
1 fennel bulb (approx. 200g)
1 onion, peeled and diced
salt and freshly ground black pepper, to taste
2 garlic cloves, peeled and crushed
2 tsp chilli flakes
1 tbsp fennel seeds
280g dried pasta (we used linguini)
100g reduced-fat crème fraîche
30g Parmesan, grated, plus extra to serve

This pasta dish brings together juicy sausage, warming chilli and aromatic fennel in a rich, creamy sauce. With a simple spice mix and a spoonful of crème fraîche, it's the kind of dinner that tastes like it took hours. You'll have it on the table in under 30 minutes, or make ahead and store in the fridge for when you fancy some hearty comfort food in the week!

Weekly Indulgence

Using a sharp knife, make a shallow cut in each sausage and remove the casings, leaving only the sausage meat. Break up the sausages into small chunks and discard the casings.

Spray a deep frying pan with low-calorie cooking spray and place over a medium heat. Add the sausage meat and cook for 5–10 minutes until the sausage is golden and slightly crisp. Use a slotted spoon to remove the sausage meat from the pan and place it in a bowl.

Remove the stalks from the fennel bulb and trim the bottom of the bulb. Cut the fennel bulb in half lengthways, then slice thinly into half-moon shapes.

Place the same frying pan used to cook the sausage back on the heat and add the sliced fennel and onion. Season to taste with salt and pepper and cook over a medium heat for 2–3 minutes until they begin to soften. Add the garlic and cook for a further 2–3 minutes.

Place the chilli flakes and fennel seeds in a pestle and mortar and grind until you get a powder-like consistency. Add this spice mix to the cooked fennel, onion and garlic and cook for a further 2–3 minutes until the vegetables have softened and the spices are well toasted.

Meanwhile, cook the pasta in a large saucepan of boiling salted water according to the packet instructions until al dente. Once the fennel and onion are cooked and softened, add 100ml water. Stir through the vegetables and use the liquid to deglaze the bottom of the pan. This will pick up any flavour from the fennel

and sausage as it cooks. Add the crème fraîche and stir until the sauce becomes creamy.

Once the pasta is cooked, use tongs to add it straight into the sauce. Take a cup and fill it halfway with some of the pasta water. Once the pasta has been added to the sauce, add the Parmesan and a drop or two of the pasta water and toss it through. This will help bring the pasta and the sauce together.

Serve the pasta topped with extra Parmesan, if desired. The pasta will keep in the fridge for up to 3 days. Reheat the pasta in a saucepan with a splash of water over a medium heat for 5–10 minutes until piping hot. If the pasta is too dry, add another splash of water to loosen.

TIP

Some sausages can contain gluten, so be sure to check before you buy if you require a gluten-free option.

FREEZE ME

BATCH COOK

DAIRY FREE

HIGH PROTEIN

'NDUJA CHICKEN ORZO

15 MINS **VARIABLE** **SERVES 4**

PER SERVING:
487 KCAL /47G CARBS

SPECIAL EQUIPMENT
28cm (10in) round casserole dish, suitable for hob and oven

- low-calorie cooking spray
- 8 skinless, boneless chicken thighs (visible fat removed), approx. 600g in total, cut in half
- 1 onion, peeled and diced
- 4 garlic cloves, peeled and crushed
- 1 medium red pepper, halved, deseeded and sliced
- 200g mushrooms, diced
- 150g passata
- 2 tbsp tomato puree
- 50g 'nduja paste
- 300ml chicken stock (1 chicken stock cube dissolved in 300ml boiling water)
- 200g dried orzo
- 100g spinach leaves
- salt and freshly ground black pepper, to taste

Get ready for a cosy, flavour-packed pot you won't be able to get enough of! The star of this is a melty, garlicky tomato sauce, complemented by a sneaky kick from 'nduja paste. You're packing in your veg, without even thinking about it. All you need to do is sit back and enjoy the delicious aroma until dinnertime!

Weekly Indulgence

OVEN METHOD
1 HOUR

Preheat the oven to 180°C (fan 160°C/gas mark 4). We browned our chicken thighs before adding them to the casserole dish, but this isn't an essential step and they can be added without browning.

Spray a large casserole dish with low-calorie cooking spray and place over a medium heat. Add the chicken thighs and brown for 5 minutes, turning halfway through.

Add the onion, garlic, peppers, mushrooms, passata, tomato puree and 'nduja paste to the dish.

Pour the stock into the casserole dish, cover with the lid and cook in the oven for 45 minutes.

Add the orzo and spinach, then return to the oven and cook for a further 20–30 minutes. The chicken should be cooked through, show no sign of pinkness and the orzo should be tender. Season to taste with salt and pepper and serve.

The casserole will keep in the fridge for up to 3 days. Reheat in the microwave for 3–4 minutes until piping hot.

TIP

If you've frozen the casserole, once defrosted, reheat it in the microwave for 3–4 minutes until piping hot.

SLOW COOKER METHOD
3–5 HOURS

SPECIAL EQUIPMENT
3.5-litre slow cooker

We browned our chicken thighs before adding them to the slow cooker, but this isn't an essential step, and they can be added to the slow cooker without browning. Spray a large frying pan with low-calorie cooking spray and place over a medium heat. Add the chicken thighs and brown for 5 minutes, turning halfway through.

Add the chicken thighs to the slow cooker pot along with the onion, garlic, peppers, mushrooms, passata, tomato puree and 'nduja paste.

Pour the stock into the pot, cover with the lid and cook on high for 2½ hours or low for 4½ hours.

Add the orzo and spinach and cook for a further 30 minutes. The chicken should be cooked through, show no sign of pinkness and the orzo should be tender. Season to taste with salt and pepper and serve.

The casserole will keep in the fridge for up to 3 days. Reheat in the microwave for 3–4 minutes until piping hot.

VEGGIE

FREEZE ME

BATCH COOK

HIGH PROTEIN

HOT HONEY HALLOUMI FLATBREADS

20 MINS | 20 MINS | SERVES 4

PER SERVING:
480 KCAL / 59G CARBS

FOR THE PICKLED ONIONS

1 red onion, peeled and finely sliced
2 tbsp cider vinegar
1 tsp granulated sweetener

FOR THE FLATBREADS

200g self-raising flour, plus extra for dusting
200g fat-free Greek yoghurt
salt and freshly ground black pepper, to taste
low-calorie cooking spray

FOR THE HUMMUS

120g tinned chickpeas, drained and rinsed
1 tsp garlic granules
juice of ½ lemon
½ tsp ground cumin
1 tbsp tahini

TO ASSEMBLE

200g reduced-fat halloumi, sliced into 8
2 tbsp hot honey
½ tsp chilli flakes
½ tsp sriracha sauce
60g rocket
60g cucumber, sliced
80g pomegranate seeds
salt and freshly ground black pepper, to taste

These Hot Honey Halloumi Flatbreads are the kind of lunch you look forward to as soon as you wake up. They're filled with golden halloumi, a speedy homemade hummus, crunchy cucumber, peppery rocket, plus little pops of pomegranate joy. Prep your flatbreads and hummus ahead of time to make lunchtime a total breeze, then drizzle over your hot honey when it's time to dig in. They're just as tasty cold too.

Weekly Indulgence

Put all the ingredients for the pickled onions into a small bowl. Mix well, then set aside to infuse while you prep the rest of the recipe.

For the flatbreads, place the flour, yoghurt, salt and pepper to taste in a large bowl and mix together. When it starts to form a dough, lightly knead for 1 minute until you have a smooth, soft dough. Your brand of yoghurt can affect the dough, so if it is a little dry, add a few drops of water, a little at a time. Tip the dough out onto a floured work surface and divide it into four equal balls.

Place a large, non-stick frying pan over a medium heat and spray with low-calorie cooking spray.

Flour your rolling pin and roll the first ball out into a thin round shape, about 20cm (8in) in diameter. When the frying pan is hot, place the flatbread in the pan and cook for 2–2½ minutes until the underside is golden and the top is slightly puffy. Flip and cook for a further 2 minutes. While your first flatbread cooks, roll out the second and continue until all the flatbreads are cooked. You can store or freeze the flatbreads at this point (see Tips).

Put all the ingredients for the hummus in a food processor and blitz until smooth. Season to taste with salt and pepper. You can store the hummus in the fridge or freeze in individual portions until ready to assemble (see Tips).

Cut each halloumi slice in half; you should have sixteen pieces of halloumi. Spray a frying pan with low-calorie cooking spray and set over a medium heat. Add the halloumi and fry for 2 minutes on each side until lightly golden. Meanwhile, add the hot honey, chilli flakes and sriracha to a small bowl and mix well.

TIPS

You can use regular honey if you prefer and just add 1 tsp of sriracha sauce and chilli flakes or to taste.

You can prep this ahead for a lunch on the go as the halloumi is still delicious when eaten cold. It's best to drizzle over the hot honey just before serving to avoid the flatbreads going soggy.

When ready to assemble, divide the hummus between the flatbreads spreading onto one side. Top with the rocket, cucumber, pickled onions, pomegranate seeds and cooked halloumi. Drizzle over the hot honey mixture and serve!

The flatbreads, hummus and pickled onions will keep in the fridge for 4 days. Reheat the flatbreads in the microwave or hot pan until just warmed through. To freeze the flatbreads, wrap them individually and freeze, then defrost and reheat in the microwave or hot pan until just warmed through. Freeze the hummus in individual portions, then defrost in the fridge. You may need to add a splash of water to loosen.

BATCH COOK

DAIRY FREE

GLUTEN FREE

USE GF SOY SAUCE AND GF GRAIN

HIGH PROTEIN

HONEY *and* LIME GLAZED SALMON WITH HERBY GRAINS

10 MINS | VARIABLE | SERVES 4

PER SERVING:
576 KCAL /42G CARBS

- 4 salmon fillets, approx. 130g each
- 1 tbsp hot honey
- finely grated zest and juice of 2 limes
- 2 garlic cloves, peeled and crushed
- 1 tbsp reduced-salt soy sauce
- salt and freshly ground black pepper, to taste
- 500g bulgur wheat and quinoa, cooked
- 1 tbsp olive oil
- 1 tbsp honey
- 1 tsp Dijon mustard
- 10g fresh mint, chopped
- 10g fresh parsley, chopped

This zingy glazed salmon is the kind of dish that brightens up any mealtime. We've coated the salmon fillets in a spicy, sticky glaze that pairs perfectly with a herby mix of bulgur wheat and quinoa, then tossed everything in a punchy lime vinaigrette. Light, fresh and full of flavour, it's the sort of speedy meal that feels a little bit fancy without any faff.

Special Occasion

OVEN METHOD
18 MINUTES

Preheat the oven to 200°C (fan 180°C/gas mark 6). Line a baking tray with foil and carefully turn up the edges of the foil on all sides to create a shallow dish for the salmon. Place the salmon fillets inside the foil 'dish' and set aside.

Add the hot honey to a bowl along with the juice and zest of one lime, the crushed garlic, soy sauce and a pinch of black pepper. Stir well to combine.

Pour the glaze carefully over the salmon, ensuring that each fillet is well coated and any spare glaze is being held within the foil 'dish'.

Place the salmon fillets in the oven for about 18 minutes, or until the salmon is cooked through. Every 5 minutes, spoon any dressing that comes off the salmon back over it to 'glaze' it. When the salmon is cooked through and fully glazed, remove from the oven.

Place the cooked bulgur wheat and quinoa in a large bowl. In a separate bowl, add the juice and zest of the remaining lime, the olive oil, honey, mustard and a pinch of salt and pepper. Whisk to combine, then pour over the warm grains. Add the chopped mint and parsley and stir well.

To serve, place some of the herby grains on a serving plate and top with a piece of glazed salmon. Finish with a sprinkling of parsley. The salmon and grains will keep in the fridge for up to 3 days.

AIR-FRYER METHOD
12 MINUTES

SPECIAL EQUIPMENT
Air fryer

Preheat the air fryer to 160°C.

Fold a large piece of foil in half so it's around the same size as the air fryer drawer. Turn the edges up to create a shallow dish for the salmon. Place the salmon fillets inside the foil 'dish' and set aside. You might have to do this in batches depending on the size of your air fryer drawer.

Add the hot honey to a small bowl along with the juice and zest of one lime, the crushed garlic, soy sauce and a pinch of black pepper. Stir well to combine.

Pour the glaze carefully over the salmon ensuring that each fillet is well coated and any spare glaze is being held within the foil 'dish'.

Place the salmon fillets in the air fryer and air-fry at 160°C for 12 minutes, or until the salmon is cooked through. Every 3–4 minutes, spoon any dressing that comes off the salmon back over it to 'glaze' it. When the salmon is cooked through and fully glazed, remove from the air fryer.

Place the cooked bulgur wheat and quinoa in a large bowl. In a separate bowl, place the juice and zest of the remaining lime, the olive oil, honey, mustard and a pinch of salt and pepper. Whisk to combine, then pour over the warm grains. Add the chopped mint and parsley and stir well.

To serve, place some of the herby grains on a serving plate and top with a piece of glazed salmon. Finish with a sprinkling of parsley. The salmon and grains will keep in the fridge for up to 3 days.

TIPS

Use normal honey instead of hot honey to avoid spice in this recipe.

If you are making this dish gluten-free, then replace the bulgur wheat with extra quinoa or use a gluten-free grain.

This dish is best eaten cold after refrigerating. If reheating, loosely wrap the salmon in foil with a splash of water. Place in the air fryer at 160°C and slowly reheat for about 8 minutes, or until the salmon is warmed through. The herby grains can be reheated in the microwave for 1–2 minutes.

Image on page 60.

VEGAN

USE VEGAN PROTEIN ALTERNATIVE

VEGGIE

USE VEGETARIAN PROTEIN ALTERNATIVE

BATCH COOK

DAIRY FREE

GLUTEN FREE

USE GF BREAD

HIGH PROTEIN

ROMESCO-STYLE CHICKEN SALAD

10 MINS | 30 MINS | SERVES 4

PER SERVING:
375 KCAL /29G CARBS

SPECIAL EQUIPMENT
Food processor

- low-calorie cooking spray
- 4 medium skinless chicken breasts, approx. 150g each
- salt and freshly ground black pepper, to taste
- 2 tsp garlic granules
- 3 tsp smoked paprika
- 150g sourdough bread, cut into 1cm (½in) cubes
- 200g roasted red peppers
- 1 garlic clove, peeled and crushed
- 1 tbsp white wine vinegar
- ½ tsp tomato puree
- juice of 1 lemon
- 30g flaked almonds, lightly toasted
- 150g cherry tomatoes, halved
- 100g cucumber, halved lengthways and sliced
- 250g cos lettuce, chopped

Think salads are boring? This Spanish-inspired chicken number will change your mind. Made up of tender chicken tossed in a sweet and smoky red pepper sauce that tastes fancy but doesn't call for high levels of effort, it's brimming with flavour and surprisingly simple to make. Toss in some crispy croutons for a crunchy texture, and you've got an addictive light lunch or dinner that's good for you!

Everyday Light

Preheat the oven to 200°C (fan 180°C/gas mark 6).

Line a baking tray with non-stick baking paper, spray with low-calorie cooking spray and set aside.

Place the chicken breasts on a work surface and cover with a large piece of cling film. Use a rolling pin to gently flatten the chicken breasts until they all have an even thickness of about 1cm (½in).

Spray the chicken with low-calorie cooking spray and season to taste with salt and pepper. In a small bowl, mix the garlic granules with 2 teaspoons of the smoked paprika. Lightly sprinkle the spice mix over both sides of the chicken.

Spray a frying pan with low-calorie cooking spray and place over a medium heat. Add the chicken to the pan and cook for a few minutes on each side until golden brown. Place the browned chicken on the lined baking sheet and bake in the oven for 15 minutes, or until cooked through.

Put the sourdough cubes into a large bowl. Season to taste with salt and pepper, spray with a little low-calorie cooking spray and toss to coat. Place the bread on the same baking tray as the chicken and return to the oven for 10–15 minutes, until the croutons are golden and crisp. If the chicken is cooked before the bread crisps up, remove the chicken from the tray and bake the croutons for a further 5–10 minutes.

To make the romesco sauce, put the red peppers into a food processor along with the remaining 1 teaspoon of smoked paprika, the crushed garlic, vinegar, tomato puree, juice of ½ lemon, almonds and a pinch of salt and pepper. Blitz until you get a smooth, slightly thick orange sauce. If the sauce is too thick, let it down with the remaining lemon juice or a drop of water.

Place the chopped tomatoes, cucumber and lettuce in a large bowl. Add a generous spoonful of the romesco sauce and mix to ensure the salad is lightly coated in the dressing. Place on a serving plate.

Add the cooked croutons to the same bowl and add another spoonful of the romesco sauce. Stir to coat the croutons lightly in the dressing and add the croutons on top of the salad.

Cut the cooked chicken breast into thin slices and place on top of the salad. Serve with a final drizzle of romesco sauce over the top.

The romesco sauce and the chicken will keep separately in the fridge for up to 3 days. The croutons will keep at room temperature for up to a week. Bring all salad elements to room temperature and assemble as per the recipe instructions.

TIPS

We used a rolling pin to flatten out the chicken breasts in the recipe but if you don't have one you can use a wine bottle or something similar to replace the rolling pin.

Alternatively, you can cook the chicken and croutons in the air fryer, if you prefer. After pan frying, air-fry the chicken at 160°C for 5 minutes. Add the croutons to the same air fryer drawer and air-fry both the chicken and croutons for a further 8–10 minutes. Take care to check on the chicken and croutons every few minutes so they don't burn. If the chicken is cooked through before the croutons are crisp, remove from the air fryer and allow the croutons to crisp up.

Image on page 61.

VEGAN

OMIT CHICKEN, USE VEGAN CREAM AND CHEESE

VEGGIE

USE ONLY MUSHROOMS IN SAUCE

BATCH COOK

DAIRY FREE

USE DF CREAM AND CHEESE

GLUTEN FREE

USE GF PASTA

HIGH PROTEIN

CREAMY CHICKEN *and* MUSHROOM TAGLIATELLE

10 MINS 15 MINS SERVES 4

PER SERVING:
395 KCAL /32G CARBS

low-calorie cooking spray
500g skinless chicken breasts, cut into thin strips
salt and freshly ground black pepper, to taste
250g chestnut mushrooms, sliced
1 brown onion, peeled and diced
2 garlic cloves, peeled and crushed
1 tsp thyme, leaves only
1 tbsp wholegrain mustard
250ml single cream alternative
25g Parmesan, grated
280g tagliatelle

Chicken and mushroom are a classic combo, so what makes this one so special? It's lighter and healthier than your usual recipe, without skimping on flavour or texture. Tender chicken, juicy mushrooms and Parmesan all come together in a silky, comforting sauce so good it'll make you go 'Mmm!' And thanks to the use of single cream alternative, it's rich without leaving you feeling like you need a nap afterwards.

Everyday Light

Spray a frying pan with low-calorie cooking spray and set over a medium heat.

Season the sliced chicken with salt and black pepper and add to the frying pan. Cook for 5–6 minutes until the chicken is cooked through and starting to brown slightly. Once cooked, remove from the pan and set aside.

Spray the same pan with more low-calorie cooking spray and add the sliced mushrooms and diced onion. Cook for 5 minutes, or until the mushrooms and onions begin to soften and brown.

Add the crushed garlic and thyme leaves to the mushrooms and onion and fry for a further 1–2 minutes. Once the garlic and thyme have cooked, add the chicken back to the pan along with the mustard, cream and 150ml water. Stir to combine all the ingredients into a creamy sauce. Allow to reduce for 1 minute, then add half of the grated Parmesan cheese.

Cook the tagliatelle in a large saucepan of boiling water according to the packet instructions, until al dente. Reserve a cup of the cooking water and add the cooked pasta directly into the sauce. Toss through. If the sauce is too thick, let it down with a little of the reserved cooking water. Add the remaining Parmesan cheese, then give the pasta and sauce a good toss through until the pasta is well coated in the creamy sauce.

Serve topped with extra thyme leaves and a final grating of Parmesan, if desired. The pasta will keep in the fridge for up to 3 days. To reheat, place the pasta in a large pan and add a splash of water. Reheat gently over a medium heat until piping hot.

FREEZE ME

BATCH COOK

DAIRY FREE

GLUTEN FREE

USE GF SOY SAUCE

HIGH PROTEIN

THAI-STYLE CHICKEN MEATBALLS

15 MINS 30 MINS SERVES 4

PER SERVING:
306 KCAL /14G CARBS

SPECIAL EQUIPMENT
Large, deep frying pan with lid, about 28cm (11in)

FOR THE MEATBALLS:
500g minced chicken
2 garlic cloves, peeled and crushed
2cm (¾in) piece of root ginger, peeled and finely grated
2 spring onions, trimmed and finely sliced
finely grated zest of 1 lime
large handful of coriander, finely chopped, plus coriander leaves, to garnish
salt and freshly ground black pepper, to taste
low-calorie cooking spray

FOR THE MASSAMAN SAUCE
4 spring onions, trimmed and finely sliced
1 red pepper, halved, deseeded and sliced
2 garlic cloves, peeled and crushed
1 x 185g jar Massaman curry paste
1 x 400g tin light coconut milk
1 tbsp soy sauce
100g green beans, trimmed
juice of 1 lime
1 tbsp sriracha sauce

TO ACCOMPANY
50g nest of egg noodles (+173 kcal per serving) or 125g cooked basmati rice (+169 kcal per serving)

Fancy a tasty midweek hero that's full of punchy Thai-inspired flavours? Then this recipe's for you! These meatballs come together in minutes, once simmered in a creamy, lightly spiced Massaman sauce. They're mild, warming and full of fragrant lime, garlic and coconut notes. Serve with noodles or rice, and you've got a cosy fakeaway-style dinner that's perfect for busy weeknights or batch cooking for later.

Weekly Indulgence

To make the meatballs, place the minced chicken, garlic, ginger, spring onions, lime zest, coriander and a good pinch of salt and pepper in a large bowl and mix well. Use wet hands to roll the mix into twelve even-sized meatballs. The chicken mince can be quite sticky; using wet hands will prevent the meatballs from sticking to your hands and will produce a neater shape.

Spray a non-stick frying pan with low-calorie cooking spray and place it over a medium heat. Add the meatballs to the pan and brown on all sides, using tongs to turn carefully. Be gentle, to avoid breaking up the meatballs. When browned, remove from the pan and set aside.

To make the sauce, add the spring onions (reserve a few for the garnish, if you like), red pepper and garlic to the frying pan and sauté for 5 minutes. Stir in the curry paste, coconut milk and soy sauce. Add the meatballs back to the pan, bring to a simmer and cover with a lid. Cook for 5 minutes.

Add the green beans and cook for a further 5–10 minutes until the meatballs are cooked through and the beans are tender but still with a bite. Stir in the lime juice and sriracha, then taste and season with salt and pepper. Garnish with the reserved spring onions, if you wish, and a few coriander leaves, and serve. You can freeze the dish by cooling it quickly, then freezing it in individual portions for up to 3 months (see Tip).

The meatballs will keep in the fridge for up to 3 days. Reheat the meatballs in the microwave for 4–5 minutes, stirring halfway through.

TIPS

You can substitute the minced chicken with minced turkey.

If you've frozen the dish, once defrosted, reheat in the microwave for 4–5 minutes, stirring halfway through.

The Massaman sauce isn't just for meatballs. It can be used as a base for a more traditional Massaman curry. Why not double up and make a batch to freeze for days when you don't want to do much cooking, and freeze in an airtight container. You can then defrost overnight and reheat on the stove with some cooked chicken and diced new potatoes. The sauce can be stored in the freezer for up to 3 months. It will also keep for 3 days in the fridge.

VEGAN

USE MAPLE SYRUP INSTEAD OF HONEY

VEGGIE

BATCH COOK

DAIRY FREE

GLUTEN FREE

USE GF SOY SAUCE

HIGH PROTEIN

STICKY GARLIC *and* CHILLI TOFU

10 MINS 15 MINS SERVES 4

PER SERVING:
270 KCAL /21G CARBS

400g firm tofu, cut into 1cm (½in) cubes
4 tbsp cornflour
1 tbsp garlic powder
½ tbsp chilli powder
3 tbsp reduced-salt soy sauce
2 tsp rice vinegar
salt and freshly ground black pepper, to taste
1 tsp chilli flakes
2 tbsp honey
2 tsp sriracha sauce
3 garlic cloves, peeled and crushed
low-calorie cooking spray
6 spring onions, trimmed and chopped
1 red pepper, halved, deseeded and sliced
1 tbsp sesame seeds

TO ACCOMPANY
50g cooked basmati rice (+173 kcal per serving)

This Sticky Garlic and Chilli Tofu is another tasty fakeaway you can whip up at home without any faff. We've smothered crispy tofu, crunchy red pepper and slightly sweet spring onions in a sticky, spicy sauce that's seriously moreish... if we do say so ourselves! The tofu gets crispy on the outside and stays soft inside, with the veg adding just the right amount of bite.

Weekly Indulgence

Place the tofu in an airtight container and add the cornflour, garlic powder and chilli. Place the lid on top and shake well to ensure the tofu is well coated.

Place the soy sauce in a small bowl with the rice vinegar, salt and pepper to taste, chilli flakes, honey, sriracha and crushed garlic and mix well.

Spray a frying pan with low-calorie cooking spray and place over a medium heat. Place the tofu in the pan and cook for 5–10 minutes until crisp and golden. Remove the tofu from the pan and set aside.

Spray the same pan with more low-calorie cooking spray and place back over a medium heat. Reserve a few of the chopped green spring onion tops for serving, then add the rest of the spring onions and sliced red peppers to the pan and cook for 3–4 minutes until slightly softened. Add the cooked tofu and garlic and chilli sauce and toss the sauce through the tofu, peppers and spring onion to ensure everything is well coated.

Serve the tofu on top of basmati rice and finish with the remaining spring onion tops and sesame seeds.

VEGAN
USE DF FETA AND MAPLE SYRUP INSTEAD OF HONEY IN DRESSING

VEGGIE

BATCH COOK

DAIRY FREE
USE DF FETA

GLUTEN FREE

HIGH PROTEIN

ROASTED BEETROOT, LENTIL *and* FETA SALAD WITH CREAMY BALSAMIC VINAIGRETTE

15 MINS + 10 MINS COOLING | **50 MINS** | **SERVES 4**

PER SERVING:
493 KCAL /39G CARBS

SPECIAL EQUIPMENT
Food processor

600g raw beetroot, leaves and root trimmed
low-calorie cooking spray
500g cooked puy lentils
35g walnuts, chopped
60g rocket leaves
60g reduced-fat feta cheese

FOR THE CREAMY BALSAMIC VINAIGRETTE
50ml balsamic vinegar
½ garlic clove, peeled and crushed
½ tbsp honey
juice of ½ lemon
½ tsp Dijon mustard
60ml olive oil
salt and freshly ground black pepper, to taste

Now this is a salad that's anything but ordinary! We've combined earthy roasted beetroot, juicy puy lentils and crunchy walnuts for a satisfying mix of textures and flavours. Every bite is a delicious balance of sweet, savoury, nutty goodness. Prep ahead as a light lunch, side dish, part of your buffet spread, or make it a midweek meal with some sweet potato fries!

Weekly Indulgence

Preheat the oven to 220°C (fan 200°C/gas mark 7) .

Spray the beetroot with low-calorie cooking spray and wrap individually in foil. Place on a baking tray and roast in the oven for 40–50 minutes until a knife easily pierces the cooked beetroot. Remove the beetroot from the oven and leave to cool for at least 10 minutes.

Meanwhile, put all the ingredients for the balsamic vinaigrette into a food processor and blitz for 20 seconds, or until you get a rich, creamy vinaigrette. Season to taste with salt and black pepper. At this point, the dressing can be poured into an airtight jar and stored in the fridge for up to a week.

Once the roasted beets have cooled in their foils, unwrap them, gently peel away the skin on the outside and discard it. Slice one of the beetroot into wedges and chop the rest into 1cm (½in) cubes. Put the cooked lentils into a large bowl and add the chopped walnuts, rocket and beetroot cubes. Crumble in 40g of the feta cheese and stir well. Add three-quarters of the balsamic vinaigrette to the lentils and stir through to ensure all the ingredients are well coated.

Serve the lentils topped with the sliced beetroot, the remaining feta cheese crumbled over the top and a drizzle of the vinaigrette.

The the salad will keep in the fridge for up to 3 days. The vinaigrette will keep in the fridge for up to a week. The salad is best eaten at room temperature after refrigeration.

TIPS

Use rubber gloves when peeling the beetroot to prevent staining.

You can cook the beetroot in the air fryer if you prefer. Air-fry at 180°C for 35–40 minutes.

If necessary, use dried lentils, cooking according to packet instructions.

VEGGIE

USE VEGETARIAN ITALIAN HARD CHEESE

FREEZE ME

BATCH COOK

GLUTEN FREE

USE GF FLOUR

HIGH PROTEIN

HERBY COURGETTE FRITTERS *and* TZATZIKI

15 MINS | 25 MINS | SERVES 4

PER SERVING:
352 KCAL / 33G CARBS

- 800g courgettes, grated
- salt and freshly ground black pepper, to taste
- 20g fresh mint, finely chopped
- 20g fresh parsley, finely chopped
- 4 spring onions, trimmed and finely chopped
- 4 garlic cloves, peeled and crushed
- 4 eggs, beaten
- 60g Italian hard cheese, grated
- 120g plain flour
- low-calorie cooking spray
- 400g fat-free Greek yoghurt
- finely grated zest and juice of 1 lemon
- 240g cucumber, grated

Crispy, herby and seriously moreish, these Courgette Fritters are the kind of tasty bites that make you look forward to getting your veggies in. Each one is golden-fried and then oven-baked to perfection, packed with flavour and tastes even better dunked into our cool, garlicky, slimming-friendly tzatziki. They're quick to rustle up and light enough to tuck into any time of day. Make them for a speedy lunch, fun side, or a cheeky snack when you're feeling peckish.

Everyday Light

Preheat the oven to 200°C (fan 180°C/gas mark 6) and line a large baking tray with non-stick baking paper.

Place the grated courgette in a large bowl with a large pinch of salt. Stir through and leave to stand for 10 minutes.

Put the grated courgette into a clean kitchen towel. Gather the ends of the towel together and twist until you have squeezed all the excess water out of the courgette. Place the courgette back in a clean bowl. Set half of the chopped herbs aside and add the remaining mint and parsley to the bowl along with the spring onions, 1 crushed garlic clove, eggs, grated cheese and flour. Use a spoon to combine the mixture thoroughly.

Spray a frying pan with low-calorie cooking spray and place over a medium heat. Place 3 or 4 heaped tablespoonfuls of the fritter mixture in the pan and cook for a few minutes until golden and crisp. Flip the fritters over and cook again on the other side for a few more minutes.

Once the fritters are golden, remove from the pan and place on the lined baking tray. Continue to cook the rest of the fritters in the same way until you have used all the mixture and all the fritters are on the baking tray.

Place the fritters in the oven for 10–15 minutes until cooked through. If you want to freeze them at this point, allow to cool when cooked and freeze on a tray for 2 hours until solid. Remove the fritters from the tray and place in a freezerproof bag. Store for up to 3 months in the freezer (see Tips).

TIPS

This recipe serves four people. The fritter mix should make twelve good-sized fritters.

The fritters can be finished off in the air fryer instead of the oven if preferred. Air-fry at 160°C for 10 minutes.

If you've frozen fritters, once defrosted, reheat in a frying pan sprayed with low-calorie cooking spray for 5–10 minutes until hot in the middle and crisp on the outside.

Add the yoghurt, lemon juice, zest and the remaining garlic, mint and parsley along with a pinch of salt and pepper to a large bowl and stir to combine.

Using a clean kitchen towel, remove the water from the grated cucumber and add the cucumber to the yoghurt. Mix well.

To serve, add a generous spoonful of tzatziki to a serving plate and top with three crisp fritters. The fritters and tzatziki will keep in the fridge for up to 3 days. Reheat the fritters in a frying pan sprayed with low-calorie cooking spray for 5–10 minutes until hot in the middle and crisp on the outside.

VEGAN

USE VEGAN PARMESAN CHEESE IN PESTO AND VEGAN FETA

VEGGIE

USE VEGETARIAN HARD CHEESE IN PESTO

BATCH COOK

DAIRY FREE

USE DF PARMESAN CHEESE IN PESTO AND DF FETA

GLUTEN FREE

USE GF GNOCCHI

MEDITERRANEAN-STYLE GNOCCHI TRAYBAKE

10 MINS | VARIABLE | SERVES 4

PER SERVING:
471 KCAL / 60G CARBS

low-calorie cooking spray
750g gnocchi
½ red onion, peeled and cut into wedges
1 red pepper, halved, deseeded and cut into 2.5cm (1in) pieces
1 yellow pepper, halved, deseeded and cut into 2.5cm (1in) pieces
150g courgette, sliced into discs and cut in half
200g cherry tomatoes, halved
salt and freshly ground black pepper, to taste
15g fresh basil
10g pine nuts, toasted
50ml olive oil
10g Parmesan cheese, grated
finely grated zest and juice of 1 lemon
50g reduced-fat feta cheese

TIPS

Make sure to check that shop-bought gnocchi is dairy free if you are vegan, as some can contain egg or milk powder.

This recipe requires one and a half bags of gnocchi – any unused gnocchi can be frozen.

Maybe you don't need a holiday, maybe you just need this Med-style traybake in your life! All you need to do is toss your gnocchi and colourful veggies onto a baking tray and pop everything in the oven until it's golden and crisp. You'll have instant summer vibes, no matter what the weather's doing outside! Top with a sprinkle of feta and boom… you've got a healthy yet comforting dish that feels much fancier than the effort it took to make! Exactly how we like it.

Weekly Indulgence

OVEN METHOD
35 MINS

Preheat the oven to 200°C (fan 180°C/gas mark 6). Line a large baking tray with non-stick baking paper and spray with low-calorie cooking spray.

Place the gnocchi in a large bowl, spray with low-calorie cooking spray and set aside.

Place the chopped onions, peppers, courgette and tomatoes on the lined baking tray. Spray with more low-calorie cooking spray and season with salt and pepper. Roast in the oven for 20 minutes. After 20 minutes, empty the gnocchi onto the tray of roasted vegetables and toss to combine. Return to the oven for a further 10 minutes.

Meanwhile, make the pesto by placing the basil, toasted pine nuts, olive oil, Parmesan and the lemon zest and juice in a blender and blitzing until you achieve a thick green paste.

Remove the traybake from the oven and mix half of the pesto through the gnocchi and vegetables. Return the traybake to the oven and roast for a further 5 minutes. To finish the dish, dot the traybake with spoonfuls of the remaining pesto and crumble over the feta cheese.

The traybake will keep in an airtight container in the fridge for up to 3 days. To reheat, transfer to a baking tray and sprinkle with a little water. Reheat for 10 minutes, or until the food is piping hot.

AIR-FRYER METHOD
27 MINS

SPECIAL EQUIPMENT
Air fryer

Preheat the air fryer to 160°C.

Place the gnocchi in a large bowl, spray with low-calorie cooking spray and set aside.

Place the chopped onions, peppers, courgette and tomatoes in the air fryer basket. Spray with more low-calorie cooking spray and season with salt and pepper. Air-fry at 160°C (325°F) for 15 minutes.

After 15 minutes, empty the gnocchi into the air fryer with the roasted vegetables and toss to combine. Air-fry for a further 8 minutes.

Meanwhile, make the pesto by placing the basil, toasted pine nuts, olive oil, Parmesan and the finely grated lemon zest in a blender and blitzing until you achieve a thick green paste.

Mix half of the pesto through the gnocchi and vegetables, then place back in the air fryer for a further 3–4 minutes.

To finish the dish, dot the bake with spoonfuls of the remaining pesto and crumble over the feta cheese.

The traybake will keep in an airtight container in the fridge for up to 3 days. To reheat, place in the air fryer and sprinkle with a little water. Air-fry at 160°C for 5–8 minutes until the food is piping hot.

FREEZE ME

VEGAN

USE VEGAN CREAM, CRÈME FRAÎCHE AND CHEESE

VEGGIE

BATCH COOK

DAIRY FREE

USE DF CREAM, CRÈME FRAÎCHE AND CHEESE

GLUTEN FREE

ROOT VEGETABLE STACKS

15 MINS 1 HR MAKES 9

PER SERVING:
155 KCAL /19G CARBS

SPECIAL EQUIPMENT
12-hole muffin tray, mandoline slicer

low-calorie cooking spray
400g potatoes, peeled
300g sweet potatoes, peeled
300g beetroot, peeled
150g reduced-fat crème fraîche
150g reduced-fat single cream alternative
2 garlic cloves, peeled and crushed
salt and freshly ground black pepper, to taste
10g fresh thyme
50g Italian hard cheese, finely grated

Root veggies are always great to pop in your trolley because they're low in calories, high in antioxidants, and they're even better when you add our creamy, herby, saucy cheese topping. We've taken potato, sweet potato, and beetroot and coated it in a deliciously aromatic cream-based sauce, infused with garlic and thyme. The perfect earthy light bite or side for your roast dinner!

Everyday Light

Preheat the oven to 220°C (fan 200°C/gas mark 7) and spray a 12-hole muffin tin with low-calorie cooking spray. This recipe should make nine portions. Use a mandoline to slice the vegetables into fine discs. Place each vegetable in a separate dish and set aside.

Place the crème fraîche in a medium saucepan along with the cream, crushed garlic and salt and pepper to taste. Pick the leaves from half of the thyme and add to the cream mix. Place the saucepan over a medium heat and cook for 10 minutes, until the cream is lightly bubbling and the garlic and thyme have infused the sauce. Add half of the grated cheese to the sauce and mix well.

To assemble, pick up one or two slices of each vegetable and stack them in the prepared holes of the muffin tin. Do this 2–3 times until each muffin hole is half filled and repeat the process until you have nine stacks. Add 2 teaspoons of the creamy garlic and thyme sauce to each stack so it is well covered in the sauce. Using the remaining sliced vegetables, create more stacked vegetables and place on top of each sauce-covered stack so they sit about 1cm (½in) higher than the muffin tin. Cover each stack with another 2 teaspoons of sauce. Loosely cover the tray with foil and bake in the oven for 35–40 minutes, until the vegetables are cooked through.

Take the muffin tin out of the oven, remove the foil and cover each stack with the remaining sauce. Sprinkle each stack with the rest of the grated cheese and some more thyme leaves. Return the tin to the oven and bake for 10–15 minutes, until the stacks are golden and bubbling with cheese.

The stacks will keep in the fridge for up to 3 days. Cover with foil and reheat in the oven until piping hot.

TIPS

Try to pick out similar sized root vegetables so the slices stack well.

If you don't have a mandoline slicer, you can use the slicing function of a food processor or, alternatively, slice as thinly as possible by hand.

To reheat from frozen, allow to defrost, cover with foil and bake in a preheated oven at 220°C (fan 200°C/gas mark 7) for 10–15 minutes until piping hot. Remove the foil and bake uncovered for a further 5 minutes until golden on top. (These might be slightly drier than when initially cooked, as the sauce will have absorbed.)

FREEZE ME

BATCH COOK

DAIRY FREE

USE DF CHEESE

GLUTEN FREE

USE GF WRAPS

PLOUGHMAN'S SAUSAGE ROLLS

15 MINS | 30 MINS | SERVES 8

PER SERVING:
179 KCAL /19G CARBS

- low-calorie cooking spray
- 300g 5% fat minced pork
- 1 tsp dried sage
- 1 tsp garlic granules
- 1 tsp onion granules
- salt and freshly ground black pepper, to taste
- 4 wheat and white tortilla wraps, approx. 60g per wrap
- 80g small-chunk pickle
- 40g reduced-fat Cheddar cheese, finely grated
- 1 medium egg, beaten

These sausage rolls are packed with everything we love about a Ploughman's lunch! Tangy pickle, melty cheese and herby pork, all wrapped in a soft tortilla. Oven-baked until golden, they're perfect warm or cold, and they freeze beautifully too. Ideal for lunchboxes, snacks or picnics!

Everyday Light

Preheat the oven to 210°C (fan 190°C/gas mark 6) and spray a large baking tray with some low-calorie cooking spray.

Place the minced pork in a large bowl and add the sage, garlic and onion granules. Season to taste with salt and pepper and mix well.

Divide the mixture into four equal portions, then shape into four sausage shapes approximately 20cm (8in) long and arrange on the lined baking tray. Cook in the oven for 15 minutes.

Remove them from the oven and leave until they are cool enough to handle. (Leave the oven on as you'll be using it again in a moment.)

Lay the wraps flat on the work surface. Spread the pickle onto the lower half of each wrap and sprinkle over the cheese.

Place a sausage close to the edge of the first wrap on top of the pickle and cheese and roll tightly. Brush a little beaten egg onto the last section of the wrap and place seam side down on the work surface while you repeat with the remaining wraps.

Cut the wraps in half. You can cut the ends off the wrap just to tidy them up a little if you wish. Arrange the sausage rolls on the baking tray and brush each one with the remaining egg. Bake in the oven for a further 10 minutes, or until they are golden brown and crisp. At this stage, you can freeze them in an airtight container for up to 3 months (see Tip).

The sausage rolls will keep in the fridge for up to 3 days.

TIP

If you've frozen the sausage rolls, once defrosted, they are best reheated in an oven preheated to 180°C (fan 160°C/gas mark 4) for 5–10 minutes until piping hot throughout, so they keep that crispy 'pastry' shell.

VEGGIE

FREEZE ME

BATCH COOK

DAIRY FREE

USE DF YOGHURT AND CHOCOLATE

GLUTEN FREE

CHOCOLATE ORANGE MOUSSE

15 MINS + 3 HRS OR OVERNIGHT CHILLING **NO COOK** **SERVES 4**

PER SERVING:
274 KCAL /20G CARBS

SPECIAL EQUIPMENT
Fine grater or microplane, stand mixer with whisk attachment (optional), 4 x 350ml mason jars or containers

150g 70% dark chocolate, broken into small pieces
finely grated zest and juice of 1 orange
150g fat-free Greek yoghurt
1 tsp vanilla extract
pinch of salt
3 egg whites
1 tbsp caster sugar

Looking for an easy chocolate fix? This rich yet airy mousse blends zesty orange with velvety dark chocolate and creamy Greek yoghurt for a lightened-up take on a classic dessert. With no baking needed, it's the perfect make-ahead pudding to keep in the fridge for when your sweet tooth strikes.

Everyday Light

Place the chocolate pieces in a heatproof glass bowl. Pour around 500ml water into a saucepan and place over a medium heat. Bring the water to the boil, then lower the heat so it is simmering. Sit the bowl with the chocolate over the simmering water, making sure the base of the bowl doesn't touch the simmering water, and stir until the chocolate has melted and is glossy and smooth.

Once the chocolate has melted, remove from the heat, add the orange zest and stir well. Make sure the zest of the orange is fine so as not to change the texture of the mousse too much. Set aside.

In a large bowl, add the Greek yoghurt, vanilla extract, salt and orange juice. Stir well to combine and set aside. Place the egg whites and caster sugar in the bowl of a stand mixer. If you don't have a stand mixer, use an electric whisk if possible or whisk by hand. Whisk the egg whites for a minute or two until they have reached stiff peaks. Slowly pour the yoghurt mix into the melted chocolate and stir until you get a creamy chocolate mixture.

Take one spoonful of the whisked egg white and beat into the creamy chocolate. This will help to loosen the mix and make it easier to incorporate the rest of the egg whites. Take another spoonful of egg white and gently fold into the mixture, trying not to lose too much air. Repeat this until all the egg white has been used and you have a light and airy chocolate mixture.

Spoon the mousse equally into four glasses or jars. Cover with cling film or a lid and leave to set in the fridge for at least 3 hours, or preferably overnight. The mousse will keep in the fridge for 2–3 days. You can also freeze the chocolate mousse.

Once set, remove from the fridge and serve straight from the glasses. If frozen, defrost thoroughly before eating. Note that the texture of the mousse may change after freezing.

VEGAN
USE VEGAN SPONGE FINGERS, CUSTARD AND YOGHURT

VEGGIE

BATCH COOK

DAIRY FREE
USE DF CUSTARD AND YOGHURT

GLUTEN FREE
USE GF SPONGE FINGERS

MOJITO TRIFLE

15 MINS + 2 HRS OR OVERNIGHT SETTING | **2 MINS** | **SERVES 6**

PER SERVING:
136 KCAL /15G CARBS

SPECIAL EQUIPMENT
6 small serving dishes (approx. 250ml glass or container)

FOR THE JELLY LAYER
3 strawberries, sliced
12 raspberries
24 blueberries
30ml white rum
5 sprigs of mint
finely grated zest and juice of 2 limes
6 sponge fingers, halved
1 tbsp white granulated sweetener
1 x 330ml can zero sugar lemon and limeade
1 x 6.5g sachet vegetarian gelatine

TO SERVE
200g fat-free Greek yoghurt
250g reduced-fat custard
1 tbsp white rum
reduced-fat aerosol cream
2 limes, sliced
6 raspberries
fresh mint leaves, to decorate (optional)

We've given a classic British dessert a zingy mojito makeover! These fun, fruity trifles are layered with lime and mint-infused jelly, a boozy hit of rum-soaked berries and a creamy yoghurt custard topping that feels extra indulgent. Topped with reduced-fat aerosol cream and a sprig of mint, they're light, refreshing and perfect for impressing family and friends at your next summer gathering. Just don't forget the spoons!

Everyday Light

For the jelly, add the strawberries, raspberries and blueberries to a large bowl and add the white rum. Stir to combine and leave to soak for 30 minutes to 1 hour.

Meanwhile, bring 150ml water, the mint and lime zest to the boil in a large saucepan over a high heat, then reduce to a simmer for 3–4 minutes to allow the mint and lime flavour to infuse. Strain the liquid into a jug to remove the mint and lime zest and leave to cool completely.

Place two sponge finger halves in the base of each serving dish and divide the soaked strawberries, raspberries and blueberries between the dishes. Set aside. Reserve the soaking rum for later.

Add the sweetener and half of the lime juice to the cooled mint and lime water and stir to dissolve. Pour in the lemon and limeade until you get 568ml of liquid and mix well. If you don't have 568ml of liquid, top up with cold water.

Pour the cooled liquid into a medium saucepan, add the powdered vegetarian gelatine and whisk to dissolve. Bring the mixture to boiling point over a medium-high heat, then pour the gelatine mix into a large measuring jug. Pour the jelly mixture equally over the prepared fruit in the serving dishes, then place in the fridge until set.

In a large bowl, combine the yoghurt, custard and the remaining lime juice. Add the rum and any rum reserved from soaking the fruit and mix with a balloon whisk until smooth. Once the jelly is set, divide the yoghurt and custard mixture between the glasses. Top with a swirl of aerosol cream, a lime slice, raspberries and mint. If you wish to store the jellies for a few days in the fridge, cover them (without toppings) with cling film. Add toppings when ready to serve.

TIP

If you are vegan or dairy free, omit the whipped cream.

BATCH COOK

VEGGIE
USE VEGGIE SAUSAGES

FREEZE ME

BATCH COOK

DAIRY FREE
USE DF CHEESE

GLUTEN FREE

HIGH PROTEIN

LOW CARB

SAUSAGE *and* EGG BREAKFAST SLICE

10 MINS **35 MINS** **SERVES 8**

PER SERVING:
239 KCAL / 6.1G CARBS

low-calorie cooking spray
6 reduced-fat sausages, approx. 55g per sausage
1 red onion, peeled and sliced
1 pepper, halved, deseeded and sliced (any colour)
150g cherry tomatoes, halved
1 tsp garlic granules
1 tsp onion granules
1 tsp dried mixed herbs
12 medium eggs
salt and freshly ground black pepper, to taste
50g spinach, tough stalks removed and leaves roughly chopped
40g reduced-fat Cheddar cheese, finely grated

Drive-thru who? Keep mornings simple and satisfying without the extra calories with this Sausage and Egg Breakfast Slice. Packed with protein and baked all together in one tray, it's easy to make and there's hardly any washing up to worry about, which is always a win! This recipe's super flexible too, as you can swap the sausages for a plant-based version to make things veggie-friendly without losing any flavour.

Everyday Light

Preheat the oven to 220°C (fan 200°C/gas mark 7) and spray a baking tray with low-calorie cooking spray.

Slice each sausage into six pieces and arrange on the oiled baking tray with the onion, pepper and tomatoes. Sprinkle over the garlic granules, onion granules and mixed herbs and toss to coat. Bake in the oven for 20 minutes.

Add the eggs to a large jug or bowl and beat until combined.

Season to taste with salt and pepper. Add the spinach, then pour the egg mixture into the tray and mix lightly. Roughly flatten, sprinkle over the grated cheese and return to the oven for a final 15–20 minutes. Slice into eight slices and serve. You can freeze the slices by leaving them to cool, then wrapping them in individual portions and freezing in an airtight container for up to 3 months. Reheat in the microwave until piping hot.

The cooled slices will keep in the fridge for up to 4 days.

FREEZE ME

PANCAKES ONLY

VEGGIE

BATCH COOK

GLUTEN FREE

USE GF BAKING POWDER

BANANA BUCKWHEAT PANCAKES

10 MINS 15 MINS SERVES 5

PER SERVING:
295 KCAL /52G CARBS

SPECIAL EQUIPMENT
Food processor or blender

200g buckwheat
1 tsp baking powder
2 tbsp low-calorie sweetener
1 tsp ground cinnamon
300g fat-free Greek yoghurt
1 tsp vanilla extract
200ml oat milk
2 medium eggs, beaten
3 medium bananas
low-calorie cooking spray
1 tbsp honey

TIPS

This recipe makes ten good-sized pancakes, but you can stretch the batter further if you make smaller ones.

Buckwheat flour can be bought in stores as an alternative to making it in the blender.

We used oat milk, but you can use any type of milk to make this recipe, although it will adjust the calories.

If you've frozen the pancakes, defrost them fully, then reheat in a frying pan over a medium heat until warmed through. Alternatively, pop them in the toaster for a few minutes to crisp up.

Getting out of bed is always easier when you know there's something delicious waiting for you downstairs. Made from nutty buckwheat flour, these pancakes are light and fluffy, and unbelievably naturally gluten-free (just make sure your baking powder is). Mix the batter the night before, pop it in the fridge, then pour it into your pan and stack 'em high!

Everyday Light

Make the buckwheat flour by adding the raw buckwheat to a food processor or blender and blitzing for 10–15 seconds until a flour consistency is achieved.

Place the flour in a large bowl and add the baking powder, sweetener and cinnamon. Stir to combine.

In another bowl, add 100g of the yoghurt, the vanilla extract, oat milk and beaten eggs and mix well to combine.

Peel two of the bananas and mash roughly in a bowl with a fork. Add this to the yoghurt mixture, then using a whisk, slowly add the wet mixture to the dry mixture to make a light and fluffy batter.

Spray a large frying pan with low-calorie cooking spray and place over a medium heat. Add ½ ladleful of the batter to the pan per pancake and cook for 2–3 minutes on one side. You can cook 2–3 pancakes at a time, depending on the size of your pan. When bubbles begin to appear on the top of the batter, the pancakes are ready to flip. Turn the pancakes over and cook for a further 1–2 minutes until fluffy and cooked through. Remove from the pan and put them on a plate and repeat this process with the rest of the batter.

You can freeze the pancakes at this stage (see Tips).

In a separate bowl, combine the remaining 200g yoghurt with the honey. Finely slice the remaining banana.

Serve two warm pancakes per person and top with a spoonful of yoghurt and some sliced banana. The pancakes will keep in the fridge for up to 3 days.

VEGAN

VEGGIE

FREEZE ME

SAUCE AND RICE SEPARATELY

BATCH COOK

DAIRY FREE

GLUTEN FREE

USE GF STOCK POTS

KORMA-STYLE CAULIFLOWER *with* CORIANDER RICE

20 MINS   40 MINS   SERVES 4

PER SERVING:
487 KCAL /69G CARBS

SPECIAL EQUIPMENT
Large, deep, non-stick deep frying pan (about 28cm/11in) or large, shallow casserole dish with a tight-fitting lid, suitable for oven and hob, food processor or blender

FOR THE CAULIFLOWER KORMA

1 onion, peeled and roughly diced
6 garlic cloves, peeled
5cm (2in) piece of fresh root ginger, peeled and roughly chopped
low-calorie cooking spray
½ tsp ground cinnamon
½ tsp ground turmeric
½ tbsp garam masala
½ tbsp ground coriander
½ tbsp ground cumin
1 x 400g tin chopped tomatoes
1 x 400g tin light coconut milk
1 vegetable stock pot
2 tbsp ground almonds
1 large cauliflower, trimmed and cut into bite-sized florets
salt and freshly ground black pepper, to taste
juice of ½ lemon
1 tbsp mango chutney
1 x 400g tin chickpeas, rinsed and drained

This creamy, crowd-pleasing curry delivers all the richness of a classic korma, without the heavy ingredients. Roasting the cauliflower brings out its natural nuttiness, while the chickpeas add texture. Finished with a blend of coconut, spices, mango chutney and lemon, it's packed with depth and just the right amount of warmth. Served with coriander rice, this one's a fragrant, flavour-filled dish you'll want to make again and again!

Weekly Indulgence

Preheat the oven to 200°C (fan 180°C/gas mark 6).

To make the korma, place the onion, garlic and ginger in a food processor and blitz to a paste.

Spray the frying pan or casserole dish with low-calorie cooking spray and place over a low-medium heat. Add the paste and gently fry for 10–15 minutes without colouring. Add all the spices and cook for a further minute until fragrant.

Add the chopped tomatoes, coconut milk and stock pot to the pan, turn the heat up to medium and stir until the sauce is bubbling. Stir the ground almonds through and turn the heat down to a gentle simmer. Cover with a lid and cook for 20 minutes, stirring occasionally.

Meanwhile, cook the cauliflower. Scatter the florets onto a baking tray and spray with low-calorie cooking spray. Season with salt and pepper and roast in the oven for 20 minutes. The cauliflower should be golden and lightly crisp around the edges.

While the cauliflower roasts, cook the coriander rice. Rinse the rice under running cold water and drain well.

Spray a large saucepan with low-calorie cooking spray and place over a medium heat. Add the garlic and cook for 30 seconds, then add the rice and cook for 2–3 minutes. Pour in 400ml water, then add the salt and bring to the boil. Turn the heat down to a simmer and cover with a lid. Cook for 10 minutes, then remove from the heat. Let the pan stand for 5 minutes, then

FOR THE CORIANDER RICE

200g basmati rice
low-calorie cooking spray
1 garlic clove, peeled and crushed
good pinch of salt
juice of ½ lemon
large handful of fresh coriander, chopped

uncover. All the liquid should be absorbed. Fluff the rice up with a fork, then stir through the lemon juice and coriander.

When the korma sauce has bubbled away for 20 minutes, uncover and add the lemon juice and mango chutney. Stir through the chickpeas and the roasted cauliflower and cook for a further 5 minutes, or until the chickpeas are heated through. Season to taste with salt and pepper and serve with the coriander rice.

The korma will keep in the fridge for up to 3 days. Cool the rice as soon as possible after cooking and refrigerate immediately for 1 day. Reheat the korma in the microwave for 3–4 minutes, stirring halfway through. Reheat the rice for 1 minute 30 seconds, or until piping hot throughout. You can also freeze the korma and rice separately (see Tips).

TIPS

You can swap the stock pot for a stock cube. No need to dissolve in water, just crumble it straight in the pan.

If you've frozen the korma and rice, once defrosted, reheat the korma in the microwave for 3–4 minutes, stirring halfway through. Reheat the rice for 1 minute 30 seconds, or until piping hot throughout.

The korma sauce works well with most proteins. Why not make a batch to freeze for days when you don't want to do much cooking. Freeze in an airtight container before adding the cauliflower. You can then defrost overnight and simply reheat and add some ready cooked chicken or tofu. The sauce can be stored in the freezer for up to 3 months. It will also keep for 3 days in the fridge.

FREEZE ME

BATCH COOK

GLUTEN FREE

USE GF STOCK

HIGH PROTEIN

SPICY CHICKEN CHOWDER

20 MINS 50 MINS SERVES 6

PER SERVING:
208 KCAL /16G CARBS

SPECIAL EQUIPMENT
Stick blender (optional)

- low-calorie cooking spray
- 2 skinless chicken breasts, about 150g each
- 1 onion, peeled and diced
- 2 carrots, peeled and cut into 1cm (½in) dice
- 3 garlic cloves, peeled and crushed
- 1 litre chicken stock (1 chicken stock cube dissolved in 1 litre boiling water)
- ½ tsp dried dill
- 1–2 tbsp hot sauce, depending on taste (we used Frank's RedHot Buffalo Wings)
- 300g potatoes, peeled and cut into 1cm (½in) dice
- 100g sweetcorn, frozen or tinned
- 75g reduced-fat cream cheese
- 75g blue Stilton, crumbled (or swap for reduced-fat Cheddar cheese, grated)
- freshly ground black pepper, to taste
- 2 spring onions, trimmed and sliced (optional)

TO ACCOMPANY (OPTIONAL)
60g wholemeal bread roll (+146 kcal per serving)

TIP

If you've frozen the soup, once defrosted, reheat in the microwave for 3–5 minutes, stirring halfway through, until piping hot.

If you're craving a warming bowlful with a bit of a kick, this is going to hit the spot. It's creamy and comforting, with a chunky base of potatoes and sweetcorn. We've given chowder a bold buffalo-style twist using garlic, hot sauce and a hint of blue cheese (swap for Cheddar if you prefer). Instead of double cream, we've opted for reduced-fat cream cheese to keep things lighter without losing that lush texture. Seriously satisfying, this is one soup you'll want on repeat.

Everyday Light

Spray a large saucepan with low-calorie cooking spray and place over a medium-high heat. When the pan is hot, add the chicken breasts and cook for a minute on each side, until sealed. Remove from the pan and set aside.

Return the pan to the heat and add the onion and carrots. Fry for 5 minutes, or until the onion is soft. Add the garlic and cook for a further minute. Add the chicken stock, dill, hot sauce, potatoes and sweetcorn and bring to the boil. Turn the heat down to a simmer and return the chicken to the pan. Cover with a lid and cook for 40 minutes, or until the chicken is cooked through and the potatoes and carrots are tender.

Use a slotted spoon to remove the chicken breasts from the pan and use two forks to pull the meat into shreds. Set aside.

Stir the cream cheese and the Stilton (or Cheddar) into the pan, until it is all melted and well combined. If you want a thicker soup, take two or three ladlefuls into a jug and blitz with a stick blender.

Return to the pan along with the shredded chicken. Season with black pepper and sprinkle with sliced spring onions before serving with bread rolls, if you wish. You can freeze the soup in individual portions in airtight containers for up to 3 months (see Tips).

The soup will keep in the fridge for up to 3 days. Reheat in the microwave for 3–5 minutes, stirring halfway through, until piping hot.

FREEZE ME

BATCH COOK

GLUTEN FREE

USE GF STOCK CUBES

HIGH PROTEIN

GREEK-STYLE SHEPHERD'S PIE *with* FETA MASH

15 MINS | 1 HR 35 MINS | SERVES 4

PER SERVING:
484 KCAL /48G CARBS

SPECIAL EQUIPMENT
Ovenproof dish, about 28 x 24cm (11 x 9½in)

- low-calorie cooking spray
- 1 onion, peeled and diced
- 2 carrots, peeled and sliced
- 400g lean diced lamb
- 2 garlic cloves, peeled and crushed
- 1 tsp dried oregano
- 1 x 400g tin chopped tomatoes
- 450ml stock (1 lamb or chicken stock cube dissolved in 450ml boiling water)
- 1 red wine stock pot
- 2 cinnamon sticks
- 2 bay leaves
- 1 tbsp tomato puree
- 1 x 400g tin chickpeas, drained and rinsed

FOR THE FETA MASH

- 600g potatoes, peeled and cut into chunks
- salt and freshly ground black pepper, to taste
- 90g reduced-fat feta cheese
- 2 tbsp fat-free Greek yoghurt
- juice of ½ lemon

TO ACCOMPANY

- 80g steamed vegetables (+38 kcal per serving)

If you love a classic Shepherd's Pie but fancy mixing things up, this Greek-inspired version is a total game-changer. We've swapped the usual flavours for a herby lamb and chickpea filling, then topped everything off with a creamy mashed potato, made extra special with crumbled feta and a hint of lemon. It's that little bit different and perfect when you want classic comfort food with a twist!

Special Occasion

Spray a large saucepan with low-calorie cooking spray and place over a medium heat. Add the onion and carrots and sauté for 5 minutes, or until beginning to brown. Add the lamb and cook for a further 3 minutes to seal the meat.

Add the garlic and oregano and cook for another minute, then stir in the tomatoes, stock and red wine stock pot. Add the cinnamon sticks and bay leaves to the pan. Bring to the boil, then turn the heat down to a simmer. Cover with a lid and cook for 30 minutes.

After 30 minutes, stir in the tomato puree and chickpeas and cook for a further 30 minutes.

Meanwhile, place the potatoes in a large saucepan of cold salted water and bring to the boil. Cook for 15–20 minutes until soft. Drain the potatoes, then return to the pan with the feta, yoghurt and lemon juice and mash well. Season with salt and pepper.

Preheat the oven to 200°C (fan 180°C/gas mark 6).

When the lamb is cooked, remove the cinnamon sticks and bay leaves and discard. Pour the lamb mixture into the ovenproof dish and top with the lemon and feta mash. You can freeze the pie at this stage – it's easier to do so in individual servings. Assemble the pie in individual ovenproof dishes (foil trays are ideal) and freeze for up to 3 months (see Tip).

Bake the pie in the oven for 25 minutes, or until the top is browned. Serve with steamed vegetables. If there are any leftovers, cool as soon as possible after cooking, then divide into individual portions and freeze in airtight containers for up to 3 months.

TIPS

If you've frozen the pie, defrost each portion fully overnight in the fridge, then place the dishes on a baking tray and cook according to the recipe.

If you've frozen any leftovers, once defrosted, loosely cover and reheat in the microwave for 4–5 minutes until piping hot.

The pie can be prepped up to 3 days ahead and kept in the fridge. Assemble and cover, then follow the recipe instructions for cooking. You may need to cook the pie for an extra 10 minutes to ensure it is piping hot throughout.

VEGAN

VEGGIE

FREEZE ME

BATCH COOK

DAIRY FREE

GLUTEN FREE

USE GF STOCK CUBES

ROASTED CAULIFLOWER *and* SESAME SOUP

10 MINS | 45 MINS | SERVES 4

PER SERVING:
190 KCAL / 14G CARBS

SPECIAL EQUIPMENT
Stick blender

600g frozen cauliflower
2 tsp sesame oil
1 onion, peeled and chopped
1 carrot, peeled and diced
4 garlic cloves, peeled and crushed
5cm (2in) piece of fresh root ginger, peeled and grated
400ml plant-based coconut drink
800ml vegetable stock (1 vegetable stock cube dissolved in 800ml boiling water)
1 tbsp miso paste
2 tbsp tahini paste
juice of ½ lime
salt and freshly ground black pepper, to taste

TO ACCOMPANY (OPTIONAL)
60g wholemeal bread roll (+146 kcal per serving)

TIPS

You can swap plant-based coconut drink for 200ml of tinned coconut milk and 200ml of water. Alternatively, use any other plant-based milk, such as almond.

If you've frozen the soup, once defrosted, reheat in the microwave for 3–4 minutes, stirring halfway through, until piping hot.

This velvety soup is smooth, satisfying and packed with nutty, savoury flavours. We've roasted cauliflower until tender, then blended it with a creamy coconut drink, miso and a swirl of tahini for extra depth. It's a rich, plant-based bowlful that's easy to batch-cook, simple to freeze and deliciously cosy on chilly days! Make sure to cook the cauliflower from frozen. If you let it defrost it can become watery and soggy and you won't get the charred edges.

Everyday Light

Preheat the oven to 200°C (fan180°C/gas mark 6). Scatter the frozen cauliflower florets over a baking tray, drizzle with 1 teaspoon of the sesame oil and roast in the oven for 15 minutes. Toss around and return to the oven for a further 15 minutes, or until the cauliflower is soft and lightly golden.

Meanwhile, place a large saucepan over a low-medium heat. Add the remaining teaspoon of sesame oil, then add the onion and carrot and sauté for 10 minutes, or until the onion is soft and golden. Add the garlic and ginger and cook for a further 1–2 minutes. Add the coconut drink and stock and bring to the boil. Stir in the roasted cauliflower, then turn the heat down to a simmer. Cover with a lid and simmer for 15 minutes, or until all the vegetables are soft. Stir in the miso paste, tahini and lime juice.

Remove the pan from the heat and use a stick blender to blitz into a smooth soup. Taste and season with salt and pepper, if needed. Serve with bread rolls, if you wish. You can freeze the soup in individual portions at this stage for up to 3 months (see Tips).

The soup will keep in the fridge for 3–4 days. Reheat in the microwave for 3–4 minutes, stirring halfway through, until hot.

FREEZE ME

BATCH COOK

DAIRY FREE

USE DF CREAM CHEESE AND CHEDDAR

GLUTEN FREE

USE GF STOCK CUBE AND BREADCRUMBS

HIGH PROTEIN

CHICKEN, BROCCOLI *and* MUSHROOM GRATIN

15 MINS | 45 MINS | SERVES 4

PER SERVING:
354 KCAL / 32G CARBS

SPECIAL EQUIPMENT
Large ovenproof dish, about 18 x 27cm (7 x 10½in)

500g potatoes, peeled and cut into 2cm (¾in) dice
100g broccoli, cut into florets
low-calorie cooking spray
1 onion, peeled and chopped
2 garlic cloves, peeled and crushed
200g white mushrooms, sliced
500g diced chicken breast
350ml chicken stock (1 chicken stock cube dissolved in 350ml boiling water)
1 tsp mustard powder
1 tsp dried thyme
1 tsp dried parsley
100g reduced-fat cream cheese
freshly ground black pepper, to taste

FOR THE TOP
15g panko breadcrumbs
20g reduced-fat mature Cheddar cheese, finely grated

This hearty gratin is proper midweek comfort food! Packed with juicy chicken, earthy mushrooms, tender broccoli and fluffy diced potatoes, everything comes together in a velvety, herby sauce, made silky smooth with a spoonful of reduced-fat cream cheese. Topped with a scattering of breadcrumbs and Cheddar, it's finished under the grill for a golden brown, bubbly finish that gets better with every bite.

Everyday Light

Place the potatoes in a medium saucepan and cover with cold water. Being careful not to overcook the potatoes, bring to the boil and cook for 3 minutes. Add the broccoli and cook for a further 3 minutes. The potatoes should be just cooked but still holding their shape, and the broccoli should still be crisp and green. Drain well and set aside.

Spray a large frying pan with low-calorie cooking spray and place over a medium heat. Add the onion and cook gently for 10 minutes, or until soft and golden. Add the garlic and mushrooms and cook for 5 minutes. Add the chicken and cook for 5 minutes, or until browned on all sides. Pour in the chicken stock and add the mustard powder, thyme and parsley. Stir, then cover and simmer for 10 minutes, or until the chicken is cooked through and shows no sign of pinkness.

Remove from the heat and stir in the cream cheese until completely blended. The sauce should be fairly runny at this stage as the potatoes will thicken it slightly. Add the cooked potatoes and broccoli and stir in. Season to taste with pepper.

Preheat the grill on a medium setting. Transfer the mixture into the ovenproof dish and spread it out evenly. Sprinkle the panko breadcrumbs and grated cheese evenly over the top.

Place under the hot grill for 5 minutes, or until bubbling and golden brown on top. Serve.

The gratin will keep in the fridge for up to 2 days, or freeze in individual portions for up to 3 months.

TIP

If you've frozen the gratin, once defrosted, reheat until it is piping hot throughout.

FREEZE ME

BATCH COOK

DAIRY FREE

HIGH PROTEIN

GREEK-STYLE CHICKEN *with* BUTTER BEANS

15 MINS + 1–2 HRS MARINATING | 30 MINS | SERVES 4

PER SERVING:
315 KCAL /17G CARBS

SPECIAL EQUIPMENT
28cm (11in) shallow, non-stick casserole dish

FOR THE MARINADE
1 tbsp olive oil
juice of 1 lemon
2 garlic cloves, crushed
1 tsp each dried oregano
1 tsp dried basil
½ tsp dried rosemary
½ tsp ground cinnamon
black pepper, to taste

FOR THE CHICKEN AND BUTTER BEANS
4 skinless chicken breasts (approx. 150g each)
300ml chicken stock (1 chicken stock cube dissolved in 300ml boiling water)
1 small red onion, peeled and sliced
1 rounded tbsp plain flour
1 x 400g tin butter beans in water, rinsed and drained
80g fine green beans, trimmed
30g pitted black olives, halved

TO ACCOMPANY
80g steamed vegetables (+38 kcal per serving)

TIP

If you've frozen the dish, once defrosted, cover and reheat in the microwave for 3–5 minutes, stirring halfway through.

Bring a taste of the Mediterranean to your dinner table with this creamy chicken dish. We've marinated tender chicken breasts in sunny flavours of garlic, citrus, oregano and cinnamon, before cooking everything in a lemon-infused sauce and adding tangy olives for even more flavour. With the butter beans packed with fibre, this is a lunch that'll definitely tide you over until your evening meal, or you can pair it with steamed veg and have it for dinner.

Everyday Light

Mix all the marinade ingredients together in a large, glass or plastic bowl. If your chicken breasts are particularly thick, place them between two pieces of cling film and flatten slightly with a mallet or rolling pin. Add the chicken breasts to the marinade and mix to coat well. Cover and chill in the fridge for 1–2 hours.

Place a non-stick frying pan over a medium-high heat. When the pan is hot, add the chicken breasts and brown each side for 2 minutes, or until golden. You don't need to spray the pan with cooking spray as there is olive oil in the marinade.

Remove the chicken breasts to a plate and set aside. Turn the heat down to medium. If there are any brown crispy bits in the pan, add a splash of stock and scrape off the bottom of the pan, then add the onion and sauté for 5 minutes until soft. Stir in any marinade that's left in the bowl, then remove the pan from the heat. Stir the flour into the onion, then add the stock, a little at a time, stirring quickly to prevent lumps. Return the pan to the heat and stir until the sauce begins to bubble and thicken.

Return the chicken breasts to the pan, cover with a lid and simmer for about 10 minutes. Flip the chicken over in the sauce to ensure even cooking, then add the butter beans, green beans and olives.

Stir well and cook for a further 5–10 minutes until the chicken is cooked through. Season with pepper (you shouldn't need any salt) and serve with steamed vegetables. If freezing, divide the cooked dish into individual portions then freeze as soon as possible for up to 3 months. The dish will keep in the fridge for 3–4 days.

FREEZE ME

BATCH COOK

DAIRY FREE

HIGH PROTEIN

BEEF, BEETROOT *and* BARLEY STEW

15 MINS | VARIABLE | SERVES 4

PER SERVING:
409 KCAL /36G CARBS

SPECIAL EQUIPMENT
28cm (11in) shallow, non-stick casserole dish, suitable for oven and hob

low-calorie cooking spray
500g lean diced beef
salt and freshly ground black pepper, to taste
1 onion, peeled and diced
1 small leek, trimmed and sliced
150g carrots, peeled and sliced
2 garlic cloves, peeled and crushed
1½ tsp ground cinnamon
1.2 litres beef stock (2 beef stock cubes dissolved in 1.2 litres boiling water)
100g pearl barley
few sprigs of thyme
350g precooked beetroot, cut into chunks
2 tbsp balsamic vinegar

TO ACCOMPANY (OPTIONAL)
80g steamed vegetables (+38 kcal per serving)

This is the kind of stew you put on for when the weather is grey and drizzly. Tender, slow-cooked beef with earthy beetroot and thyme ticking away in the background, finished off with a splash of balsamic vinegar to give everything a little lift. Prep all your ingredients and let them bubble away gently, then come back to a delicious dinner that tastes as good as it smells.

Weekly Indulgence

OVEN METHOD
3 HOURS

Preheat the oven to 160°C (fan 140°C/gas mark 3).

Spray the casserole dish with low-calorie cooking spray and place over a high heat.

Season the diced beef with salt and pepper and add to the hot pan. Fry the beef for 2 minutes, or until browned and sealed on all sides. Remove the beef to a plate and set aside. Turn the heat down to medium and spray the pan again if needed.

Add the onion, leek and carrots to the pan and sauté for 5 minutes, or until beginning to soften. Return the beef to the pan and add the crushed garlic and cinnamon. Cook for 1 minute, then add the stock and bring to the boil. Add the pearl barley and turn the heat down to a simmer. Add the thyme sprigs, cover with the lid and place in the oven. Cook for 1 hour 30 minutes.

Remove from the oven and add the beetroot, including any juices from the packet. Stir in the balsamic vinegar, then return to the oven and cook for a further hour, or until the vegetables are soft and the beef is fall-apart tender. Season with salt and pepper, if needed, and serve with steamed vegetables, if you wish. You can freeze the stew at this stage by cooling it as quickly as possible, then freezing in individual airtight containers for up to 3 months (see Tips).

The stew will keep in the fridge for up to 3 days. Reheat individual portions in the microwave for 3–4 minutes, stirring halfway through.

SLOW COOKER METHOD
4–8 HOURS

SPECIAL EQUIPMENT
Casserole dish suitable for the hob, 3.5-litre slow cooker

Spray the casserole dish with low-calorie cooking spray and place over a high heat. Season the diced beef with salt and pepper and add to the hot pan. Fry the beef for 2 minutes, or until browned and sealed on all sides.

Place the beef in the slow cooker pot. Add the onion, leek, carrots, garlic and cinnamon. Stir in the stock and pearl barley. Add the thyme sprigs on top, then cover with the lid and cook for 3½ hours on high or 6–7 hours on low.

Add the beetroot, including any juice, and stir in the balsamic vinegar. Replace the lid and cook for a further 1–1½ hours until the beef is tender and the vegetables are cooked. Season with salt and pepper, if needed, and serve with steamed vegetables, if you wish. You can freeze the stew by cooling as quickly as possible, then freezing in individual airtight containers for up to 3 months (see Tips).

The stew will keep in the fridge for up to 3 days. Reheat individual portions in the microwave for 3–4 minutes, stirring halfway through. Alternatively, reheat the whole dish in a large saucepan, stirring gently over a medium heat until piping hot, adding a splash of water if needed.

TIPS

Keep an eye on the liquid in your stew. If your lid isn't quite as tight fitting as it could be, cover the top of the casserole dish with foil before placing the lid on top. This will help prevent excess evaporation. The barley will also absorb some of the stock. Add a little extra water to the pan if it seems to be drying out.

If you've frozen the stew, once defrosted, reheat in the microwave for 3–4 minutes, stirring halfway through. You may need to add a splash of water, as the stew can dry out a little in the freezer.

Image overleaf.

VEGAN
USE VEGAN RICOTTA

VEGGIE

FREEZE ME
GNOCCHI ONLY

BATCH COOK

DAIRY FREE
USE DF RICOTTA

SWEET POTATO GNOCCHI *with* BROCCOLI *and* RICOTTA

20 MINS + 10 MINS COOLING | 1 HR | SERVES 4

PER SERVING:
356 KCAL /53G CARBS

- 600g sweet potatoes
- 250g ricotta cheese
- salt and freshly ground black pepper, to taste
- 150g plain flour, plus a little extra for dusting
- low-calorie cooking spray
- 200g Tenderstem broccoli, trimmed and halved
- 1 garlic clove, peeled and crushed
- juice of 1 lemon
- 1 tsp chopped fresh basil

Fancy a meal that's comforting, colourful and ridiculously delicious? This ticks all the boxes: light, fluffy dumplings made from humble ingredients, crisped up in the pan and tossed with garlicky broccoli. Making gnocchi from scratch at home is easier than you'd think. With just a few simple steps, you'll have soft, pillowy dumplings in no time at all. Top the dish with drops of lemon and basil ricotta to add a fresh, creamy flavour. Then enjoy any leftovers as a fibre-packed lunch; it's a batch-cook dream!

Everyday Light

Preheat the oven to 220°C (fan 200°C/gas mark 7) and line a baking tray with non-stick baking paper.

Using a fork, prick the skins of the sweet potatoes all over. Place the potatoes on the lined baking tray and bake in the oven for 40 minutes, or until they are cooked through and soft inside. Remove from the oven and leave to cool for 10 minutes.

When the sweet potatoes are cooled, scoop the flesh from the potatoes and place in a large bowl. You should have about 300–350g cooked potato without the skins. Use a fork or a potato masher to mash the sweet potato until it becomes smooth.

Add 100g ricotta to the sweet potato mash and mix well. Season with salt and pepper. Next, add the flour a few spoonfuls at a time and mix until you get a dough. Be careful not to overwork the dough; it should be soft but not wet or sticky.

Flour a baking tray and set aside, then dust the work surface with a little more flour. Divide the dough into four pieces. Gently roll one piece into a long sausage shape, about 2.5cm (1in) thick. Use a sharp knife to cut the gnocchi into 2.5cm (1in) pieces. Place on the floured tray and set aside. Repeat this method with the rest of the dough. Each quarter will be enough for one portion. You can freeze the gnocchi at this stage by spreading the gnocchi out on a baking tray and freezing them for 1 hour. Then, place them in a sealed bag or container and freeze for up to 3 months (see Tip). The uncooked gnocchi will also keep in the fridge for up to 2 days.

Spray a large frying pan with low-calorie cooking spray and place over a medium heat. Add the Tenderstem broccoli and cook for a minute or two. Season with salt and pepper and add the crushed garlic. Cook for a further 2 minutes, or until slightly softened, then empty into a large bowl. Wipe the pan clean, spray with more low-calorie cooking spray and place over a low heat.

Place a large pot of boiling salted water over a medium heat next to the frying pan. Add the gnocchi to the boiling water and cook for 2–3 minutes. If cooking four portions, do this in two batches. When the gnocchi float to the surface, they are cooked.

Use a slotted spoon to scoop the cooked gnocchi out of the boiling water and into the warmed frying pan and cook for 2–3 minutes, until they start to become brown and crisp. Add half of the broccoli, a pinch of salt and pepper and a squeeze of lemon juice. Toss the broccoli and gnocchi together for a few more minutes.

Place the remaining ricotta in a medium bowl with a pinch of salt and pepper, a squeeze of lemon juice and the chopped basil and mix well to combine.

To serve, place the gnocchi and broccoli in a serving dish and top with drops of the lemon and basil ricotta.

TIPS

Use a potato ricer to make the sweet potato as smooth as possible.

If you've frozen the uncooked gnocchi, cook them straight from frozen by placing them into a large saucepan of boiling water. They are cooked when they float to the surface after a few minutes.

Image on page 109.

VEGGIE

FREEZE ME

GLUTEN FREE

USE GF PASTA, FLOUR AND BREAD

CARAMELIZED ONION MAC *and* CHEESE

15 MINS · 1 HR 10 MINS · SERVES 6

PER SERVING:
479 KCAL / 76G CARBS

SPECIAL EQUIPMENT
28cm (11in) casserole dish, suitable for oven and hob

- low-calorie cooking spray
- 3 onions, peeled and finely sliced
- salt and freshly ground black pepper, to taste
- 2 tbsp finely chopped fresh thyme
- 1 tbsp Henderson's relish
- 1 tbsp granulated sweetener
- 500g macaroni
- 2 tbsp plain flour
- 500ml skimmed milk
- 120g reduced-fat Cheddar cheese, finely grated
- 60g reduced-fat spreadable cheese
- 2 tsp Dijon mustard
- ¼ tsp sriracha sauce
- 1 sliced wholemeal bread, approx. 37g, made into breadcrumbs

Give your usual mac and cheese an upgrade with this French onion-inspired version. Sweet onions are slowly caramelized until soft and golden, with a sprinkle of fresh thyme adding even more depth to the rich flavour. Meanwhile, the creamy cheese sauce comes together quickly in the pan, soaking up all that savoury goodness from the onions. It's comfort food that feels fancy without any fuss!

Weekly Indulgence

Spray the casserole dish with low-calorie cooking spray and place over a low heat. Add the onions and season to taste with salt. Fry for 20 minutes, stirring occasionally. You may need to add a few splashes of water to stop them catching.

Add the thyme, Henderson's relish and sweetener and fry for 20 minutes, stirring and adding water if needed. The onions should be glossy, softened and turning golden brown. Add the macaroni to a large saucepan of boiling water and cook according to the packet instructions. We cooked ours for 8 minutes.

Scrape the onions into a large bowl. Add the flour and a little milk to the onion pan and whisk until smooth and combined. Add the remaining milk, then place over a medium heat and whisk occasionally until thickened. Add 100g of the grated cheese, the spreadable cheese, mustard and sriracha and whisk until the cheese has melted. Season to taste with salt and pepper.

Add the cooked macaroni and half the onions to the cheese sauce. Mix until combined and the pasta is coated in the sauce. Transfer to the ovenproof dish (if using). Spread the remaining onions on top of the macaroni.

Preheat the grill on the medium setting. In a medium bowl, mix the breadcrumbs with the remaining cheese and scatter over the top of the macaroni.

Place the dish under the hot grill until golden brown and the cheese has melted. Serve or leave to cool and freeze for up to 3 months. The dish will keep in the fridge for up to 4 days. Reheat in the microwave for 3 minutes, or until piping hot.

TIPS

If you've frozen the dish, once defrosted, reheat in the microwave for 3 minutes, or until piping hot.

FREEZE ME

FILLING ONLY

BATCH COOK

GLUTEN FREE

USE GF PASTRY AND STOCK POT

HIGH PROTEIN

CHICKEN POT PIE

15 MINS | 1 HR 10 MINS | SERVES 6

PER SERVING:
415 KCAL /23G CARBS

SPECIAL EQUIPMENT
23cm (9in) casserole dish, suitable for oven and hob

low-calorie cooking spray
500g diced chicken breast
2 leeks, trimmed and finely sliced
3 garlic cloves, peeled and crushed
2 carrots, peeled and diced
2 celery sticks, diced
150g mushrooms, diced
2 tsp dried thyme
2 tsp onion granules
200ml boiling water
1 chicken stock pot
270ml light double cream alternative
100g reduced-fat cream cheese
2 tsp Dijon mustard
1 tbsp cornflour
salt and freshly ground black pepper, to taste

TO SERVE
160g ready-rolled reduced-fat puff pastry sheet
1 tsp skimmed milk

TO ACCOMPANY
80g steamed vegetables (+38 kcal per serving)

TIP

If you've frozen the filling, once defrosted, reheat the filling for 3–4 minutes until piping hot, then following the remaining steps of the recipe.

You don't have to give up pie night even if you're watching what you eat. This chicken pie is creamy, comforting, full to the brim with tender chicken and good-for-you vegetables, and still under 500 calories (believe it!). You can make a big pot of the filling and stash it in your fridge or freezer until you're ready to crown it with golden, flaky pastry. Hearty yet simple, it's a winner, winner, chicken dinner for sure!

Weekly Indulgence

Spray a large frying pan with low-calorie cooking spray and place over a medium heat. Add the chicken and fry for 5 minutes, or until browned on all sides. Remove to a plate.

Add the leeks, garlic, carrots, celery and mushrooms to the pan and fry for 5 minutes. Return the chicken to the pan and sprinkle over the thyme and onion granules.

Pour the boiling water into a heatproof jug, then add the stock pot and stir until dissolved.

Pour the stock into the pan along with the cream alternative, cream cheese and mustard. Stir until blended.

In a small bowl, combine the cornflour and 1 tablespoon cold water and stir until smooth. Pour into the pan and stir. Bring to the boil, then turn the heat down to low and simmer for 20 minutes. Season to taste with salt and pepper. The sauce should be thickened and vegetables softened. This is the point where you can store or freeze the pie filling ready to top with the pastry when ready to serve (see Tip).

Preheat the oven to 200°C (fan 180°C/gas mark 6). Scrape the pie filling into the ovenproof dish or casserole dish. Top with the pastry and brush with the milk. Decorate the top however you like, then use a knife to add a few steam holes in the centre. Cook in the oven for 35–40 minutes until the top is golden brown and the pie filling is heated through. Serve with steamed vegetables.

The whole pie can be kept in the fridge, but we think it's best to prepare the filling, cool and store for up to 3 days in an airtight container. Reheat the filling for 3–4 minutes until piping hot, then follow the remaining steps of the recipe.

VEGGIE

FREEZE ME

BATCH COOK

RHUBARB *and* CUSTARD ARCTIC ROLL

20 MINS + 3 HRS FREEZING | 40 MINS + 1 HR COOLING | SERVES 10

PER SERVING:
148 KCAL /29G CARBS

SPECIAL EQUIPMENT
Baking tray, about 30 x 20cm (12 x 8in), electric hand whisk

- 300g reduced-calorie vanilla ice cream
- 150g reduced-fat custard
- 4 medium eggs
- 50g granulated sweetener
- 50g caster sugar
- 1 tsp vanilla extract
- 100g self-raising flour
- 1 tbsp custard powder

FOR THE RHUBARB

- 200g rhubarb
- 20g granulated sweetener
- 1 tsp vanilla extract

We've given this arctic roll a rhubarb and custard twist to make it extra tasty. Soft sponge meets silky smooth ice cream, with fruity rhubarb and sweet custard giving it that classic flavour combo we all know and love. It's a fab make-ahead dessert; prepare it in advance, pop it in the freezer and simply slice whenever you're ready to serve. You'll want this one on hand for entertaining… or even just having a treat tucked away for later. Go on, you deserve it.

Everyday Light

Cut a sheet of non-stick baking paper and a sheet of cling film from each roll, each approximately 50cm (20in) in length. Lay each sheet out separately on the work surface.

Place the ice cream in a large bowl and break it up a little with a spoon. Leave to soften slightly for 5 minutes, then add the custard and stir through the slightly softened ice cream.

Working quickly, spoon the ice cream lengthways down the centre of the non-stick baking paper sheet. Roughly shape the ice cream into a 20cm (8in) long cylinder shape. Roll the ice cream cylinder up tightly in the non-stick baking paper and twist the ends to seal tightly. Place the wrapped roll lengthways down the centre of the cling film sheet and roll up tightly, twisting the ends to seal. Freeze for 3 hours until solid.

Meanwhile, start making the sponge cake. Preheat the oven to 180°C (fan 160°C/gas mark 4). Line the baking tray with non-stick baking paper.

Place the eggs, sweetener, caster sugar and vanilla extract in a large bowl. Use an electric whisk to whisk on high speed for 5 minutes, or until very thick, pale and creamy. The mixture should hold a 'ribbon' trail when the whisk is lifted out.

Sift the flour and custard powder into the mixture a little at a time and use a large spoon to gently fold it in until just combined. Scrape into the prepared tray and spread out evenly. Bake in the oven for 10–15 minutes, until golden. Gently press the centre of the sponge, it should spring back when it's ready and leave no indent. Meanwhile, cut another sheet of non-stick baking paper approximately 50cm (20in) in length. Turn the cooked sponge out of the tray onto the sheet of non-stick baking paper. Carefully peel off the lining paper and discard. While the sponge is still warm, roll it up to form a Swiss roll, starting with one of the short sides. Place seam side down and leave to cool completely rolled on the paper sheet (approx. 1 hour).

Meanwhile, turn the oven temperature up to 200°C (fan 180°C/ gas mark 6) and line a baking tray with non-stick baking paper. Place the rhubarb in a large bowl, sprinkle over the sweetener and vanilla essence and stir to combine. Spread the rhubarb over the lined baking tray and bake in the oven for 20–25 minutes, until tender. Remove from the oven and leave to cool completely.

Gently unroll the cooled sponge and spread the rhubarb evenly over the surface. Remove the ice cream roll from the freezer and quickly unwrap. Place the solid ice cream roll onto the sponge. Quickly roll and ease the sponge around the ice cream roll; the edges of the sponge should just meet underneath.

Place the arctic roll on a fresh sheet of non-stick baking paper and twist the ends to seal, then wrap in fresh cling film, wrapping tightly. Quickly give it a little roll to help make a good cylinder shape and immediately place it in the freezer. Freeze for approx. 1½–2 hours until solid throughout.

When ready to serve, unwrap and use a large, serrated knife to cut into 10 even slices. Serve at once. Once assembled, the arctic roll will keep in the freezer for up to 3 months.

Image overleaf.

VEGAN

USE VEGAN CHOCOLATE

VEGGIE

FREEZE ME

BATCH COOK

DAIRY FREE

USE DF CHOCOLATE

GLUTEN FREE

USE GF CHOCOLATE

BANANA CRUNCH ICE CREAM

15 MINS + OVERNIGHT FREEZING **NO COOK** **SERVES 6**

PER SERVING:
168 KCAL /27G CARBS

SPECIAL EQUIPMENT
Food processor or blender, 1-litre freezer-proof container

6 ripe bananas, approx. 100g each, peeled and sliced
30g milk chocolate chips or chopped milk chocolate
30g pecans, chopped
2 tbsp toffee flavour dessert topping

If you love easy treats, this ice cream is about to become your new obsession. With just four ingredients and 15 minutes, you'll whip up something seriously creamy and utterly irresistible. Got a few bananas turning brown in the fruit bowl? This is the perfect way to use them. Swirl through pecans and chocolate chips for that gorgeous crunch in every scoop. Simply freeze overnight, and you'll have a big tub of sweet, silky ice cream waiting whenever the craving hits.

Everyday Light

Line a baking tray with a sheet of non-stick baking paper. Place the sliced bananas on the lined baking tray in a single layer and freeze for 2½–3 hours, until frozen.

When you're ready to make the ice cream, remove the bananas from the freezer and leave them to soften for 5 minutes.

Place the bananas in a food processor or blender and blitz for a minute or two until thick, pale, smooth and creamy. You may need to do this in two batches, depending on the size of your food processor or blender. At this stage, you can freeze the blitzed bananas overnight, then store in the freezer in an airtight container until ready to use (up to 3 months).

Add the chocolate and nuts and fold them into the ice cream using a silicone spatula. Scrape into a 1-litre freezer-proof container, roughly spread out and return to the freezer for 4 hours, or until frozen.

When ready to serve, remove from the freezer and leave to soften for about 10 minutes before scooping. Drizzle over the toffee topping and serve.

The ice cream will keep in the freezer for up to 3 months. Remove from the freezer and leave to stand at room temperature for 10 minutes to make it easier to scoop.

ON
THE
GO

VEGGIE

BATCH COOK

GLUTEN FREE

USE GF OATS AND CUSTARD

APPLE CRUMBLE BREAKFAST POTS

15 MINS 30 MINS SERVES 4

PER SERVING:
286 KCAL /47G CARBS

SPECIAL EQUIPMENT
4 x 350ml mason jars, or reusable yoghurt pots

6 eating apples, peeled, cored and diced
juice of ½ lemon
1 tsp ground cinnamon
2–3 tsp granulated sweetener (optional)

FOR THE CRUNCHY TOPPING
1 tbsp reduced-fat spread
1 tbsp honey
40g rolled porridge oats
10g flaked almonds

FOR THE CUSTARD YOGHURT
300g fat-free Greek yoghurt
150g ready-to-use light custard
2 tsp honey
1–2 tsp vanilla bean paste

Dessert for breakfast? Don't mind if we do! This cosy make-ahead brekkie has all the best bits of an apple crumble, only we've made some smart swaps to lighten things up. Think gently spiced apples with a sprinkling of cinnamon and a splash of lemon that brings out their natural sweetness as they caramelize in the oven. Prep your pots the night before, then pop them in the fridge, and wake up to layers upon layers of tasty goodness with no extra effort required.

Everyday Light

Preheat the oven to 200°C (fan 180°C/gas mark 6). Line a small baking tray with greaseproof paper.

Add the diced apples, lemon juice, cinnamon, 3 tablespoons water and the sweetener (if using) to a roasting tray and mix well. Cover loosely with foil and cook in the oven for 20 minutes.

Meanwhile, make the crunchy topping. Place the spread and honey in a small bowl and give it a 20-second burst in the microwave to melt. Add the oats and almonds and mix well. Spread the mix out on the lined baking tray in a layer about 5mm (¼in) thick.

When the apples have been cooking for 20 minutes, uncover and stir well. Return to the oven, uncovered, and pop the oat mix in alongside. Cook for a further 10–12 minutes until the apples are soft and the oats are golden and crisp around the edges.

Remove from the oven. Break the oats into clumps and leave to cool.

While the apples and oats cool, mix the yoghurt, custard, honey and vanilla bean paste together in a bowl.

When everything is cool, divide the apples between the jars or containers and top with the custard yoghurt. Seal or cover and store in the fridge for up to 4 days.

Store the crunchy topping in an airtight container (no need to refrigerate) and sprinkle on the top of the yoghurt the morning you are ready to eat.

VEGAN

USE VEGAN YOGHURT, CHOCOLATE AND MAPLE SYRUP

VEGGIE

BATCH COOK

DAIRY FREE

USE DF YOGHURT AND CHOCOLATE

GLUTEN FREE

USE GF OAT MILK AND OATS

CHOCOLATE OVERNIGHT OATS

5 MINS + OVERNIGHT CHILLING **NO COOK** **SERVES 4**

PER SERVING:
414 KCAL / 61G CARBS

SPECIAL EQUIPMENT
4 x 350ml mason jars or containers

240g rolled porridge oats
4 tbsp cocoa powder
1 tbsp chia seeds
300ml oat milk
200g fat-free Greek yoghurt
3 tbsp honey
2 tsp vanilla extract
12 raspberries
20g dark chocolate, grated

Kickstart your day the choccy way with these Chocolate Overnight Oats. We've filled them with fibre-rich chia seeds to see you through to lunchtime and support your digestion. The clue is in the title: make them the night before so they can soak up all the yummy flavours in the fridge, and you can roll out of bed and tuck into a creamy, chocolatey breakfast that's filling and good for you.

Weekly Indulgence

Mix the oats, cocoa powder and chia seeds together in a bowl. In a separate bowl, mix the oat milk, yoghurt, honey and vanilla together.

Pour the yoghurt mixture into the dry ingredients and stir to combine. Divide the mix between the bowls, jars or containers.

Cover with a lid or cling film and chill in the fridge overnight.

To serve, top each with three raspberries and some dark chocolate shavings.

The overnight oats will keep in the fridge for up to 5 days.

TIP

If you are making this vegan, use maple syrup instead of honey.

FREEZE ME

BATCH COOK

GLUTEN FREE

USE GF MUFFINS

HIGH PROTEIN

SMOKY BREAKFAST SANDWICH

15 MINS | 25 MINS | SERVES 4

PER SERVING:
433 KCAL / 36G CARBS

SPECIAL EQUIPMENT
28 x 20cm (11 x 8in) baking tin, food processor

FOR THE EGG LAYER

- 150g reduced-fat cottage cheese
- 6 medium eggs
- salt and freshly ground black pepper, to taste
- 40g spinach leaves

FOR THE TOMATOES

- low-calorie cooking spray
- 200g cherry tomatoes, halved
- 1 tbsp chipotle paste
- 1 tsp smoked paprika
- 1 tsp garlic granules
- 1 tsp onion granules
- 1 tsp granulated sweetener

FOR THE PORK

- 200g 5% fat minced pork
- 1 tsp dried sage
- 1 tsp garlic granules

TO SERVE

- 4 English muffins, sliced in half
- 4 reduced-fat processed cheese slices
- 4 tsp reduced-sugar ketchup

Skip the drive-through and get ahead of your week with these grab-and-go breakfast sandwiches. These sandwiches are a meal prep dream! Stack up soft English muffins with roasted tomatoes, and protein-packed egg, pork and cheese. Don't forget to add chipotle paste to the tomatoes if you're looking for a smoky kick. Make a batch, wrap them up and stash them in the fridge or freezer. You'll be buzzing every morning when you've got a tasty, speedy breakfast ready to go.

Weekly Indulgence

Preheat the oven to 200°C (fan 180°C/gas mark 6) and line the tin with non-stick baking paper.

Add the cottage cheese and eggs to the food processor and blitz until smooth. Season to taste with salt and pepper, then add the spinach and mix well. Pour the egg mixture into the prepared tin and bake in the oven for 25 minutes, or until the egg mixture is set. Remove from the oven and cut the egg mixture into four squares.

Meanwhile, spray a baking tray with low-calorie cooking spray and add all the ingredients for the tomatoes, mixing well to coat. Bake in the oven for 20 minutes, or until softened and the tomatoes have begun to break down.

In a large bowl, add all the ingredients for the pork and mix well with your hands. Divide into four portions, then shape into pork patties approximately the size of your English muffins.

Spray a frying pan with low-calorie cooking spray and place over a medium heat. Add the patties and cook for 3–4 minutes on each side, until cooked through and browned. Remove and set aside.

Now that all elements are ready, you can make the sandwiches. Spread the tomato mix on the bottom of the muffins, then add the egg, pork and a slice of cheese. Spread the ketchup onto the top half of the muffins and place on top.

Serve straight away or wrap in non-stick baking paper and foil or cling film and freeze for up to 3 months, or keep in the fridge for up to 4 days (see Tips).

TIPS

The chipotle gives these sandwiches a smoky heat. If you prefer, you can omit this from the tomato mixture.

If you've frozen or stored the sandwiches, you can reheat either in the microwave or the air fryer. To microwave, unwrap the sandwich, place onto a paper towel and microwave for 2 minutes, or until piping hot. To air-fry, unwrap the sandwich and air-fry at 160°C for 5 minutes, or until piping hot.

BANANA CHIA BREAKFAST BOWL

10 MINS + OVERNIGHT CHILLING | NO COOK | SERVES 4

VEGAN
USE VEGAN YOGHURT, MILK AND CHOCOLATE

VEGGIE

BATCH COOK

DAIRY FREE
USE DF YOGHURT, MILK AND CHOCOLATE

GLUTEN FREE
USE GF OATS

HIGH PROTEIN

PER SERVING:
464 KCAL /33G CARBS

SPECIAL EQUIPMENT
4 x containers with lids, about 10 x 14cm (4 x 5½in)

- 2 medium bananas, peeled and mashed
- 250g fat-free Greek yoghurt
- 250ml skimmed milk
- 60g rolled porridge oats
- 4 tbsp chia seeds
- 2 tsp vanilla extract
- 60g pecan nuts, chopped
- 30g dark chocolate chips
- 4 tbsp pumpkin seeds
- 2 tbsp peanut butter powder

When you're half awake and need a nourishing breakfast that'll give you the motivation to get out the door, you need this breakfast bowl in your morning rotation. You can whip it up in minutes, then pop it in the fridge, ready for you to dig your spoon in whenever you need a solid start to the day. No pan, no faff and enough fibre and protein to keep you going until lunchtime!

Weekly Indulgence

Add the mashed banana, yoghurt, milk, oats, chia seeds and vanilla to a large bowl and mix until combined.

Divide the mixture between the plastic containers, then sprinkle over the pecans, chocolate and pumpkin seeds.

In a small bowl, combine the peanut butter powder with 2 tablespoons cold water and mix until smooth. Drizzle over the top of the chia mixture, then cover the containers with the lids and leave in the fridge overnight.

The breakfast bowls will keep in the fridge for up to 4 days.

TIP

You can swap the dark chocolate for milk chocolate, if you prefer!

VEGAN

USE VEGAN SPREAD, YOGHURT, CHOCOLATE AND MAPLE SYRUP

VEGGIE

FREEZE ME

BATCH COOK

DAIRY FREE

USE DF SPREAD, YOGHURT AND CHOCOLATE

BREAKFAST COOKIES

10 MINS **8–10 MINS** **MAKES 12**

PER SERVING:
136 KCAL / 24G CARBS

- 100g plain flour
- 100g rolled porridge oats
- 80g brown granulated sweetener (you can use white if you prefer)
- 40g mixed seeds (we used a four-seed mix of pumpkin, sunflower, linseed and sesame)
- 2 tbsp chia seeds
- 30g soft dried apricots, chopped
- 40g reduced-fat spread
- 40g fat-free Greek yoghurt
- 3 tbsp honey
- 1 tsp vanilla extract
- 10g dark chocolate chips or chopped dark chocolate

Cookies for breakfast? Yes, you did read that right! Instead of reaching for shop-bought biscuits, whip up a batch for the freezer. These beauties take just 10 minutes to prep and 10 minutes to cook. You'll know they're ready when they're lightly golden and your kitchen smells incredible. Packed with seeds, dried fruit and a little chocolate on top, they're a delicious boost towards your fibre goal and perfect for mornings when you need something tasty and wholesome. Simply defrost overnight and you'll be ready to roll!

Everyday Light

Preheat the oven to 190°C (fan 170°C/gas mark 5) and line a baking tray with non-stick baking paper.

Add the flour, oats, sweetener, mixed seeds, chia seeds and apricots to a large bowl and mix to combine. Add the spread, yoghurt, honey and vanilla and, using your hands, mix into a soft dough.

Divide the dough into twelve portions and shape into balls.

Arrange on the lined baking tray. Lightly press the cookies and shape into rounds. These cookies don't really spread so this will be the finished shape.

Top with the dark chocolate chips and bake in the oven for 8–10 minutes until lightly golden brown. When the cookies are completely cool, wrap individually and freeze in an airtight container for up to 3 months. There's no need to reheat, just defrost them overnight.

The cookies will keep in an airtight container for up to 4 days.

TIP

If you are making these cookies vegan, use maple syrup instead of honey.

VEGGIE

BATCH COOK

GLUTEN FREE

USE GF WEETABIX

HIGH PROTEIN

BANOFFEE OVERNIGHT WEETABIX POTS

15 MINS + OVERNIGHT STANDING   NO COOK   SERVES 4

PER SERVING:
294 KCAL /52G CARBS

SPECIAL EQUIPMENT
4 x 350ml mason jars or containers, food processor or blender

100g dates, chopped
90ml boiling water
4 Weetabix, crushed
200ml skimmed milk
160g fat-free Greek yoghurt
160g quark
2 tsp vanilla extract
1 tbsp honey
2 bananas, peeled and sliced
12g dried banana chips
4 tsp low-calorie caramel syrup

What's better than a breakfast you can just roll out of bed and dig into? These banana-infused overnight oats are a nutritious make-ahead breakfast you can prep the night before and then leave in the fridge, so you have a protein-packed, fibre-filled breakfast waiting for you when you wake up. What makes this 15-minute meal so irresistible? We've layered Weetabix with banana and dates, doused everything in slimming-friendly caramel syrup, and then topped everything with creamy yoghurt. Delish!

Everyday Light

Add the dates to a small heatproof bowl and pour over the water. Leave to soak for 10 minutes while you prepare the rest of the recipe.

Add the Weetabix and milk to a medium bowl and mix well. Divide between the serving dishes or plastic containers and press down.

Add the yoghurt, quark, vanilla and honey to a large bowl and mix well.

Once the dates have softened, add the dates and any remaining soaking water to the food processor along with half the fresh bananas and blitz into a smooth puree.

Add a layer of the date puree on top of the Weetabix layer. Layer the remaining sliced bananas on top of the date puree and finish with the yoghurt mixture.

Divide the banana chips between the yoghurt pots and drizzle over the caramel syrup. Cover and keep in the fridge for up to 3 days.

VEGGIE

FREEZE ME

BATCH COOK

DAIRY FREE

USE DF SPREAD

GLUTEN FREE

USE GF OATS, FLOUR AND BAKING POWDER

BUTTERNUT SQUASH MUFFINS

10 MINS | 35 MINS | MAKES 12

PER SERVING:
120 KCAL /16G CARBS

SPECIAL EQUIPMENT
12-hole muffin tray, 12 silicone or paper cake cases, high-speed blender or food processor

- 125g butternut squash, peeled and diced
- juice of 2 oranges, plus 1 tsp finely grated zest
- 75g reduced-fat spread
- 100g rolled porridge oats
- 100g self-raising flour
- 2 tsp baking powder
- 1 tsp mixed spice
- 2–3 tbsp granulated sweetener
- 40g soft dried apricots, finely chopped
- 1 medium egg
- ½ tsp icing sugar

If you fancy a sweet bake that feels special, these muffins are an absolute treat. The butternut squash puree keeps them deliciously moist and fluffy, while zingy orange and soft apricots add little bursts of sweetness. It's a family-friendly way to sneak more fruit and veg into your day. Made with oat flour for extra texture, they're perfect for baking on a Sunday and popping into an airtight tin, ready for grab-and-go breakfasts or an afternoon snack with a cuppa.

Everyday Light

Place the butternut squash in a small saucepan and add the orange juice and zest. Place over a high heat until it is bubbling, then turn the heat down to a simmer and cover with a lid. Cook for 10–15 minutes, until the butternut squash is soft. Remove from the heat and stir in the spread until it has melted. Leave to cool for 5 minutes, then mash with a fork.

While the squash cools, preheat the oven to 200°C (fan 180°C/ gas mark 6) and line the muffin tray with silicone or paper cupcake cases.

Put the oats into the high speed blender or food processor and blitz to a coarse flour. Add to a large bowl, along with the flour, baking powder, mixed spice, sweetener and apricots. Stir the dry ingredients together and make a well in the centre.

Beat the egg into the butternut squash mixture, then pour the butternut squash mixture into the well in the dry ingredients and use a spatula to quickly fold together.

When combined, spoon the mixture into the muffin cases. Bake in the centre of the oven for 15–20 minutes until risen and spongy, and a skewer inserted into the middle comes out clean.

Leave to cool, then dredge with icing sugar. You can freeze the muffins in an airtight container for up to 3 months (see Tip).

The muffins will keep in the fridge for up to 5 days.

TIP

If you've frozen the muffins, once defrosted, they can be eaten cold or microwaved for 30–40 seconds to warm through.

COTTAGE CHEESE BAGELS

VEGGIE | FREEZE ME | BATCH COOK | HIGH PROTEIN

15 MINS + 20 MINS RESTING **25 MINS** **SERVES 4**

PER SERVING:
349 KCAL / 31G CARBS

FOR THE BAGELS:

- 200g reduced-fat cottage cheese
- 140g self-raising flour, plus extra for dusting
- salt and freshly ground black pepper, to taste
- ½ medium egg, beaten
- 1 tsp sesame seeds

FOR THE FILLING:

- 1 avocado, halved, stone removed and mashed
- 2 boiled eggs, peeled and mashed
- 2 tbsp reduced-fat mayonnaise
- 1 spring onion, trimmed and finely sliced
- 60g reduced-fat feta-style cheese, crumbled
- 30g cucumber, sliced
- 1 tomato, sliced
- ½ red onion, peeled and finely sliced
- 80g rocket

Looking for a quick, protein-packed breakfast or lunch? These bagels are lower in calories and higher in protein than shop-bought versions, and you can double up the batch to freeze for later. They're perfect for busy mornings or on-the-go lunches! With only 15 minutes prep time, we've filled ours with a creamy avocado egg mayo, but honestly, you can stuff them with whatever takes your fancy. Talk about versatile and fuss-free!

Everyday Light

Line a baking tray with non-stick baking paper. Add the cottage cheese to a food processor and blitz until smooth.

Scrape the cottage cheese into a large bowl and add the flour and a little salt and pepper. Mix and bring together into a rough shaggy ball. Leave to stand for 10 minutes.

Tip the dough out onto a lightly floured work surface and knead a few times to make a smooth ball of dough. Divide into four portions.

Roll one piece of dough out into a sausage about 25cm (10in) long. Join the ends by pinching together and rolling the join lightly to smooth the edges. Place on the lined baking tray and repeat to make four bagels.

Preheat the oven to 200°C (fan 180°C/gas mark 6). Cover the tray with a clean kitchen towel and leave in a warm place for 10 minutes. The dough should be slightly puffed up but won't rise or double in size like a bread dough would. Brush with egg and sprinkle over the sesame seeds. Bake in the oven for 20–25 minutes, until lightly golden brown.

When ready to serve, prepare the filling. Add the mashed avocado and egg to a large bowl along with the mayonnaise and spring onion. Mix well and season to taste.

Slice the bagels in half and spread the avocado mixture on the bottom half. Top with the feta, cucumber, tomato, red onion and rocket. Place the other bagel half on top and serve. Bagels can be frozen in a freezer-proof bag or container for up to 3 months.

The bagels will keep in an airtight container for up to 4 days. The avocado egg mayo will keep in the fridge for up to 2 days.

TIPS

The bagels alone are 172 kcal.

Alternatively, you can cook these bagels in the air fryer if you prefer. Air-fry at 160°C for 10–15 minutes.

BATCH COOK

DAIRY FREE

GLUTEN FREE

HIGH PROTEIN

COWBOY CAVIAR

20 MINS NO COOK SERVES 8

PER SERVING:
193 KCAL /33G CARBS

SPECIAL EQUIPMENT
Mini chopper or blender

2 mixed coloured peppers, deseeded and diced
1 red onion, peeled and diced
1 cucumber, halved, deseeded and diced
6 salad tomatoes, stalk removed, deseeded and cut into dice
250g cooked sweetcorn, tinned or frozen (drained)
2 x 400g tins mixed beans, rinsed and drained
1 tsp salt
freshly ground black pepper, to taste
mixed leaves, to serve

FOR THE DRESSING
3 tbsp olive oil
juice of 3 limes
2 tbsp honey
1 red chilli, deseeded and chopped
good handful of fresh coriander, roughly chopped, including stalks

TO ACCOMPANY
100g cooked chicken breast (+148 kcal per serving) or 100g tin tuna in spring water, 72g drained (+72 kcal per serving) or 75g reduced-fat vegetarian feta (+138 kcal per serving)

Say howdy to a recipe all the way from Texas! This fresh and zingy mixed bean salad is packed with colourful, crunchy veggies and flavoured with a mild chilli, honey and lime dressing. The beauty of this dish is its adaptability: it's perfect as a side for summer BBQs or you can pair it with a burger for some midweek magic. We like to make a batch on a Sunday and use it for lunches throughout the week!

Everyday Light

Place the peppers, red onion, cucumber and tomatoes in a large bowl. Add the sweetcorn and mixed beans.

Place all the dressing ingredients into the mini chopper or blender and blitz for a few seconds to form a dressing.

Add the dressing to the bowl and toss together. Season with the salt and pepper to taste.

Store in a large airtight container or divide into eight individual portions for a prep-ahead lunch. On the day, top with your chosen protein (we have given some easy suggestions) and a handful of mixed leaves.

The dish will keep in the fridge for up to 4 days.

TIPS

The vegetables will release juices as the salad is stored. Make sure to scoop up the liquid that will accumulate at the bottom of the tub, as this is where most of the flavour is.

Removing the seeds from the cucumber and tomatoes reduces the amount of liquid in the salad and keeps it fresher for longer.

To remove the seeds, cut the cucumber in half lengthways and use a teaspoon to scoop them out.

To prepare the tomatoes, cut the tomato in half horizontally and scoop out the seeds with a teaspoon. Remove the stalk as you dice.

VEGGIE
USE TOFU OR HALLOUMI

FREEZE ME

BATCH COOK

DAIRY FREE
USE DF YOGHURT AND MAYONNAISE

GLUTEN FREE

HIGH PROTEIN

CHICKEN SHAWARMA SKEWERS

20 MINS + 1–2 HRS MARINATING   20 MINS   SERVES 4

PER SERVING:
331 KCAL /12G CARBS

SPECIAL EQUIPMENT
8 metal or bamboo skewers

650g skinless chicken breast, diced into 2.5cm (1in) cubes
400g fat-free Greek yoghurt
3 garlic cloves, peeled and crushed
1 tsp ground turmeric
2 tsp ground coriander
1 tsp paprika
1 tbsp ground cumin
1 tsp sumac
1 tsp ground allspice
salt and freshly ground black pepper, to taste
4 lemons, finely grated zest and juice of 2 lemons
1 red onion, peeled and cut into wedges
low-calorie cooking spray
50g light mayonnaise

TO ACCOMPANY (OPTIONAL)
mixed salad (+15 kcal per serving)

TIP

You can cook the skewers on a BBQ or under a preheated hot grill. Be sure to turn the skewers every 3–4 minutes to prevent burning.

If using bamboo skewers, soak them in water for 10 minutes first to prevent burning in the oven.

If you've frozen the skewers, defrost thoroughly in the fridge, then cook as above.

You really can't beat a good old chicken shawarma, especially when it's homemade and a fraction of the usual calories! For this dish, we've marinated tender chicken breast in creamy yoghurt with an aromatic six-spice blend. Lightly charred on the outside and juicy on the inside, the chicken tastes even better after you've drizzled over the light and tangy garlicky sauce. Serve with a crisp side salad to keep things on the lighter side, or you could pile everything into a warm flatbread with some couscous on the side.

Everyday Light

Place the chicken in a large bowl and add 200g of the Greek yoghurt, 2 crushed garlic cloves and all the spices. Season with salt and pepper and add the finely grated zest and juice from 1 lemon. Mix all the ingredients well to combine, making sure that the chicken is coated all over in the marinade. Cover the bowl with cling film and leave to marinate in the fridge for 1–2 hours.

Preheat the oven to 220°C (fan 200°C/gas mark 7) and line a baking tray with non-stick baking paper.

Cut two of the lemons into thin slices and pull apart the red onion wedges into separate layers.

To assemble the skewers, add a cube or two of chicken to a skewer. Fold the lemon slice in half and add it to the skewer along with a slice of red onion. Repeat this process again, finishing the skewer with a final piece of chicken. You should get eight skewers out of this recipe. You can freeze the uncooked skewers on a baking sheet for a few hours at this stage, then store them in an airtight container for up to 3 months (see Tips).

Place the skewers on the lined baking tray and spray with low-calorie cooking spray. Roast the skewers in the oven for 15–20 minutes until cooked all the way through. Turn every 5 minutes or so to ensure the chicken browns all over.

To make the garlic sauce, add the remaining yoghurt to a large bowl along with the mayonnaise, the zest and juice of the remaining lemon, the remaining crushed garlic and a good pinch of salt and pepper, and mix well to combine.

Serve the cooked chicken shawarma skewers with a mixed salad and a drizzle of the garlic sauce.

The cooked chicken skewers will keep in the fridge for up to 3 days. The garlic sauce will keep in the fridge for 3–4 days. The chicken can be eaten at room temperature but you can also reheat it in the oven. Preheat the oven to 180°C (fan 160°C/gas mark 4) and cook for 5–10 minutes until the chicken is piping hot on the inside.

VEGAN

USE VEGAN MEAT ALTERNATIVE AND DF CHEESE

VEGGIE

USE VEGETARIAN MEAT ALTERNATIVE

BATCH COOK

DAIRY FREE

USE DF CHEESE

GLUTEN FREE

USE GF TORTILLAS

HIGH PROTEIN

CHICKEN *and* CHORIZO QUESADILLAS

10 MINS **20 MINS** **SERVES 4**

PER SERVING:
484 KCAL /33G CARBS

300g skinless chicken breast, cut into 2.5cm (1in) pieces
salt and freshly ground black pepper, to taste
2 tsp smoked paprika
2 tsp garlic granules
low-calorie cooking spray
60g chorizo, diced into small cubes
1 onion, peeled and thinly sliced
1 medium red pepper, halved, deseeded and sliced
handful of fresh parsley, chopped
juice of 1 lime
80g reduced-fat mozzarella, grated
80g reduced-fat Cheddar cheese, grated
4 wholemeal tortillas, approx. 60g each

Hola, Mexican night! Chicken and chorizo are a match made in heaven in this flavour-packed dish. We've marinated the meat in a sweet and smoky seasoning, with added pepper and onion creating a caramelized, crunchy taste. Everything's sandwiched between two soft tortilla wraps and held together with an oozy mixture of mozzarella and Cheddar. Make as a speedy and simple dinner option for the whole family or prepare and enjoy cold as a lunchbox treat.

Weekly Indulgence

Place the diced chicken in a large bowl and season with salt and pepper. Add the smoked paprika and garlic granules and mix until well combined.

Spray a frying pan with low-calorie cooking spray and place over a medium heat. Add the chicken and cook for 5 minutes, or until the chicken is cooked through and beginning to brown. Remove from the pan and set aside.

Wipe the frying pan down and spray again with low-calorie cooking spray. Place back over a medium heat and add the cubed chorizo. Cook for 3–4 minutes, keeping it moving around the pan so it does not burn. The chorizo should begin to release its own paprika-flavoured oil.

Once the chorizo is starting to crisp up and has released its oils, add the sliced onions and peppers and cook for a further 4–5 minutes, until the peppers and onions have softened and taken on the chorizo oil. Put the chicken back in the pan along with the chopped parsley and a squeeze of lime juice. Stir everything together. Put the chicken and chorizo mix in a bowl and set aside.

Place the grated mozzarella and Cheddar cheese in a separate bowl and mix to combine.

Place a tortilla in a dry frying pan and top with a quarter of the cheese mix. Spoon half of the chicken and chorizo filling on top and spread out in an even layer. Top with another quarter of

TIPS

If you are making vegetarian quesadillas, then use a vegetarian meat alternative or use only the peppers and onions in the filling.

Use a pizza-style mozzarella in these quesadillas as any soft mozzarella balls will release too much water and make the quesadillas wet.

To flip the quesadilla, slide onto a plate or chopping board. Turn the frying pan over to cover the uncooked side of the quesadilla and quickly flip the plate/board and the pan at the same.

the cheese. Place another tortilla wrap on top of the filling and place the pan over a low-medium heat. Toast the quesadilla for 3 minutes on one side or until the bottom of the tortilla is golden brown and the cheese is starting to melt inside. Flip the quesadilla over in the pan and cook for a further 2–3 minutes until the bottom tortilla is toasted and the cheese in the quesadilla is completely melted. Repeat this process with the remaining ingredients to make a second quesadilla.

Quarter the quesadillas and serve two quarters per person.

The chicken, chorizo and pepper filling will keep in the fridge for up to 3 days. When ready to use, assemble the quesadillas as per the recipe guidelines. Bring the filling to room temperature and place between the tortillas with a sprinkling of cheese and gently toast in a pan until the filling and cheese is warm.

VEGAN

OMIT CHICKEN AND USE VEGETABLE STOCK CUBE

VEGGIE

OMIT CHICKEN AND USE VEGETABLE STOCK CUBE

BATCH COOK

DAIRY FREE

GLUTEN FREE

USE GF SOY SAUCE AND STOCK CUBE

HIGH PROTEIN

NOODLE POTS

10 MINS + 10 MINS RESTING | **NO COOK** | **SERVES 4**

PER SERVING:
340 KCAL /53G CARBS

SPECIAL EQUIPMENT
4 x 500ml jars with lids (mason jars are ideal)

1 chicken stock cube, crumbled
1 tsp garlic granules
½ tsp ground ginger
4 tbsp soy sauce
120g cooked sweetcorn
120g cooked, shelled edamame beans
2 carrots, peeled and finely shredded or grated
4 spring onions, trimmed and finely sliced
160g cooked chicken breast, cut into small dice
4 x 50g nests of thin rice noodles

Say goodbye to boring lunches! These handy Noodle Pots are our lighter, homemade twist on shop-bought cup noodles, but without any hidden nasties. Layered up in a mason jar with chicken, crunchy veg, and flavourings like garlic, ginger and soy, all you need to do is top with boiling water when you're ready to eat. They're quick to prep, fridge-friendly for up to four days, and completely customizable!

Everyday Light

Divide the ingredients between the jars and layer up in the order they are listed, keeping the wetter items away from the noodles.

Break the noodles up a little, then press everything down so you can fasten the lid. Store in the fridge for up to 4 days.

To prepare, bring the jar out of the fridge for at least 30 minutes to allow it to come to room temperature. Top up with boiling water, straight from the kettle. Reseal the jar and leave to stand for 10 minutes.

Stir well with a fork, making sure you get right down to the flavourings at the bottom of the jar, and enjoy!

The assembled jars will keep in the fridge for 3–4 days. Once prepared, use immediately.

TIP

If you want to make this recipe vegan and vegetarian, swap the chicken for extra edamame beans.

HARISSA AUBERGINE *and* HALLOUMI SALAD

15 MINS | **45 MINS** | **SERVES 4**

VEGAN
USE VEGAN CHEESE, YOGHURT AND MAPLE SYRUP

VEGGIE

BATCH COOK

DAIRY FREE
USE DF HALLOUMI AND YOGHURT

GLUTEN FREE

HIGH PROTEIN

PER SERVING:
379 KCAL / 30G CARBS

- low-calorie cooking spray
- 2 aubergines, approx. 400g, trimmed
- 90g harissa paste
- salt and freshly ground black pepper, to taste
- 225g reduced-fat halloumi, cut into 1cm (½in) cubes
- 250g cooked quinoa
- 15g fresh mint leaves, chopped
- 50g rocket
- 80g pomegranate seeds
- juice of 1 lemon
- 1 tbsp olive oil
- 1 tbsp honey
- 1 tsp Dijon mustard
- 1½ tbsp pomegranate molasses
- 100g fat-free Greek yoghurt

We've roasted creamy, meaty aubergine in a harissa coating until it's deliciously sticky, then paired it with tangy halloumi for the ultimate contrast. Quinoa brings a nutty boost of protein, while fresh mint, peppery rocket and pomegranate seeds add colour and crunch. Finished with a slimming-friendly sweet and tangy dressing, this rainbow of a salad is packed with flavour!

Everyday Light

Preheat the oven to 220°C (fan 200°C/gas mark 7) and spray a baking tray with low-calorie cooking spray.

Slice the aubergine lengthways and then again into wedges. You should get around eight to ten wedges per aubergine.

Place the wedges on the prepared baking tray and spoon the harissa on top. Use your hands to coat the aubergine well. Season with salt and pepper and roast in the oven for 35–45 minutes. Turn the wedges halfway through cooking. If they are looking dry, spray with a little low-calorie cooking spray. The aubergine is ready when the wedges are soft, golden and sticky with harissa. Remove from the oven and set aside.

Put the halloumi into a dry frying pan and cook over a medium heat for 5–10 minutes until golden. Remove the pan from the heat.

Place the cooked quinoa in a large bowl along with the chopped mint, rocket and pomegranate seeds. Add the halloumi and stir.

To make the dressing, place half of the lemon juice in a bowl along with the olive oil, honey, mustard and pomegranate molasses. Add a pinch of salt and pepper to season and whisk to combine. Add two-thirds of the dressing to the quinoa and halloumi and stir through. Place the yoghurt in a separate bowl with the remaining lemon juice and a good pinch of salt and pepper. Mix to combine.

To serve, place the halloumi and quinoa salad on a serving plate and top with the harissa aubergine wedges. Finish with a drizzle of lemon yoghurt and any remaining dressing, if preferred. The salad and dressing will keep in separate containers in the fridge for up to 3 days.

TIPS

Different brands of harissa can have different spice strengths. Taste your harissa before coating the aubergine to make sure the spice strength is to your taste. We used Tesco's own brand harissa, which is not too spicy.

Once cooked, this salad is best eaten at room temperature, but the aubergines can be reheated in a 180°C (fan 160°C/gas mark 5) oven for 5–10 minutes until piping hot.

VEGAN

USE VEGAN YOGHURT AND FETA

VEGGIE

BATCH COOK

DAIRY FREE

USE DF YOGHURT AND FETA

GLUTEN FREE

USE GF COUSCOUS

HIGH PROTEIN

MAPLE-ROASTED CARROTS *with* WHIPPED FETA *and* GIANT COUSCOUS

15 MINS   40 MINS   SERVES 4

PER SERVING:
294 KCAL / 34G CARBS

SPECIAL EQUIPMENT
Food processor

- low-calorie cooking spray
- 550g medium carrots, about 10, washed thoroughly and cut lengthways in half
- salt and freshly ground black pepper, to taste
- 2 tbsp maple syrup
- 250g giant couscous
- 10g fresh parsley, chopped, plus extra to garnish
- 10g fresh mint, chopped
- 1 tbsp extra virgin olive oil
- 1 tsp Dijon mustard
- juice of 1 lemon
- 150g reduced-fat feta cheese
- 100g reduced-fat Greek yoghurt
- ½ tbsp honey

We bet you never thought you'd be fantasizing about carrots for lunch, but with this recipe up your sleeve, you just might! We've made the most of this humble veg's natural sweetness by drizzling it with maple syrup and then roasting it for a sticky, caramelized effect. The addition of creamy whipped feta and nutty giant couscous brings everything together!

Everyday Light

Preheat the oven to 220°C (fan 200°C/gas mark 7) and line a baking tray with non-stick baking paper. Spray with low-calorie cooking spray and set aside.

Place the halved carrots on the baking tray, spray with low-calorie cooking spray and season with salt and pepper. Roast in the oven for 15 minutes.

Place 1 tablespoon of the maple syrup in a bowl and, once the carrots have roasted for 15 minutes, use a pastry brush to brush the syrup over the carrots. Return the carrots to the oven and roast for a further 20–25 minutes until sticky and golden. Remove from the oven and set aside.

Cook the couscous according to packet instructions. Drain and place in a large bowl. Add the chopped herbs and stir through.

To make the dressing, whisk the remaining maple syrup in a small bowl with the olive oil, mustard, half of the lemon juice and a pinch of salt and pepper. Add the dressing to the couscous and mix.

Put the feta cheese in the food processor with the yoghurt, honey and remaining lemon juice, add 1 tablespoon water to loosen the mix and blitz to a thick and creamy white sauce.

To serve, add a spoonful or two of the whipped feta to a serving plate and top with the couscous. Place the carrots on top of the couscous and garnish with a little fresh parsley. The carrots and couscous will keep in the fridge for up to 3 days. The whipped feta will keep in the fridge for up to 3 days.

TIPS

If you are making this dish vegan, leave out the honey from the whipped feta.

Alternatively, you can cook these carrots in the air fryer, if you prefer. Air-fry at 160°C for 30–35 minutes, making sure to add the maple glaze after 10 minutes.

This salad is best eaten at room temperature after storing in the fridge.

VEGAN
USE VEGAN RICOTTA AND HARD CHEESE AND VEGAN MILK INSTEAD OF EGG

VEGGIE
USE VEGETARIAN HARD CHEESE

BATCH COOK

DAIRY FREE
USE DF RICOTTA AND HARD CHEESE

GLUTEN FREE
USE GF PUFF PASTRY

COURGETTE, LEMON *and* RICOTTA TART

10 MINS **30 MINS** **SERVES 6**

PER SERVING:
329 KCAL /24G CARBS

SPECIAL EQUIPMENT
Food processor

- 320g light ready-rolled puff pastry, chilled
- 250g ricotta cheese
- juice of 1 lemon
- 20g fresh mint, chopped
- 20g fresh basil, chopped
- 2 garlic cloves, peeled and crushed
- salt and freshly ground black pepper, to taste
- 500g courgette, trimmed and sliced into very thin rounds
- low-calorie cooking spray
- 1 medium egg, beaten
- 20g Italian hard cheese, grated
- 15g pine nuts, toasted
- 1 tbsp extra virgin olive oil
- 90g pea shoots, to serve

In this cheesy vegetable tart, pre-rolled pastry saves you precious time in the kitchen. Top it with lemony ricotta and seasonal veg for a light, fresh filling that keeps calories down without compromising on flavour. Bookmark this one when you want to be the host with the most without actually doing the most. Take leftovers to work for lunch (if there are any!)

Everyday Light

Preheat the oven to 220°C (fan 200°C/gas mark 7) and line a large baking tray with non-stick baking paper.

Unroll the pre-rolled pastry and lay it on the lined baking tray. Use a knife to gently score a line approximately 1cm (½in) from the edge of the pastry to create a border for the tart. Take care not to cut the pastry all the way through.

Place the ricotta in a large bowl along with half of the lemon juice and half of the chopped mint and basil leaves. Add a crushed garlic clove and a pinch of salt and pepper and mix well to combine. Spoon the ricotta mix on the inner part of the pastry sheet, taking care not to cover the pastry border.

Place the courgette rounds in rows on top of the ricotta until it is completely covered, taking care not to cover the pastry border. Spray the courgettes with low-calorie cooking spray. Use a pastry brush to brush the beaten egg over the pastry border until it is well coated. Bake in the oven for 30 minutes, or until the pastry is golden brown and the courgette rounds are cooked.

Place the remaining chopped mint and basil in the food processor along with the grated hard cheese, toasted pine nuts, the remaining crushed garlic clove and the olive oil. Add 1 tablespoon warm water, the remaining lemon juice and a pinch of salt and pepper. Blitz until you get a smooth green sauce. If the sauce is too thick, let it down slightly with another tablespoon of warm water.

Use a pastry brush to brush the green sauce gently over the tart to cover the courgette slices. Serve topped with pea shoots and an extra drizzle of the herby green sauce. The tart will keep in the fridge for up to 2 days.

TIPS

Use a mandoline to get the courgette rounds extra thin.

Most supermarket-bought rolled puff pastry is vegan but be sure to check before you buy.

To store the tart, portion it into six and wrap in foil, then keep in the fridge. It can be eaten at room temperature or you can reheat in in a 180°C (fan 160°C/gas mark 5) oven for 5–10 minutes until warmed through.

BATCH COOK

GLUTEN FREE

USE GF WRAP

HIGH PROTEIN

NEW YORK DELI WRAP

15 MINS | NO COOK | SERVES 4

PER SERVING:
372 KCAL /37G CARBS

FOR THE MUSTARD COLESLAW

150g lighter than light mayonnaise
2 tsp English mustard
¼ tsp dill
2 tsp pickle juice
100g red cabbage, shredded
1 carrot, peeled and cut into matchsticks or coarsely grated
2 spring onions, trimmed and finely sliced
good pinch of freshly ground black pepper

FOR THE WRAPS

4 x 60g tortilla wraps
200g sliced pastrami
4 x 25g Dutch Edam slices, cut in half
4 pickled gherkins, sliced lengthways
good handful of rocket leaves

Bring a bite of the Big Apple to your lunchtimes with this make-ahead pastrami feast. Peppery pastrami pairs with mild and smooth Edam, with creamy mustard coleslaw adding a satisfying crunch. We've also included tangy pickles to give the whole thing a welcome 'zing!' that perfectly balances all the other flavours. The best part? You don't even have to make it on the day; assemble a couple and stick them in the fridge, ready to grab on your way out the front door.

Everyday Light

Place the mayonnaise, mustard, dill and pickle juice in a large bowl and mix well. Remove 2 tablespoons and reserve for assembling the wraps.

Add the cabbage, carrot and spring onions to the mayo and mix until well combined. Season well with pepper.

Now assemble the wraps. Lay the tortilla in front of you and use the reserved mustard mayo to spread thinly on each one.

Distribute the filling evenly along the lower half of the wrap, leaving a 2cm (¾in) gap at the edges for folding. Start with the pastrami, then cheese, coleslaw, sliced gherkins and top with a handful of rocket leaves.

Bring the sides of the wrap in, to hold the filling, then roll tightly from the bottom to fully enclose.

Wrap the wrap in greaseproof paper, twisting the ends like a cracker to seal, or wrap in foil. Repeat with the other wraps. The wraps will keep in the fridge for 3–4 days.

TIP

You can swap pastrami for sliced beef.

BUTTERNUT SQUASH, CARROT *and* COCONUT SOUP

20 MINS | 45 MINS | SERVES 4

VEGAN

VEGGIE

FREEZE ME

BATCH COOK

DAIRY FREE

GLUTEN FREE

USE GF STOCK CUBES

PER SERVING:
187 KCAL /18G CARBS

SPECIAL EQUIPMENT
Stick blender or food processor

low-calorie cooking spray
1 onion, peeled and diced
400g butternut squash, peeled and chopped (prepared weight)
250g carrots, peeled and diced
1 red chilli, deseeded and chopped
2 garlic cloves, peeled and crushed
1 x 400ml tin light coconut milk
600ml vegetable stock (1 stock cube dissolved in 600ml boiling water)
juice of ½ lime
salt and freshly ground black pepper, to taste
1 tbsp pumpkin seeds

TO ACCOMPANY (OPTIONAL)
60g wholemeal bread roll (+146 kcal per serving)

This vibrant soup is everything we love about autumn. The butternut squash and carrots turn silky and sweet as they cook, and the coconut milk brings a gorgeous creamy richness that feels super comforting without being heavy. It's the perfect soup to batch at the weekend. Portion it up, chill or freeze it and you've got cosy lunches ready to grab.

Everyday Light

Spray a large saucepan with low-calorie cooking spray and place it over a medium heat. Add the onion, butternut squash and carrots and sauté for 10 minutes, or until the onion is soft. Add the chilli and garlic and cook for a further minute to release the flavours. Stir in the coconut milk and vegetable stock and bring to the boil. Turn the heat down to a simmer, cover with a lid and cook for 30 minutes, or until the vegetables are soft.

Remove the pan from the heat and use a stick blender to blitz to a smooth soup. Alternatively, transfer to a food processor, then return the soup to the pan.

Add the lime juice and season to taste with salt and pepper.

Ladle into bowls, sprinkle with the pumpkin seeds and serve, with bread rolls on the side if you like.

You can freeze the soup at this stage for up to 3 months (see Tips). The soup will keep in the fridge for up to 3 days. Reheat in the microwave for 3–5 minutes until piping hot.

TIPS

The pumpkin seeds add a nutty crunch, but if you leave them out, it is 169 kcal per serving.

If you've frozen the soup, once defrosted, reheat in the microwave for 3–5 minutes until piping hot.

VEGGIE

FREEZE ME

BATCH COOK

GLUTEN FREE
USE GF PASTRY

CHEESE *and* BEAN PINWHEELS

5 MINS | 20–25 MINS | MAKES 16

PER SERVING:
127 KCAL /14G CARBS

- 375g light, ready-rolled puff pastry
- 70g reduced-fat mature Cheddar cheese, finely grated
- 2 x 200g tins reduced sugar and salt baked beans
- ¼ tsp freshly ground black pepper

These Cheese and Bean Pinwheels are about to become your new favourite easy bake! With just five ingredients, they're super simple to make. They need less than half an hour in the oven, and when they're ready, you'll have gloriously golden puff pastry swirls packed with cheesy baked beans. Perfect for lunchboxes, buffets, your next picnic or simply as an on-the-go snack.

Everyday Light

Preheat the oven to 200°C (fan 180°C/gas mark 6) and line a baking tray with non-stick baking paper.

Unroll the pastry sheet, leaving it on the greaseproof paper backing, and place on the work surface. Sprinkle over half the grated cheese, leaving a 1cm (½in) gap along the long edges.

Spoon over the beans, trying to get an even coverage. Add the remaining cheese and sprinkle over the black pepper.

Roll up the pastry, starting with the long edge closest to you, using the paper backing to help you. Keep rolling until you have made a 'Swiss roll'. When you have finished rolling the pastry up, make sure it is seam side down. Use a large, serrated knife to cut it into sixteen spiral-shaped slices.

Place the swirls flat on the lined baking tray, leaving gaps between each swirl. Bake in the oven for 20–25 minutes until golden and crisp. Place on a wire rack to cool or serve warm fresh from the oven. You can freeze the cooled pinwheels at this stage by placing them in a freezerproof container between layers of non-stick baking paper. Freeze for up to 3 months (see Tips). The pinwheels will keep in an airtight container for 3 days.

TIPS

Alternatively, you can cook these swirls in the air fryer if you prefer. Air-fry at 160°C for 10–15 minutes until golden and crisp.

If you find the pastry difficult to slice, wrap the roll up in the greaseproof paper packaging and pop back into the fridge to chill for 10 minutes. The pastry will firm up and be easier to slice.

If you've frozen the pinwheels, defrost overnight in the fridge. They can be eaten cold or re-reheated in a 200°C (fan 180°C/gas mark 6) oven for 10 minutes until warmed through.

VEGGIE

FREEZE ME

BATCH COOK

GLUTEN FREE

USE GF FLOUR

BLUEBERRY CRUMBLE SQUARES

10 MINS | 40 MINS | MAKES 16

PER SERVING:
108 KCAL /19G CARBS

SPECIAL EQUIPMENT
20cm (8in) square baking tin, food processor

300g self-raising flour
60g granulated sweetener
60g reduced-fat spread
1 medium egg
1 tsp almond extract
150g reduced-fat cottage cheese
1 tsp vanilla extract
1 tbsp honey
100g blueberries, halved
10g flaked almonds

Meet your new favourite sweet treat that almost tastes too good to be slimming-friendly: blueberry crumble in bite-sized form! You won't believe how simple this is to make. Bake a batch and pop it into your fridge and they'll keep for up to three days, so you have a ready-made treat waiting for your afternoon cuppa!

Everyday Light

Preheat the oven to 200°C (fan 180°C/gas mark 6) and line the square baking tin with non-stick baking paper.

First, make the crumble. In a large bowl, add the flour and sweetener and stir to combine. Using your fingertips, rub the spread into the flour mixture until it forms a breadcrumb texture.

Add the egg and almond extract to the flour mixture and use your hands to bring it together until it's just starting to stick together in a larger breadcrumb texture.

Add the cottage cheese, vanilla and honey to the food processor and blitz until smooth.

Add half the crumble mixture to the prepared tin and firmly press flat with your fingers, covering the bottom of the tin. Spread the cottage cheese mixture onto the base and scatter over the halved blueberries. Add the remaining crumble mixture over the top and press with your fingers to encase the blueberries between the two layers.

Sprinkle over the flaked almonds and bake in the oven for 35–40 minutes, until the top is golden brown and the blueberries are soft when a knife is inserted.

Leave to cool completely in the tin, then cut into sixteen squares and serve! You can freeze the squares in an airtight container for up to 3 months (defrost overnight), or the squares will keep in an airtight container for up to 4 days.

VEGGIE

FREEZE ME

BATCH COOK

DAIRY FREE

USE DF YOGHURT AND MILK

GLUTEN FREE

USE GF OATS AND FLOUR

TRIPLE BERRY BAKES

10 MINS **20–25 MINS** **SERVES 4**

PER SERVING:
450 KCAL /68G CARBS

SPECIAL EQUIPMENT
4 x ovenproof and freezer-proof containers with lids (10 x 14cm /4 x 5½in)

80g rolled porridge oats
160g self-raising flour
2 tbsp chia seeds
160g fat-free Greek yoghurt
160ml skimmed milk
4 medium eggs
2 tbsp granulated sweetener
4 tbsp honey
2 tsp vanilla extract
200g raspberries, fresh or frozen
120g blackberries, fresh or frozen
40g blueberries, fresh or frozen

Wake up to something sweet and surprisingly healthy with these. Packed with juicy berries, 21g of protein, and 8g of fibre per pot, they're designed to give your mornings a proper boost. We've made them in individual pots so they're great for grabbing on the go, prepping ahead for the week or freezing for later. We went for raspberries, blackberries and blueberries, but feel free to sub in your favourites, and you've got a fruity breakfast that's fluffy and golden on the outside and soft and sweet on the inside.

Weekly Indulgence

Preheat the oven to 200°C (fan 180°C/gas mark 6).

In a large bowl, add the oats, flour, chia seeds, yoghurt, milk, eggs, sweetener, 2 tablespoons of the honey and vanilla and mix well. Divide between the containers and top with the raspberries, blackberries and blueberries. Place the containers on a baking tray and pop into the oven for 20–25 minutes until slightly risen and golden brown on top.

Remove from the oven and drizzle over the remaining honey. Leave to cool completely before covering with lids and storing in the freezer for up to 3 months or in the fridge for up to 4 days. Reheat in the microwave for 2–3 minutes until piping hot.

TIPS

Swap for other berries if you prefer.

If you've frozen the dish, once defrosted, reheat in the microwave for 2–3 minutes until piping hot.

VEGGIE

FREEZE ME

BATCH COOK

DAIRY FREE

USE DF SPREAD

BANANA CRUMBLE MUFFINS

10 MINS | 20–25 MINS | MAKES 12

PER SERVING:
121 KCAL /26G CARBS

SPECIAL EQUIPMENT
12-hole muffin tray, 12 muffin cases, electric hand whisk

FOR THE MUFFINS
60g reduced-fat spread
100g brown granulated sweetener, you can use white if you prefer
1 medium egg
180g self-raising flour
½ tsp baking powder
1 tsp vanilla extract
½ tsp ground cinnamon
2 medium bananas, peeled and mashed

FOR THE CRUMBLE TOPPING
30g self-raising flour
15g brown sugar
15g reduced-fat spread

Get ready for these effortless Banana Crumble Muffins to make your kitchen smell amazing! We've flavoured these beauties with cinnamon and vanilla, then finished them with a simple crumble topping. Think banana bread, but in a grab-and-go muffin form. Ready in 30 minutes, you'll bake a big batch and have a lovely pick-me-up whenever you fancy something sweet.

Everyday Light

Preheat the oven to 200°C (fan 180°C/gas mark 6) and line the muffin tray with the cases.

For the muffins, add the spread and sweetener to a large bowl. Mix using an electric whisk for 1 minute, or until pale and combined. Add the egg, flour, baking powder, vanilla, cinnamon and mashed bananas and mix until fully combined.

Divide the batter between the muffin cases.

For the crumble topping, in a small bowl, combine the flour and sugar. Add the spread, then rub it in with your fingertips until it forms a breadcrumb texture.

Sprinkle the crumble topping over each muffin. Bake in the oven for 20–25 minutes until a skewer inserted comes out clean and the tops are lightly golden brown. Leave to cool before freezing for up to 3 months or storing in an airtight container for up to 4 days.

TIPS

Save those brown, spotty bananas for this recipe, as they are best!

If you've frozen the muffins, then defrost overnight.

VEGGIE

FREEZE ME

BATCH COOK

GLUTEN FREE

USE GF PASTRY

CHOCOLATE CUSTARD SWIRLS

10 MINS + 15 MINS CHILLING **15–20 MINS** **MAKES 16**

PER SERVING:
99 KCAL /13G CARBS

100g light custard
½ tsp vanilla extract
1 tsp cornflour
320g light ready-rolled puff pastry sheet
50g milk chocolate chips

Have you been eyeing up the chocolate twists in the supermarket bakery aisle recently? Say hello to our slimming-friendly version! We've taken fluffy puff pastry and filled it with light custard, then added milk chocolate chips to sweeten the deal even more. They're flaky on the outside and soft in the middle, and just what you need when you're craving something sweet but don't want to go overboard.

Everyday Light

Line a baking tray with non-stick baking paper.

Add the custard to a small bowl, then add the vanilla and cornflour and mix until smooth.

Unroll the chilled pastry sheet on a chopping board, leaving it on the greaseproof paper backing, and spread the custard evenly over the pastry sheet, leaving a 1cm (½in) gap along one long edge. Scatter the chocolate chips evenly over the custard.

Roll the pastry up, starting with the long edge without the gap, using the greaseproof paper backing to help you. Keep rolling until you've made a 'Swiss roll', finishing seam side down. Place the roll still on the chopping board in the fridge and chill for 15 minutes to firm up.

Preheat the oven to 200°C (fan 180°C/gas mark 6).

Use a large, serrated knife to carefully cut into sixteen spiral-shaped slices. Don't worry if the spirals aren't perfectly shaped, you can reshape them on the baking tray, if needed.

Lay the slices flat on the lined baking tray, leaving gaps between each and gently press the seam on each to seal.

Bake in the oven for 15–20 minutes until golden and crisp. You can freeze the cooled swirls at this stage by placing them in a freezerproof container between layers of non-stick baking paper. Freeze for up to 3 months (see Tips).

The swirls will keep in the fridge for up to 4 days.

TIPS

Alternatively, you can cook these swirls in the air fryer if you prefer. Air-fry at 160°C for 10–15 minutes, until crisp and golden.

If you've frozen the swirls, defrost overnight in the fridge. They can be eaten cold or re-reheated in a 200°C (fan 180°C/gas mark 6) oven for 10 minutes until warmed through.

FREEZE AND GO

FREEZE ME

STEW ONLY

BATCH COOK

DAIRY FREE

HIGH PROTEIN

CITRUS CHICKEN STEW

15 MINS 35 MINS SERVES 4

PER SERVING:
499 KCAL /63G CARBS

SPECIAL EQUIPMENT
28cm (10in) casserole dish, suitable for hob and oven

- 1 onion, peeled and diced
- 1 red pepper, deseeded and diced
- 1 carrot, peeled and diced
- 2 celery sticks, diced
- 4 garlic cloves, peeled and crushed
- 480g diced chicken breast
- 1 tsp garlic granules
- 1 tsp ground turmeric
- ½ tsp chilli powder
- 1 tbsp tomato puree
- salt and freshly ground black pepper, to taste
- low-calorie cooking spray
- juice of 1 grapefruit, approx. 150ml
- juice of 1 orange, approx. 50ml
- 1 tbsp cornflour
- 1 tbsp cold water
- 1 vegetable stock cube
- 200g couscous
- 200ml boiling water
- 200g sweetcorn
- 200g frozen peas
- 100g spinach, stalks removed, washed and completely dried

Zesty and ready in a flash, this stew is pure sunshine in a pan. The orange and grapefruit juice combine to give it a lovely tang that really lifts all the flavours, bubbling away with a rainbow of veggies for added crunch and even more colour. It's all done on the hob too, so you stick it all in one pan and you won't have to worry about a big pile of washing up. Serve with fluffy couscous because trust us, you'll want to soak up every last drop!

Weekly Indulgence

Add the onion, red pepper, carrot, celery, garlic and diced chicken to a large freezer-proof bag. Sprinkle in the garlic granules, turmeric, chilli powder, tomato puree and season to taste with salt and pepper. Give the bag a good shake, then seal and label. Freeze for up to 3 months.

When ready to cook, defrost the bag overnight in the fridge.

Spray a large casserole dish with low-calorie cooking spray and place over a medium heat. Add the contents of the bag and fry for 10 minutes, or until the chicken is browned on all sides and the vegetables are starting to soften.

Add the grapefruit and orange juices. In a small bowl, mix the cornflour with the cold water until smooth. Pour into the casserole dish with the stock cube, stirring well. Cover with a lid and simmer for 20 minutes, or until the vegetables are soft and the chicken is cooked through.

Meanwhile, place the couscous in a heatproof bowl and pour over the boiling water. Cover with a plate and set aside until ready to serve.

Add the sweetcorn and peas to the casserole dish and cook uncovered for 5 minutes, or until heated through. Add the spinach and stir until wilted. Serve the stew with the couscous. You can freeze the chicken stew for 3 months, but make the couscous when you are ready to serve. Reheat in the microwave for 3–4 minutes until piping hot.

The chicken stew will keep in the fridge for up to 3 days.

VEGAN

VEGGIE

FREEZE ME

BATCH COOK

DAIRY FREE

GLUTEN FREE

USE GF STOCK CUBES

SPICY CHICKPEA SOUP

15 MINS **VARIABLE** **SERVES 4**

PER SERVING:
218 KCAL /32G CARBS

- 1 x 400g tin chickpeas, drained and rinsed
- 1 onion, peeled and diced
- 1 medium pepper, any colour, halved, deseeded and diced
- 3 garlic cloves, peeled and crushed
- 1–2 tbsp harissa paste, depending on how spicy you like it
- 1 tsp ground cumin
- 1 x 400g tin chopped tomatoes
- 2 tbsp tomato puree
- juice of ½ lemon
- 1 vegetable stock cube
- 40g dried apricots, finely chopped
- 150g sweet potato, peeled and cut into 1cm (½in) dice
- handful of fresh coriander, chopped
- salt and freshly ground black pepper, to taste

TO ACCOMPANY (OPTIONAL)

- 60g wholemeal bread roll (+146 kcal per serving)

Need something warming, hearty, and full of flavour? This Spicy Chickpea Soup, packed with Moroccan-inspired flavours like harissa, cumin and sweet bursts of apricot, brings a little taste of sunshine to even the greyest winter day. It's loaded with veggies and tender chickpeas, making it filling enough to enjoy just as it is, or you can pair it with a wholemeal bread roll if you fancy something a bit more substantial. Comforting, colourful and seriously satisfying!

Everyday Light

HOB-TOP METHOD
50 MINS

Place all the ingredients, except the coriander and salt and pepper, in a large freezer-proof bag, seal well, label and freeze for up to 3 months.

Remove the bag from the freezer the day before you want to cook and defrost it overnight in the fridge.

When ready to cook, empty the contents of the bag into a large saucepan with a tight-fitting lid. Add 800ml water and stir well.

Bring to the boil, then turn the heat down to a simmer. Cover with a tight-fitting lid and cook for 45 minutes until the vegetables are tender, stirring occasionally.

When cooked, stir in the coriander, then season to taste with salt and pepper, if needed. You can freeze the soup at this stage, if you like for up to 3 months (see Tips). Serve with a bread roll, if you wish.

The soup will keep in the fridge for up to 3 days. Reheat, covered, in the microwave for 3–5 minutes, stirring halfway through, until piping hot.

SLOW COOKER METHOD
4–7 HOURS

SPECIAL EQUIPMENT
3.5-litre slow cooker

Place all the ingredients, except the coriander and salt and pepper, in a large freezer-proof bag, seal well, label and freeze for up to 3 months.

Remove the bag from the freezer the day before you want to cook and defrost it overnight in the fridge.

When ready to cook, empty the contents of the bag into the slow cooker pot. Add 800ml water and stir well. Cover with the lid and cook on high for 3–4 hours or on low for 6–7 hours.

When cooked, stir in the coriander, then season to taste with salt and pepper, if needed. You can freeze the soup at this stage, if you like (see Tips). Serve with a bread roll, if you wish.

The soup will keep in the fridge for up to 3 days. Reheat, covered, in the microwave for 3–5 minutes, stirring halfway through, until piping hot.

TIPS

If you want to cook this without the freezer prep, just fry the onions, peppers and garlic in a little low-calorie cooking spray in a large saucepan for 5 minutes, then add the remaining ingredients and cook for 45 minutes.

If you are slow cooking this soup and you want to cook this without the freezer prep, just add everything, except the coriander, to the slow cooker pot and follow the rest of the recipe.

If you've frozen the soup, once defrosted, cover and reheat in the microwave for 3–5 minutes, stirring halfway through, until piping hot.

Image overleaf.

VEGAN

VEGGIE

FREEZE ME

BATCH COOK

DAIRY FREE

GLUTEN FREE

USE GF STOCK CUBES

MEXICAN-STYLE RICE SOUP

20 MINS · VARIABLE · SERVES 6

PER SERVING:
216 KCAL / 36G CARBS

1 onion, peeled and diced
2 mixed peppers, halved, deseeded and diced
2 carrots, peeled and diced
2 red chillies, chopped
4 garlic cloves, peeled and crushed
2 tsp ground cumin
2 tsp dried oregano
1 tsp smoked sweet paprika
2 tbsp tomato puree
1 x 400g tin chopped tomatoes
1.2 litres vegetable stock (2 vegetable stock cubes dissolved in 1.2 litres boiling water)
1 x 198g tin sweetcorn, drained (160g drained weight)
1 x 400g tin kidney beans, rinsed and drained (240g drained weight)
125g long-grain rice
juice of ½ lime
handful of fresh coriander leaves, roughly chopped
salt and freshly ground black pepper, to taste

TO ACCOMPANY (OPTIONAL)
60g wholemeal bread roll (+146 kcal per serving)

If you're a fan of big, bold flavours, then you'll be wanting a big bowl of this soup. Cosy and comforting, we've packed it with tomatoes, beans and a colourful array of vegetables, thickening it with rice to make it wonderfully filling. What makes it extra special is the combination of garlic, cumin, smoky paprika and a gentle touch of chilli, giving every spoonful a gentle kick that warms you from the inside out.

Everyday Light

HOB-TOP METHOD
1 HOUR 5 MINS

Place the onion, peppers, carrots, chillies, garlic, cumin, oregano, paprika, tomato puree, chopped tomatoes, stock cubes, sweetcorn and kidney beans in a large freezer-proof bag, seal well, label and freeze for up to 3 months.

Remove the bag from the freezer the day before you want to cook and defrost it overnight in the fridge.

When ready to cook, empty the contents of the bag into a large saucepan. Add the stock and stir well. Bring to the boil, then turn the heat down to a simmer and cover with a tight-fitting lid. Cook for 50 minutes.

Rinse the rice under a cold tap and stir into the soup. Replace the lid and cook for a further 15 minutes, or until the rice is cooked.

Add the lime juice and coriander, and season to taste with salt and pepper. You can freeze the soup in individual portions for up to 3 months (see Tips). Serve with a bread roll, if you wish.

The soup will keep in the fridge for 1–2 days. Reheat individual portions in the microwave for 3–4 minutes, stirring halfway through, until piping hot.

SLOW COOKER METHOD
4½–8 HOURS

SPECIAL EQUIPMENT
3.5-litre slow cooker

Place the onions, peppers, carrots, chillies, garlic, cumin, oregano, paprika, tomato puree, chopped tomatoes, stock cubes, sweetcorn and kidney beans in a large freezer-proof bag, seal well, label and freeze for up to 3 months.

Remove the bag from the freezer the day before you want to cook and defrost it overnight in the fridge.

When ready to cook, empty the contents of the bag into the slow cooker pot. Add 1.2 litres boiling water and stir well. Cover with the lid and cook for 4 hours on high or 7–7½ hours on low.

Rinse the rice under a cold tap and stir into the soup. Replace the lid and cook for a further 25 minutes, or until the rice is cooked.

Add the lime juice and coriander, and season to taste with salt and pepper. You can freeze the soup in individual portions for up to 3 months (see Tips). Serve with a bread roll, if you wish.

The soup will keep in the fridge for 1–2 days. Reheat individual portions in the microwave for 3–4 minutes, stirring halfway through, until piping hot.

TIPS

You can make this as spicy as you want. For a mild heat, remove all the seeds and white membrane from inside the chillies. For more heat, chop it all up, seeds and all. We removed the seeds from one chilli and left some in the other for a medium-spiced soup.

If you are cooking this soup in advance, it will thicken up when left as the rice continues to absorb the liquid. Add a splash of water or stock when reheating, to thin it down, if you prefer.

If you are not preparing this as a Freeze and Go bag, add the onions, peppers, carrots, chillies, garlic, cumin, oregano, paprika, tomato puree, chopped tomatoes, stock cubes, sweetcorn and kidney beans to a large saucepan, then follow rest of the recipe.

If you've frozen the soup, once defrosted, reheat in the microwave for 3–4 minutes, stirring halfway through, until piping hot. The soup may dry when frozen, as the rice will absorb liquid as it defrosts. If it becomes too dry, add a splash of water or stock when reheating.

Image on page 175.

FREEZE ME

BATCH COOK

HIGH PROTEIN

GLUTEN FREE

USE GF ROLLS

SHREDDED TURKEY ROLLS

15 MINS | VARIABLE | SERVES 8

PER SERVING:
317 KCAL /33G CARBS

SPECIAL EQUIPMENT
Large casserole dish, suitable for oven and hob

- 2 tsp garlic granules
- 2 tsp onion granules
- 2 tsp dried mixed herbs
- 1 tsp mustard powder
- 400g turkey breast or turkey breast steaks
- 190g reduced-fat green pesto
- juice of 1 lemon
- 1 pepper, halved, deseeded and sliced (any colour)
- 100g spinach leaves
- 50g reduced-fat cream cheese

TO SERVE:

- 200g cherry tomatoes, diced
- 2 tsp finely sliced fresh basil
- salt and freshly ground black pepper, to taste
- 8 bread rolls, approx. 60g per roll, sliced in half
- 125g reduced-fat mozzarella
- 10g reduced-fat spread
- 1 tsp dried mixed herbs

TO ACCOMPANY (OPTIONAL)

- 75g mixed salad (+15 kcal per serving)

More often than not, simple ingredients can go a long way, and this is proof of just that! Juicy shredded turkey meat is mixed with pesto and cream cheese, creating a herby, smooth savoury filling with just the right amount of zing. This fresh take on your regular sandwich always hits the spot. The real bonus is how easy they are to make ahead! Prep this bag in advance and it's there whenever you're ready to cook.

Everyday Light

HOB-TOP METHOD
1 HOUR 10 MINS

Add the garlic granules, onion granules, mixed herbs and mustard powder to a small bowl and mix to combine. Add the turkey to a large freezer-proof bag, sprinkle over the herb mixture and rub it into the turkey. Add the pesto and rub it into the turkey. Seal the bag, label and freeze for up to 3 months.

Remove the bag from the freezer the day before you want to cook and defrost it overnight in the fridge.

When ready to cook, preheat the oven to 180°C (fan 160°C/gas mark 4). Empty the contents of the bag into the casserole dish, add the lemon juice, 25ml water and the peppers. Mix well, cover with a lid and cook in the oven for 35–45 minutes.

Remove the turkey to a plate and, using two forks, shred the meat. Return the turkey meat to the pan. Add the spinach and return to the oven for 5 minutes, or until wilted. Add the cream cheese and mix until combined. You can freeze the turkey mixture or store it in an airtight container at this stage for up to 3 months and assemble the rolls when ready to serve. Add the tomatoes and basil to a large bowl and season to taste with salt and pepper.

Place the bottom halves of the bread rolls on an ovenproof tray and pack the rolls quite tightly together. Spoon the turkey mixture onto the bottom half of the rolls, then divide the tomato mixture between the rolls and tear the mozzarella on top. Pop into the oven for 10 minutes.

Add the reduced-fat spread to a small bowl and melt for 30 seconds in the microwave. Stir in the dried herbs.

Replace each lid on top of the turkey and brush the top of each roll with the spread and herb mixture. Pop back into the oven for a further 8–10 minutes, covering the rolls with foil if they are beginning to brown too much. Serve with a mixed salad, if you wish.

The turkey will keep in the fridge for up to 4 days. Reheat the turkey in the microwave for 4 minutes, or in a frying pan until heated through, then assemble the rolls fresh.

SLOW COOKER METHOD

2 HOURS 20 MINS

SPECIAL EQUIPMENT

3.5-litre slow cooker

Add the garlic granules, onion granules, mixed herbs and mustard powder to a small bowl and mix to combine. Add the turkey to a large freezer-proof bag, sprinkle over the herb mixture and rub it into the turkey. Add the pesto and again rub it into the turkey. Seal the bag, label and freeze for up to 3 months.

Remove the bag from the freezer the day before you want to cook and defrost it overnight in the fridge. When ready to cook, empty the contents of the bag into the slow cooker pot, then add the lemon juice, 25ml water and the peppers. Mix well, cover with a lid and cook on high for 1½–2 hours. Remove the turkey to a plate and, using two forks, shred the meat.

Return the turkey meat to the pot. Add the spinach and cover with a lid until wilted. Add the cream cheese and mix until combined. You can freeze or store the turkey mixture at this stage and assemble the rolls when ready to serve. Add the tomatoes and basil to a large bowl and season to taste with salt and pepper.

Preheat the oven to 180°C (fan 160°C/ gas mark 4).

Place the bottom halves of the bread rolls on an ovenproof tray and pack the rolls quite tightly together. Spoon the turkey mixture onto the bottom half of the rolls, then divide the tomato mixture between the rolls and tear the mozzarella on top. Pop into the oven for 10 minutes.

Add the reduced-fat spread to a small bowl and melt for 30 seconds in the microwave. Stir in the dried herbs.

Replace each lid on top of the turkey and brush the top of each roll with the spread and herb mixture. Pop back into the oven for a further 8–10 minutes, covering the rolls with foil if they are beginning to brown too much.

Serve with a mixed salad, if you wish. The turkey will keep in the fridge for up to 4 days.

Reheat the shredded turkey in the microwave for 4 minutes, or in a frying pan until heated through, then assemble the rolls fresh.

TIPS

Alternatively, if you prefer not to prepare as a freeze and go bag, skip freezing the turkey and follow the recipe as above.

If you've frozen the cooked turkey, once defrosted, reheat the turkey in the microwave for 4 minutes, or in a frying pan until heated through.

FREEZE ME

BATCH COOK

DAIRY FREE

GLUTEN FREE

USE GF SOY SAUCE

HIGH PROTEIN

FIVE-SPICE BEEF *with* PLUMS

10 MINS **VARIABLE** **SERVES 4**

PER SERVING:
386 KCAL /37G CARBS

SPECIAL EQUIPMENT
28cm (11in) shallow casserole dish with a tight-fitting lid

- 1 onion, peeled and sliced
- 2 carrots, peeled and sliced
- 6 plums, stones removed and diced
- 4 garlic cloves, peeled and crushed
- large piece of fresh root ginger, peeled and grated
- 2 tsp Chinese five-spice
- 4 tbsp soy sauce
- 2 tbsp honey
- 1 x 400g tin chopped tomatoes
- 500g lean diced beef
- 2 tbsp cornflour mixed to a slurry with 2 tbsp water (optional)

TO ACCOMPANY
50g raw/125g cooked basmati rice (+173 kcal per serving)

Craving something rich, comforting and effortlessly impressive? This Five-spice Beef with Plums is a brilliant prep-ahead winner! Just defrost, pop everything into your pot, then let it gently simmer away while you put your feet up. The beef slow-cooks until it's melt-in-the-mouth tender in a fragrant garlic, ginger and five-spice sauce, with sticky-sweet plums. We love this fakeaway served with rice, noodles or even chips.

Special Occasion

OVEN METHOD

3 HOURS

Place all the ingredients, except the cornflour, in a large freezer-proof bag, then seal, label and freeze for up to 3 months. Remove the bag from the freezer the day before you want to cook and defrost it overnight in the fridge.

When ready to cook, preheat the oven to 180°C (fan 160°C/gas mark 4). Empty the contents of the bag into the casserole dish, stir in 200ml water and cover with a tight-fitting lid. Cook in the oven for 3 hours, or until the beef is tender and the carrots are cooked.

Stir after 90 minutes and add more water if it seems to be drying out. If the sauce needs thickening, stir the cornflour slurry into the pan, until the sauce thickens. You can freeze the dish at this stage for up to 3 months (see Tips). Serve with rice.

The stew will keep in the fridge for up to 3 days. Reheat, covered, in the microwave for 3–5 minutes, stirring halfway through, until piping hot.

SLOW COOKER METHOD

6–8 HOURS

SPECIAL EQUIPMENT
3.5-litre slow cooker

Place all the ingredients, except the cornflour, in a large freezer-proof bag, then seal, label and freeze for up to 3 months. Remove the bag from the freezer the day before you want to cook and defrost it overnight in the fridge.

TIPS

If you are not preparing this as a Freeze and Go bag, add all the ingredients straight into a casserole dish and cook as above.

If you've frozen the cooked stew, once defrosted, cover and reheat in the microwave for 3–5 minutes, stirring halfway through, until piping hot.

When you are ready to cook, empty the contents of the bag into the slow cooker pot, stir in 200ml water and cover with the lid. Cook on high for 5–6 hours or low for 8 hours until the beef is tender and the carrots are cooked. If the sauce needs thickening, stir the cornflour slurry into the stew, until the sauce thickens. You can freeze the dish at this stage for up to 3 months (see Tips). Serve with rice.

The stew will keep in the fridge for up to 3 days. Reheat, covered, in the microwave for 3–5 minutes, stirring halfway through, until piping hot.

TIPS

When defrosting, place the bag in a tray, to catch any drips.

If the contents of the freezer bag are still frosty, you may have to increase the cooking time.

FREEZE ME

BATCH COOK

DAIRY FREE

LOW CARB

HIGH PROTEIN

TERIYAKI-STYLE CHICKEN DRUMSTICKS

10 MINS | 35–45 MINS | SERVES 10

PER SERVING:
186 KCAL /4.5G CARBS

2 tbsp soy sauce
2 tbsp tomato puree
2 tbsp granulated sweetener
1 tbsp rice vinegar
1 tbsp fish sauce
1 tbsp honey
2 tsp garlic granules
¼ tsp ground ginger
½ tsp chilli flakes
juice of ½ lime
1kg skinless chicken drumsticks, about 10 drumsticks
low-calorie cooking spray

TO ACCOMPANY
75g mixed leaf salad (+15 kcal per serving)

How does something sweet, sticky and seriously tasty sound? That's exactly what you're in for with these Teriyaki-Style Chicken Drumsticks. The homemade teriyaki marinade brings together soy, honey, garlic and ginger to create rich, savoury-sweet flavours that really mingle together with the chicken in the freezer bag. After baking your drumsticks to golden perfection, you'll get a delicious and glossy glaze that'll have you licking your fingers.

Everyday Light

Place all the ingredients, except the chicken and low-calorie cooking spray, into a large freezer-proof bag and mix together. Add the chicken drumsticks to the bag and mix to coat. Seal well, label and freeze for up to 3 months.

Remove the bag from the freezer the day before you want to cook and defrost it overnight in the fridge.

When ready to cook, preheat the oven to 210°C (fan 190°C, gas mark 6) and spray a baking tray with low-calorie cooking spray. Remove the chicken drumsticks from the bag and place on the tray. Discard any leftover marinade.

Cook in the oven for 35–45 minutes, until the chicken is cooked through, there is no sign of pinkness and the juices run clear when the tip of a sharp knife or skewer is inserted into the thickest part of the meat. You can freeze the dish at this stage, if you like, for up to 3 months. Serve with a mixed salad.

The dish will keep in the fridge for up to 3 days. You can enjoy it cold or reheat (see Tips).

TIPS

If not preparing as a Freeze & Go bag, put everything, except the chicken and low-calorie cooking spray, in a large, non-reactive bowl and mix well. Add the chicken and mix to coat. Cover with cling film or another plate and leave in the fridge to marinate overnight. Follow the rest of the recipe.

If you've frozen the chicken, once defrosted, enjoy cold, or reheat by placing on a baking tray, covering with foil and reheating in an oven preheated to 210°C (fan 190°C, gas mark 6).

FREEZE ME

BATCH COOK

DAIRY FREE

GLUTEN FREE

HIGH PROTEIN

GAMMON *and* PINEAPPLE CHILLI

15 MINS **VARIABLE** **SERVES 6**

PER SERVING:
341 KCAL / 31G CARBS

750g unsmoked gammon joint, any visible fat removed, chopped into large chunks
1 red onion, peeled and sliced
2 peppers, halved, deseeded and sliced (any colour)
2 garlic cloves, peeled and crushed
1 x 400g tin mixed beans in tomato sauce
400g tin chopped tomatoes
2 tsp onion granules
2 tsp garlic granules
2 tsp mild chilli powder
2 tsp dried oregano
1 tsp smoked paprika
1 tbsp chipotle paste
1 tbsp tomato puree
1 tbsp sriracha sauce
2 tbsp granulated sweetener
50g dried apricots, diced
1 x 425g tin pineapple chunks (this should give you 260g fruit and 180ml pineapple juice)

TO ACCOMPANY
50g raw/125g cooked basmati rice (+173 kcal per serving)

TIP

If you are not preparing this as a Freeze and Go bag, add everything to the casserole dish or slow cooker pot and cook as above.

If you love a dump-it-all-in and let it do its thing kind of dinner, this chilli is going to be right up your street! Once everything's added to the pot, you can walk away while it works its magic. Sweet and smoky flavours come from pineapple, dried apricots and pineapple juice, all mixed through tender, shredded gammon, veggies and beans. With just a few short steps and budget-friendly ingredients, it honestly doesn't get easier!

Special Occasion

HOB-TOP METHOD
3 HOURS

Place all the ingredients, except the pineapple and juice, in a large freezer-proof bag, label and freeze for up to 3 months.

Remove the bag from the freezer the day before you want to cook and defrost it overnight in the fridge. When ready to cook, preheat the oven to 180°C (fan 160°C/gas mark 5).

Empty the contents of the bag into the casserole dish, then add the pineapple and juice. Cover with the lid and cook over a low heat for 3 hours, stirring halfway through. Remove the gammon from the casserole dish when the gammon is tender and starting to fall apart. Using two forks, shred the meat and return it to the dish.

You can freeze the dish at this stage for up to 3 months (see Tips). Serve with rice. The chilli will keep in the fridge for up to 3 days. Microwave for 4–7 minutes until piping hot throughout.

SLOW COOKER METHOD
4–6½ HOURS

SPECIAL EQUIPMENT
3.5-litre slow cooker

Place all the ingredients, except the pineapple and juice, in a large freezer-proof bag, label and freeze for up to 3 months. Remove the bag from the freezer the day before you want to cook and defrost it overnight in the fridge.

When ready to cook, empty the contents of the bag into the slow cooker pot. Add the pineapple and juice. Cover with the lid and

cook on high for 4 hours or low for 6½ hours. Remove the gammon from the slow cooker when the gammon is tender and starting to fall apart. Using two forks, shred the meat and return it to the dish.

You can freeze the dish at this stage for up to 3 months (see Tips). Serve with rice.

The chilli will keep in the fridge for up to 3 days. Microwave for 4–7 minutes until piping hot.

TIP

If you've frozen the cooked chilli, once defrosted, cover and reheat in the microwave for 4–7 minutes until piping hot.

FREEZE ME

BATCH COOK

DAIRY FREE

GLUTEN FREE

USE GF STOCK POT

BOSTON BEANS

15 MINS · VARIABLE · SERVES 4

PER SERVING:
310 KCAL /40G CARBS

- 1 onion, peeled and diced
- 2 garlic cloves, peeled and crushed
- 4 smoked bacon medallions, diced
- 2 x 400g tins haricot beans, approx. 520g, drained and rinsed
- 400g tin of chopped tomatoes
- 200g passata
- 2 tbsp tomato puree
- 2 tsp dried thyme
- 1 tsp smoked paprika
- 1 tbsp Henderson's relish
- 1 tsp sriracha sauce
- 3 tbsp black treacle
- 1 bay leaf
- 1 red wine stock pot
- salt and freshly ground black pepper, to taste

TO ACCOMPANY (OPTIONAL)
60g wholemeal bread roll (+146 kcal per serving)

Say hello to our take on classic Boston Beans. We've kept things simple by using tinned beans, which means less prep and cooking time without skimping on taste. Sweet treacle, smoky diced bacon and rich tomatoes all mingle together to create a glorious, sticky sauce that clings beautifully to every bean. This is a brilliant source of iron, protein and fibre, making it a wholesome choice for any mealtime. Serve it with a crusty roll, a jacket spud, or even a slice of toast for a cosy, satisfying meal.

Everyday Light

HOB-TOP METHOD
60 MINS

Add all the ingredients, except for the stock pot and salt and pepper, to a large freezer-proof bag, label and freeze for up to 3 months.

When ready to cook, defrost the bag in the fridge overnight. Tip the contents of the bag into a large casserole dish. Add the stock pot and 150ml boiling water, cover with a lid and cook over a low-medium heat for 1 hour. The sauce should be rich and thickened and the beans and vegetables cooked through. Season to taste with salt and pepper and serve with a bread roll, if you wish. You can also freeze the dish for up to 3 months. The dish will keep in the fridge for up to 3 days.

SLOW COOKER METHOD
2½–5 HOURS

SPECIAL EQUIPMENT
3.5-litre slow cooker

Add all the ingredients, except for the stock pot and salt and pepper, to a large freezer-proof bag, label and freeze for up to 3 months.

When ready to cook, defrost the bag in the fridge overnight. Tip the contents of the bag into the slow cooker pot. Add the stock pot and 150ml boiling water and cook on high for 2½ hours or low for 5 hours. The sauce should be rich and thickened and the beans and vegetables cooked through. Season to taste with salt and pepper and serve with a bread roll, if you wish. You can also freeze the dish in an freezer-proof container for up to 3 months. The dish will keep in the fridge for up to 3 days.

TIPS

If not prepared as a Freeze and Go bag, add everything to the casserole dish or slow cooker pot and follow the method above.

If you've frozen the finished dish, reheat in the microwave for 3–4 minutes until piping hot.

MULTI
SERVE

BASE RECIPE

VEGAN
USE VEGAN MAYO

VEGGIE

BATCH COOK

DAIRY FREE

GLUTEN FREE
USE GF NOODLES

HIGH PROTEIN

CRUNCHY ASIAN-STYLE SALAD

20 MINS **35 MINS** **SERVES 2 (+ 2 PORTIONS SALAD)**

PER SERVING:
386 KCAL / 22G CARBS

FOR THE CRUNCHY ASIAN-STYLE SALAD

50g nest of wholemeal noodles
salt
1 tsp sesame oil
120g white cabbage, shredded
1 large carrot, peeled and cut into matchsticks or grated
1 red pepper, halved, deseeded and cut into slices
80g mangetout, trimmed and sliced
100g shelled edamame beans, cooked according to the packet instructions
large handful of fresh coriander leaves, roughly chopped

FOR THE CRISPY TOFU

200g firm tofu
1 tsp garlic granules
½ tsp onion granules
1 tsp Chinese 5 spice
2 tsp sesame oil
1 tbsp dark soy sauce
a pinch of salt (optional)

FOR THE DRESSING

40g light mayonnaise
1 tbsp sriracha sauce
½ lime, juice only

TIP

A single serving of crunchy salad, without topping or dressing, is 100 kcal and 11g carbs.

Made up of crisp veggies, nutty edamame beans, fresh herbs and soft wholewheat noodles, this Crunchy Asian-Style Salad makes a versatile dish that forms the base for two additional recipes. The toasty sesame oil adds an authentic, aromatic twist, then all that's left to do is take the base salad and add your topping and dressing! If you're stuck for topping ideas, this recipe uses a third of the salad topped with crispy tofu and sriracha mayo but you can use the remainder to make Peanut and Lime Salmon Salad on page 195 and Sweet Chilli Chicken Noodle Salad on page 196.

Everyday Light

First, make the salad. Cook the noodles according to the packet instructions, usually about 4 minutes in a saucepan of boiling salted water. Drain and rinse well under cold water to cool the noodles and stop them overcooking, and rinse away any starch.

Drain the noodles well, then place in a large bowl. Use scissors to snip the noodles into smaller, easier-to-manage lengths. Add the teaspoon of sesame oil and toss the noodles to coat. This will add flavour and prevent them sticking. Add the prepared vegetables to the bowl, toss together and stir through the coriander.

At this point you can divide the salad into 3. Use one third for the crispy tofu salad. The remainder can be stored for up to 4 days, to use as a base for the salads on pages 195 and 196.

To make the crispy tofu, preheat the oven to 200°C (180°C fan/ gas mark 5). Line a baking tray with foil.

Wrap the block of tofu in kitchen paper and give it a good squeeze to remove excess moisture. No need to press it. Grate the tofu into a bowl, using the coarse side of the grater. Sprinkle the garlic granules, onion granules and Chinese 5 spice over the tofu. Add the 2 teaspoons of sesame oil and the soy sauce and toss gently to coat, being careful to not break up the shreds of tofu.

Spread the tofu over the prepared baking tray, season with a little salt if required, and place in the oven for 30 minutes, stirring gently every 10 minutes to ensure even crispness.

While the tofu cooks, make the dressing by mixing the mayo, sriracha and lime juice together until smooth.

When the tofu is cooked, allow to cool then assemble the salads. Divide 2 portions of the crunchy salad into 2 bowls. Drizzle the sriracha mayo over, then pile the crispy tofu on top.

Serve. The crunchy salad base will keep for 4–5 days. Once topped with the tofu and dressing, it is best used within 24 hours.

PEANUT *and* LIME SALMON SALAD

15 MINS + 20 MINS CHILLING | 15 MINS | SERVES 2

VEGAN

VEGGIE

BATCH COOK

DAIRY FREE

GLUTEN FREE

USE GF SOY SAUCE AND RICE NOODLES

PER SERVING:
443 KCAL /19G CARBS

FOR THE DRESSING

25g smooth peanut butter
1½ tbsp light soy sauce
juice of ½ lime
2cm (¾in) piece of fresh root ginger, peeled and grated
1 garlic clove, peeled and crushed
1 tsp runny honey
1 tsp sriracha or other hot sauce

FOR THE SALAD

2 x 110g skinless, boneless salmon fillets
⅓ Crunchy Asian-Style Salad base recipe (page 192)

Get ready for a flavour explosion in the form of this salad! The star of the show is the satay sauce, a delicious blend of savoury, sweet and spicy. Creamy and complex, the dressing perfectly complements the rich and flaky salmon, with the sriracha packing a subtle punch. Made using the Crunchy Asian-Style Salad on page 192 as a base, this dish is simple and speedy to prep ahead and pop in the fridge for light lunches you can plate up on repeat!

Weekly Indulgence

Whisk all the dressing ingredients together in a bowl until smooth. Place the salmon fillets on a plate. Use 2 tablespoons of the dressing to rub into the salmon fillets. Cover with cling film and chill in the fridge for 20 minutes.

Preheat the oven to 200°C (fan 180°C/gas mark 6) and line a baking tray with foil.

Place the salmon fillets on the lined baking tray and bake in the oven for 15 minutes, or until it is opaque and flaky.

Pile the Crunchy Asian-Style Salad into serving bowls, lay a cooked salmon fillet on top and drizzle the dressing over. Serve.

The crunchy salad base will keep for 4–5 days. Once topped with the salmon and dressing, it is best used within 24 hours.

TIP

A single serving of crunchy salad, without topping or dressing, is 100 kcal and 11g carbs.

BATCH COOK

DAIRY FREE

GLUTEN FREE

USE GF SOY SAUCE AND RICE NOODLES

HIGH PROTEIN

SWEET CHILLI CHICKEN NOODLE SALAD

15 MINS **20 MINS** **SERVES 2**

PER SERVING:
290 KCAL /19G CARBS

FOR THE DRESSING
- 2 tbsp light sweet chilli sauce
- 1½ tbsp light soy sauce
- juice of ½ lime
- 2cm (¾in) piece of fresh root ginger, peeled and grated
- 1 garlic clove, peeled and crushed

FOR THE SALAD
- 2 skinless chicken breasts, approx. 150g each
- ⅓ Crunchy Asian-Style Salad base recipe (page 192)

We're constantly brainstorming new ways to assemble our greens, and trust us, you'll be rushing back for seconds when you try this zingy number. The dish uses the Crunchy Asian-Style Salad on page 192 as a base, topped with tender chicken in a light sweet chilli sauce you'll find easily on your local supermarket shelves. We've used wholemeal noodles because they're lower in calories and higher in fibre and protein, keeping you fuller for longer.

Everyday Light

Whisk all the dressing ingredients together in a bowl until smooth.

Use 1 tablespoon of the dressing to rub into the chicken breasts. Place them on a plate and cover with cling film. Refrigerate for 20 minutes.

Preheat the oven to 200°C (fan 180°C/gas mark 6) and line a baking tray with foil.

Place the chicken breasts on the lined baking tray and bake in the oven for 20 minutes, or until thoroughly cooked and no pink remains.

Pile the crunchy salad into serving bowls, slice the cooked chicken and place on top. Drizzle with the dressing and serve.

The crunchy salad base will keep in the fridge for 4–5 days. Once topped with the chicken and dressing, it is best used within 24 hours.

BASE RECIPE

VEGAN
SERVE WITHOUT EGG

VEGGIE

FREEZE ME

BATCH COOK

DAIRY FREE

GLUTEN FREE
USE GF BREADCRUMBS

NUTTY MUSHROOM STUFFING POTATO HASH

20 MINS + 30 MINS SOAKING | 1 HR 20 MINS | SERVES 6

PER SERVING:
464 KCAL /50G CARBS

SPECIAL EQUIPMENT
Ovenproof dish, about 28 x 20cm (11 x 8in)

FOR THE STUFFING
30g dried porcini mushrooms
low-calorie cooking spray
1 large leek, trimmed, halved and thinly sliced
3 garlic cloves, peeled and crushed
500g chestnut mushrooms, chopped
1 tsp finely chopped fresh sage
1 tsp finely chopped fresh thyme
4 sprigs of rosemary, leaves removed from stalks and finely chopped
salt and freshly ground black pepper, to taste
180g chestnuts, roughly chopped
100g walnuts, roughly chopped
200g ciabatta, made into breadcrumbs

FOR THE HASH
300g new potatoes, cubed
300g sweet potato, peeled and cubed
low-calorie cooking spray
salt and freshly ground black pepper, to taste
1 tbsp chopped fresh rosemary
6 medium eggs

This herby stuffing potato hash is rich and earthy, with fluffy rosemary-roasted potatoes combined with sunshine-coloured sweet potatoes, and a jammy fried egg on top. Before turning this into a hearty hash, you can make up a batch of Nutty Mushroom Stuffing and save half to turn into our Veggie Wellington on page 204, or our Stuffed Butternut Squash on page 202. So many possibilities… and yes, it's freezer-friendly too!

Weekly Indulgence

Preheat the oven to 220°C (fan 200°C/gas mark 7) and line a baking tray with non-stick baking paper.

To make the stuffing, begin by rehydrating the porcini mushrooms. Place the dried mushrooms in a heatproof bowl and pour over 300ml boiling water. Allow the mushrooms to soak in the water for 30 minutes. Once soaked, drain the mushrooms (reserving the liquid for later) and finely chop. Set aside.

Meanwhile, for the hash, place all the potatoes in a large bowl and spray with low-calorie cooking spray. Season to taste with salt and pepper, add the chopped rosemary and toss to coat. Arrange in a single layer on the lined baking tray and roast in the oven for 25–30 minutes until golden and crisp.

For the stuffing, spray a large frying pan with low-calorie cooking spray and place over a medium heat. Add the sliced leek and garlic and gently cook for a few minutes until beginning to soften. Add the chopped chestnut mushrooms to the leek and cook for a further 10 minutes, or until softened and any liquid has evaporated. Add the porcini mushrooms along with the chopped herbs. Season to taste with salt and pepper and cook for a further 5 minutes.

In a dry frying pan, warm the chestnuts and walnuts gently over a medium heat for 5 minutes until they are toasted and beginning to release their aroma. Add the toasted nuts to the mushroom mix and cook for a further minute, then remove the pan from the heat and leave to cool.

Once the mushroom and nut mixture is cooled, add the bread crumbs and stir through.

Strain the reserved mushroom liquid to remove any grit. Add half of the liquid to the mushrooms and breadcrumbs and stir through until you get a slightly moist (but not too wet) mixture. If the mixture is too dry add a few more drops of the mushroom liquid. At this point, you can cool and store the stuffing if you wish to make the Veggie Wellington (page 204) or the Stuffed Butternut Squash (page 202).

You can also freeze or store the stuffing at this point for later. Place the prepared stuffing in a baking dish and leave to cool. Cover with foil so it is airtight and freeze for up to 3 months or in the fridge for up to 3 days (see Tips).

To make the hash, lightly crush the potatoes with a fork and toss through the stuffing mix. Place in the ovenproof dish, cover with foil and bake in the oven for 20 minutes. Remove the foil and return to the oven for a further 10 minutes, or until the hash is golden and crisp. Remove from the oven. Divide the hash mix between six plates.

Spray a frying pan with low-calorie cooking spray and place over a medium low heat. Once the pan is hot, add the eggs (you may need to do these in batches) and gently fry for 2–3 minutes, until the white is cooked and starting to crisp up around the edges and the yolk is still runny.

Serve the freshly cooked egg on top of the hash immediately. Break open the yolk to add a rich sauce to your hash.

TIPS

We have used ciabatta bread in this recipe, but you can use any white bread. Breadcrumbs are best made with bread that is at least one or two days old and slightly stale.

As this is a multi-serve recipe, be sure to only bake the prepared mushroom mix if it is to be used for the stuffing potato hash. If it is being prepared to go into a Veggie Wellington (page 204) or Stuffed Butternut Squash (page 202), prepare the stuffing up to adding the toasted chestnuts and walnuts to the stuffing mix and allowing it to cool. For each multi-serve recipe, you will need half of this base recipe (so this recipe will make enough stuffing to create both the Veggie Wellington and the Stuffed Butternut Squash).

You can use leftover roast potatoes in this dish.

If you've stored or frozen the stuffing, preheat the oven to 200°C (fan 180°C/gas mark 6). Place the foil-covered dish in the oven and cook for 25 minutes, or until the stuffing is hot in the middle. Remove the foil and cook for a further 5–10 minutes until the top is crisp and golden.

VEGAN

VEGGIE

BATCH COOK

DAIRY FREE

GLUTEN FREE

USE GF BREADCRUMBS

STUFFED BUTTERNUT SQUASH

10 MINS 50 MINS SERVES 4

PER SERVING:
444 KCAL /66G CARBS

2 butternut squash, halved and deseeded
low-calorie cooking spray
salt and freshly ground black pepper, to taste
½ Nutty Mushroom Stuffing base recipe, unbaked (page 198)
finely grated zest of 1 orange
60g dried cranberries, chopped
20g fresh parsley, chopped

TO ACCOMPANY
80g steamed veg (+38 kcal per serving)

This vibrant veggie main makes the most of our Nutty Mushroom Stuffing (page 198), turning it into a hearty filling for tender roasted butternut squash. It's packed with plenty of texture and flavour. Whether you're cooking up a meat-free showstopper for the veggies/vegans in your life or using up a batch of stuffing, this easy dish looks impressive and tastes even better!

Weekly Indulgence

Preheat the oven to 220°C (fan 200°C/gas mark 7) .

Spray the four butternut squash halves with low-calorie cooking spray and season to taste with salt and pepper. Place the squash halves flat on a baking tray with skin side up. Bake in the oven for 25–30 minutes until softened and the skin has become golden and brown.

Once the squash has cooked, turn the halves so the inside is facing up. Use a spoon to create a crevice in the long section of the butternut squash for the stuffing to go into. Take care not to remove too much squash. Place any scooped-out squash in a bowl. Repeat this with all the butternut squash halves.

Place the unbaked Nutty Mushroom Stuffing in a large bowl and add any squash that has been scooped out. Add the orange zest, chopped cranberries and three-quarters of the chopped parsley and mix well to combine.

Use a spoon to fill each butternut squash half with the stuffing mix. Spray each stuffed squash with a little more low-calorie cooking spray and return to the oven for 15–20 minutes until the squash and stuffing are golden and crisp.

Place one butternut squash half on each serving plate and sprinkle with the remaining chopped parsley. Serve with steamed vegetables.

The stuffed squash will keep in the fridge for up to 3 days. Reheat in an oven preheated to 200°C (fan 180°C/gas mark 5) for 10–15 minutes, until the squash and filling is hot.

VEGAN

USE VEGAN MILK AND PASTRY

VEGGIE

FREEZE ME

BATCH COOK

DAIRY FREE

USE DF PASTRY

VEGGIE WELLINGTON

35 MINS + 1 HR CHILLING **1 HR** **SERVES 8**

PER SERVING:
332 KCAL /41G CARBS

500g butternut squash, peeled and cubed
300g sweet potato, peeled and cubed
salt and freshly ground black pepper, to taste
low-calorie cooking spray
½ Nutty Mushroom Stuffing base recipe, unbaked (page 198)
1 tbsp plain flour, for dusting
500g puff pastry block
1 egg, beaten

TO ACCOMPANY
80g steamed veg (+38 kcal per serving)

This stunning Veggie Wellington is the ultimate plant-based centrepiece. Wrapped in crisp, golden pastry and filled with sweet roasted veg and our Nutty Mushroom Stuffing (page 198), it's packed with herby, nutty flavour and just the right amount of festive flair. Whether it's for a Sunday roast or Christmas Day, this impressive showstopper is guaranteed to be a hit around the dinner table.

Everyday Light

Preheat the oven to 220°C (fan 200°C/gas mark 7) and line a baking tray with non-stick baking paper. Place the cubed squash and potato on the baking tray, season to taste with salt and pepper, spray with low-calorie cooking spray and bake in the oven for 25–30 minutes, until soft and slightly golden.

Place the cooked vegetables in a large bowl and use a fork to roughly mash them. Add the Nutty Mushroom Stuffing and mix well to combine. Set aside to cool completely (this takes 15–20 minutes in the fridge).

Dust the work surface with the flour and rub a little over the rolling pin. Place the pastry block on the floured surface and begin to roll out the pastry into a large square. Give the pastry a quarter turn each time you roll to make it as equally square as possible. You want the square to be approximately 40 x 40cm (16 x 16in).

Once you have a large square measuring 40 x 40cm (16 x 16in), cut it in half so you have two long rectangles. Place one pastry rectangle on a sheet of non-stick baking paper (this will help you move the prepared wellington). Spoon the mushroom mix into a loaf shape that runs the length of the pastry. The filling should be about 10cm (4in) wide, allowing for a wide border around the edge. Brush the border with beaten egg and carefully lay the second rectangle of pastry on top of the wellington. Using your hand, gently push the pastry down around the filling so as to 'tuck' it in and leave no air pockets.

Once the filling has been well covered by the pastry and there are no air pockets, use the back of a fork to gently press the two sheets of pastry together to seal them. Use a sharp knife to trim the excess pastry from the edges of the wellington, leaving a border of about 1cm (½in). Lightly score the top of the pastry with a knife to create a diamond pattern and brush the top of the wellington with beaten egg. Use the baking paper underneath the pastry to gently pull the wellington onto a large baking tray.

Place the glazed wellington in the fridge to chill for at least 30 minutes.

Once chilled, preheat the oven to 220°C (fan 200°C/gas mark 7) and bake the wellington in the oven for 30 minutes, or until the pastry is crisp and golden and the inside of the wellington is piping hot. Slice the wellington into eight generous slices and serve with steamed vegetables.

The uncooked wellington will keep in the fridge for up to 3 days. Ensure that it is tightly wrapped in cling film. Brush the wellington with egg and cook in a preheated oven following the cooking instructions above.

If the base recipe has been stored in the fridge before using, prepare the veggie wellington following the recipe instructions. Before glazing with egg and baking, wrap the wellington tightly in cling film so it is airtight and freeze for up to 3 months (see Tips).

TIPS

This recipe provides eight generous slices of wellington but you can cut smaller slices to make it go even further.

To make this vegan, use vegan milk instead of egg for brushing over the pastry.

If the base recipe has previously been frozen, this recipe is not freezable. If you've frozen the wellington, then glaze with egg and bake in an oven preheated to 220°C (fan 200°C/gas mark 7) for 45–50 minutes until the pastry is puffed and golden and the inside is piping hot.

Image overleaf.

BASE RECIPE

FREEZE ME

BATCH COOK

DAIRY FREE

GLUTEN FREE

USE GF STOCK

HIGH PROTEIN

LOW CARB

SHREDDED BEEF *in* RED WINE

15 MINS | VARIABLE | SERVES 12

PER SERVING:
190 KCAL / 8.2G CARBS

SPECIAL EQUIPMENT
4-litre deep casserole dish with tight-fitting lid, suitable for oven and hob

1.2kg silverside beef joint
salt and freshly ground black pepper, to taste
low-calorie cooking spray
750ml beef stock (1 beef stock cube dissolved in 750ml boiling water)
2 onions, peeled and sliced
3 carrots, peeled and sliced
4 garlic cloves, peeled and crushed
1 tbsp tomato puree
250ml red wine
1 tbsp Henderson's relish
3 dried bay leaves
3 tbsp cornflour, made into a slurry with 3 tbsp cold water

TO ACCOMPANY
250g mashed potato and 80g steamed vegetables (+212 kcal per serving)

It's amazing what you can achieve with a solid base recipe. Similar to a classic pot roast, this hearty beef dish features tender chunks of meat slowly simmered in a rich red wine gravy. Serve it as a comforting roast dinner with all the trimmings, then save the remaining two-thirds to make Meat and Potato Pie on page 212 and the Beef and Red Wine Lasagne on page 214. It's batch cooking that never gets boring, you can enjoy it straightaway or freeze for an easy, make-ahead dinner whenever you need it.

Weekly Indulgence

OVEN METHOD
4 HOURS

Preheat the oven to 160°C (fan 140°C/gas mark 2).

Remove any netting from the beef joint and season it well with salt and pepper.

Spray the casserole dish with low-calorie cooking spray and place over a high heat. When the pan is hot, add the beef and brown thoroughly on all sides. Remove from the pan and set aside. Turn the heat down to medium. If there are any crispy bits stuck to the pan, add a splash of stock and scrape them up with a spatula.

Add the onions, carrots and garlic to the casserole and sauté for 8–10 minutes until softened and golden. Stir in the tomato puree, then add the red wine and Henderson's relish.

Return the joint of beef to the pan and add the stock. It should almost cover the meat, with about 3–4cm (1¼–2in) of beef visible above the liquid.

Tuck the bay leaves around the pan, cover with a tight-fitting lid and place on a low shelf in the oven. Cook for 3–3½ hours, checking after 2 hours to ensure the liquid is not evaporating. You can top up with a little boiling water if the stock is reducing.

When the beef is fall-apart tender, remove the beef from the pan and place on a large plate or tray. Remove the bay leaves and discard.

Slowly stir the cornflour slurry into the pan. You shouldn't need to return the pan to the hob for this, as the residual heat from the pan should be enough to thicken the sauce.

Use two forks to pull the beef apart into shreds and return to the pan. Stir to coat with gravy.

This recipe makes 12 portions of Beef in Red Wine. We served four portions with mash and veggies and divided the remainder into two to use for Beef and Red Wine Lasagne (page 214) and Meat and Potato Pie (page 212). To freeze the dish, cool quickly, then divide the base recipe into three portions and freeze in airtight freezer bags or containers for up to 3 months (see Tips).

This dish will keep in the fridge for 3–4 days. Reheat in a covered, microwavable dish for 6–7 minutes until piping hot, stirring halfway through. Alternatively, reheat in a saucepan over a medium heat, stirring occasionally, until piping hot.

TIPS

A tight-fitting lid is important to ensure the cooking liquid does not evaporate during cooking. You can tightly cover the pan with foil before putting the lid on, to give a tighter seal.

If you've frozen the dish, once defrosted, reheat in a covered, microwavable dish for 6–7 minutes until piping hot, stirring halfway through. Alternatively, reheat in a saucepan over a medium heat, stirring occasionally, until piping hot.

SLOW COOKER METHOD
6–8 HOURS

SPECIAL EQUIPMENT
3.5-litre slow cooker

Remove any netting from the beef joint and season it well with salt and pepper.

Spray a frying pan with low-calorie cooking spray and place over a high heat. When the pan is hot, add the beef and brown thoroughly on all sides.

Place the onions, carrots, garlic, tomato puree, red wine and Henderson's relish into the slow cooker pot and stir well. Place the browned beef joint in the slow cooker and add the stock. Stir well and tuck the bay leaves around the joint. Cover with the lid and cook on high for 6 hours or low for 8 hours.

When the beef is fall-apart tender, remove it from the pot and place on a large plate or tray. Remove the bay leaves and discard.

Slowly stir the cornflour slurry into the juices left in the slow cooker pot to thicken the gravy.
Use two forks to pull the beef apart into shreds and return to the slow cooker. Stir to coat with gravy.

This recipe makes 12 portions of Beef in Red Wine. We served four portions with mash and veggies and divided the remainder into two to use for Beef and Red Wine Lasagne (page 214) and Meat and Potato Pie (page 212). To freeze the dish, cool quickly, then divide the base recipe into three portions and freeze in airtight freezer bags or containers for up to up to 3 months (see Tips).

This dish will keep in the fridge for 3–4 days. Reheat in a covered, microwavable dish for 6–7 minutes until piping hot, stirring halfway through. Alternatively, reheat in a saucepan over a medium heat, stirring occasionally, until piping hot.

DAIRY FREE

OMIT MILK

HIGH PROTEIN

MEAT *and* POTATO PIE

10 MINS | 30 MINS | SERVES 4

PER SERVING:
525 KCAL /63G CARBS

SPECIAL EQUIPMENT
28 x 24cm (11 x 9½in) ovenproof dish

- 600g potatoes, peeled and cut into 2cm (¾in) dice
- salt and freshly ground black pepper, to taste
- ⅓ Shredded Beef in Red Wine base recipe (page 208)
- 1 sheet ready-rolled puff pastry, cut to fit the ovenproof dish (we used 220g pastry)
- 1 tbsp milk

TO ACCOMPANY
80g steamed vegetables (+38 kcal per serving)

With just a few extra ingredients and steps, you can turn our Shredded Beef in Red Wine on page 208 into a completely different meal. In this pie, tender chunks of beef are coated in a rich, wine-infused gravy, combined with fluffy potatoes and a golden, crispy pastry crust. This one's great for dark and chilly winter evenings when you're in dire need of something cosy but want something low effort. All it takes is half an hour in the oven to turn your leftovers into something that tastes like it's straight from a country pub.

Special Occasion

Preheat the oven to 200°C (fan 180°C/gas mark 6).

Cook the potatoes in a large saucepan of boiling salted water for 5–10 minutes until tender. Drain and allow to air-dry for a minute or two.

Place the potatoes in a large bowl and add the Shredded Beef in Red Wine. Mix together and season with salt and pepper, if needed. Transfer the mix to the ovenproof dish.

Trim the pastry sheet to size and lay over the top of the pie mix, pressing the edges down to seal it to the dish. Crimp the edges and score decorative edges over the top if desired. Brush the top with milk, and bake in the oven for 25–30 minutes until the pastry is golden and the filling is piping hot.

Serve with steamed vegetables.

GLUTEN FREE

USE GF LASAGNE

HIGH PROTEIN

BEEF *and* RED WINE LASAGNE

10 MINS · 1 HR 5 MINS · SERVES 4

PER SERVING:
547 KCAL /47G CARBS

SPECIAL EQUIPMENT
28 x 24cm (11 x 9½in) ovenproof dish

- low-calorie cooking spray
- 350g chestnut mushrooms, sliced
- 4 garlic cloves, peeled and crushed
- 1 tsp dried mixed herbs
- 1 x 400g tin chopped tomatoes
- 80g fresh baby spinach leaves, stalks removed, washed and completely dried
- 165g reduced-fat cream cheese
- 4–5 tbsp semi-skimmed milk (or whichever type you prefer)
- ½ tsp garlic granules
- ½ tsp onion granules
- ½ tsp mustard powder
- 100g reduced-fat mature Cheddar, finely grated
- salt and freshly ground black pepper, to taste
- ⅓ Shredded Beef in Red Wine base recipe (page 208)
- 9 sheets dried lasagne (approx. 165g)

TO ACCOMPANY
75g mixed salad
(+15 kcal per serving)

TIP

Use whichever milk you have available. All work (even plant-based), and the difference in calories is minimal.

This tasty lasagne uses our Shredded Beef in Red Wine on page 208 as its base, so be sure to have it ready before you start cooking. Rich, hearty and quite literally layered with comfort, this dish combines juicy beef, earthy mushrooms and tender spinach in a thick, flavour-packed tomato sauce. Topped with a no-cook creamy cheese sauce for minimal effort and barely any washing up, it's proper comfort food without the fuss.

Special Occasion

Preheat the oven to 200°C (fan 180°C/gas mark 6).

Spray a large frying pan with low-calorie cooking spray and place over a medium-high heat. Add the mushrooms and sauté for 5–10 minutes until all the liquid they release has evaporated.

Add the crushed garlic and mixed herbs and cook for a further minute. Stir through the tomatoes and bring to a simmer. Cook for 10 minutes.

Stir the spinach into the sauce until wilted.

Place the cream cheese in a large bowl and beat in the milk, garlic and onion granules, mustard and half the cheese. Season with a little salt and plenty of pepper.

Mix the Shredded Beef in Red Wine into the mushroom and tomato sauce.

Assemble the lasagne in the ovenproof dish, starting with a third of the sauce, then three lasagne sheets. You should get three layers, ending with lasagne sheets. Spread the cheese sauce on top and sprinkle over the remaining cheese.

Bake in the oven for 35–40 minutes until the cheese is bubbling and a knife slides easily through the centre of the lasagne. Serve with a mixed salad.

BASE RECIPE

FREEZE ME

BATCH COOK

DAIRY FREE

GLUTEN FREE

USE GF STOCK CUBES

HIGH PROTEIN

LOW CARB

ROAST CHICKEN *with* LEMON GRAVY

15 MINS | 2 HRS | SERVES 8

PER SERVING:
409 KCAL / 7.6G CARBS

SPECIAL EQUIPMENT
Fine microplane grater, blender or food processor, fat separator jug (optional)

1 onion, peeled and cut into large chunks
2 carrots, peeled and cut into large chunks
6 garlic cloves, peeled
finely grated zest and juice of 2 lemons
½ tbsp olive oil
salt and freshly ground black pepper, to taste
1 extra-large whole chicken, approx. 2–2.2kg
500ml chicken stock (1 chicken stock cube dissolved in 500ml boiling water)
2 tbsp cornflour mixed to a slurry with 2 tbsp water (optional)

TO ACCOMPANY
200g simple roast potatoes (+170 kcal per serving)

Want to make a simple roast chicken dinner go even further? This Roast Chicken with Lemon Gravy does exactly that, infusing the chicken with fresh lemon and smothering it in a zingy, flavour-packed gravy that's guaranteed to have everyone hovering round the kitchen. Feed a crowd and serve all eight portions with your favourite roast trimmings, or feed four and save the rest to whip up another two family dinners. The leftovers are perfect for transforming into our Chicken Pesto Pasta Bake (page 220) and Sweet and Sour Chicken Curry (page 219), making this single roast a seriously smart, fuss-free winner.

Weekly Indulgence

Preheat the oven to 200°C (fan 180°C/gas mark 6).

Scatter the onion, carrots and whole garlic cloves in the bottom of a roasting tray.

In a small bowl, mix the lemon zest with the olive oil to form a paste. Season with a little salt and pepper. Gently loosen the skin around the chicken breast by working your fingers between the skin and the meat. You can use a spoon if you prefer, but fingers are easier and there is less likelihood of you tearing the skin. Rub half the lemon paste under the skin on the breast, then smother the rest over the outside of the whole chicken. Place the chicken in the roasting tray, on top of the chopped vegetables, and pour 200ml water into the tin. Roast in the oven for 2 hours (40 minutes per kilo plus an extra 20 minutes) until the juices run clear when a skewer is inserted into the thigh.

When cooked, transfer the chicken to a plate and cover loosely with foil to rest, while you prepare the gravy.

Use a slotted spoon to remove the veggies from the roasting tray and place them in a blender or food processor.

Pour the stock into the roasting tray, and scrape up any sticky, flavourful bits on the bottom of the tray. Pour this into a fat separator jug and allow 2–3 minutes for the juices to settle. The fat should form a layer on top. If you don't have a fat separator, pour

into a jug, allow to settle and then skim off the fat with a spoon. Carefully pour half the stock into a saucepan, and half into the blender with the vegetables, leaving behind the layer of fat. Blitz the veggies and stock until smooth and add this to the pan of stock. Add the lemon juice and heat until bubbling. The blitzed vegetables should have thickened the sauce, but if you want it thicker, stir in the cornflour slurry until you get the consistency you like. Season to taste with salt and pepper.

Carve the chicken. At this stage you can freeze the chicken or store it for another recipe. Strip the meat off the bones, wrap well in individual portions, and freeze for up to 3 months (see Tips) or store the chicken in an airtight container in the fridge for up to 3 days. Freeze or store the gravy separately to give you more options for serving. Serve the chicken with the lemon gravy and roast potatoes. If you stored the chicken in the fridge, microwave for 4–6 minutes until piping hot. Reheat the chicken and gravy together to prevent the chicken drying out.

TIPS

Use a fine microplane grater to zest the lemons, being careful not to grate down to the white pith, as this can leave a bitter taste.

If you've frozen the chicken and gravy, after defrosting, microwave for 4–6 minutes until piping hot. Reheat the chicken and gravy together to prevent the chicken drying out.

DAIRY FREE

GLUTEN FREE

HIGH PROTEIN

SWEET *and* SOUR CHICKEN CURRY

15 MINS | 20 MINS | SERVES 4

PER SERVING:
252 KCAL / 29G CARBS

low-calorie cooking spray
1 onion, peeled and diced
½ red pepper, deseeded and diced
½ green pepper, deseeded and diced
2cm (¾in) piece of fresh root ginger, peeled and grated
4 garlic cloves, peeled and crushed
2 tsp garam masala
2 tsp ground coriander
1 tsp ground turmeric
1 tsp paprika
2 tbsp tomato puree
2 tsp tamarind paste
250g passata
3 tbsp mango chutney
1 tbsp lemon juice
¼ cooked chicken from Roast Chicken and Lemon Gravy base recipe (page 216)
handful of fresh coriander, chopped
salt and freshly ground black pepper, to taste

TO ACCOMPANY
50g raw/125g cooked basmati rice (+173 kcal per serving)

Got leftover roast chicken to use up? This tasty fakeaway will transform it into a dinner you'll want to make again and again. This mildly spiced curry gets its sweetness from mango chutney and a gentle tang from tamarind paste, creating a rich sauce that's full of flavour. Quick to cook and ideal for feeding the whole family, it's delicious served with fluffy rice or warm naan. If you fancy a bit more heat, just add a fresh chilli or a sprinkle of chilli flakes before serving.

Weekly Indulgence

Spray a large frying pan with low-calorie cooking spray and place over a medium heat. Add the onion, peppers, ginger and garlic and sauté for 5 minutes, or until the onion begins to soften.

Add the spices and cook for a further minute until fragrant. Stir in the tomato puree and tamarind paste. Add the passata, mango chutney, lemon juice and 100ml water and stir until the sauce begins to bubble. Cook for 5 minutes.

Add the chicken to the pan and stir well. Cook for a further 5 minutes, or until the chicken is thoroughly reheated and piping hot.

Add the coriander and season to taste with salt and pepper. Serve with rice.

GLUTEN FREE

USE GF PASTA AND STOCK CUBE

HIGH PROTEIN

CHICKEN PESTO PASTA BAKE

15 MINS 40 MINS SERVES 4

PER SERVING:
470 KCAL /42G CARBS

SPECIAL EQUIPMENT
Blender, 26 x 18cm (10¼ x 7in) ovenproof dish

- 200g small pasta shapes, such as fusilli or penne
- salt and freshly ground black pepper, to taste
- 160g baby spinach
- 30g fresh basil sprigs
- 165g reduced-fat cream cheese
- juice of 1 lemon
- 100ml chicken stock (1 chicken stock cube dissolved in 100ml boiling water)
- 1 tsp garlic granules
- 30g Parmesan, finely grated
- 150g frozen peas
- ¼ cooked chicken from Roast Chicken and Lemon Gravy base recipe (page 216)
- 125g light mozzarella cheese

TO ACCOMPANY (OPTIONAL)
75g mixed salad (+15 kcal per serving)

This easy, cheesy pasta dish is a brilliant way to turn leftovers into something totally delicious. Using Roast Chicken with Lemon Gravy on page 216 (or any cooked chicken you've got), this vibrant green bake is packed with spinach and basil, blended into a sauce so it's full of goodness and family-friendly too! Sweet peas perfectly complement the herby flavours, making this a comforting, crowd-pleasing dinner that's guaranteed to go down a treat.

Weekly Indulgence

Preheat the oven to 200°C (fan 180°C/gas mark 6).

Cook the pasta according to the packet instructions (usually 9–12 minutes in a pan of boiling salted water). Drain well and place in a large bowl.

While the pasta cooks, make the sauce. Place a frying pan over a medium heat and add the spinach. Stir for around a minute until it has wilted. Place in a sieve and squeeze out any excess water.

Place the spinach in a blender, along with the basil, cream cheese, lemon juice, stock, garlic granules and Parmesan, and blitz to a smooth sauce.

Stir the sauce into the pasta, along with the peas and chicken.

Season to taste with salt and pepper. Transfer to the ovenproof dish. Tear the mozzarella into pieces and dot evenly over the top.

Bake in the oven for 25 minutes, or until the cheese is bubbling and the pasta bake is thoroughly heated through. Serve with a mixed salad, if you wish.

TIP

You can prep ahead a batch of the pesto sauce. It will keep for 3 days in the fridge or up to 3 months in the freezer. You can then reheat it and stir through any pasta. Why not try it stirred through some cooked spaghetti and roasted vegetables.

BASE RECIPE

FREEZE ME

DAIRY FREE

USE DF FETA-STYLE CHEESE

GLUTEN FREE

HIGH PROTEIN

CHIPOTLE CHICKEN TRAYBAKE

10 MINS | 30 MINS | SERVES 8

PER SERVING:
202 KCAL /11G CARBS

- 3 tbsp chipotle paste
- 2 tbsp tomato puree
- 1 tbsp honey
- 1 tbsp granulated sweetener
- 1 tbsp smoked paprika
- 2 tsp onion granules
- 1 tsp ground cumin
- juice of 1 lime
- 1kg skinless chicken breasts
- 2 red onions, peeled and cut into 2cm (¾in) slices
- 2 peppers, deseeded and cut into 2cm (¾in) slices (any colour)
- 4 garlic cloves, peeled and crushed
- 4 sweetcorn cobs, approx. 250g
- low-calorie cooking spray

TO SERVE

- 40g reduced-fat feta-style cheese, crumbled
- 1 tsp chopped fresh coriander (optional)

TO ACCOMPANY

150g sweet potato mash and 80g steamed vegetables (+124 kcal per serving)

We love a traybake because it's easy, low-effort and all in one pan. For this recipe, juicy chicken roasts alongside tender veg, with a touch of mild chipotle paste adding a gentle kick. Honey gives everything a delicious caramelized finish, bringing the dish together perfectly. Serve it with sweet potato and steamed veg or use it as a base for Chipotle Chicken Enchiladas on page 224 and Creamy Chipotle Chicken on page 227.

Everyday Light

Preheat the oven to 200°C (fan 180°C/gas mark 6).

In a small bowl, mix the chipotle paste, tomato puree, honey, sweetener, paprika, onion granules, cumin and lime juice until smooth.

Place the chicken breasts on a large baking tray and spread half the chipotle mix over them. Bake in the oven for 15 minutes.

After 15 minutes, remove the tray from the oven and add the onions, peppers, garlic and sweetcorn. Add the rest of the paste and mix to coat the vegetables. Spray with low-calorie cooking spray and return to the oven for a further 15 minutes.

Remove the chicken breasts from the tray and, using two forks, shred the meat. Cut the sweetcorn off the cobs. Return the chicken and sweetcorn to the tray and mix to combine. You can allow to cool, then divide into individual servings and freeze in airtight containers for up to 3 months (see Tip).

Sprinkle over the feta and coriander, if using, and serve with sweet potato mash and steamed vegetables.

The traybake will keep in the fridge for up to 4 days. Reheat in the microwave for 3–4 minutes until piping hot, then top with feta and coriander.

TIP

If you've frozen the traybake, after defrosting, reheat in the microwave for 3–4 minutes until piping hot, then top with feta and coriander.

FREEZE ME

BATCH COOK

DAIRY FREE
USE DF CHEESE

GLUTEN FREE
USE GF TORTILLA WRAPS

HIGH PROTEIN

CHIPOTLE CHICKEN ENCHILADAS

10 MINS 25 MINS SERVES 4

PER SERVING:
482 KCAL / 51G CARBS

SPECIAL EQUIPMENT
Ovenproof dish, about 25 x 30cm (9 x 12in)

½ Chipotle Chicken Traybake base recipe (page 222)
1 x 400g tin black beans, approx. 240g, drained and rinsed
200g passata
8 soft tortilla wraps, approx. 30g per wrap
40g reduced-fat Cheddar cheese, finely grated
5g fresh coriander, finely chopped

TO ACCOMPANY (OPTIONAL)
75g mixed salad (+15 kcal per serving)

When life gives you a Chipotle Chicken Traybake (page 222), make enchiladas! Using the traybake as a base, we came up with this Mexican-inspired dish to save you time, money and a whole lot of mental energy. Wrapped in tortillas and topped with gooey, melty cheese, it's the kind of meal that brings everyone to the table. We like to serve ours with a crisp side salad.

Weekly Indulgence

Preheat the oven to 200°C (fan 180°C/gas mark 6).

Add the Chipotle Chicken Traybake mixture to a large frying pan and place over a medium heat. Add the black beans and passata and bring to the boil. Turn the heat down and simmer for 10–15 minutes until heated through and thickened.

Microwave the tortilla wraps for 30 seconds; this will make them easier to roll. Spoon the chicken mixture down the middle of each tortilla wrap, then roll the wrap over the filling to encase.

Place the enchiladas in the ovenproof dish and sprinkle over the cheese. Bake in the oven for 10 minutes, or until the cheese is bubbly, melted and golden. Sprinkle over the coriander and serve with a mixed salad.

This dish will keep in the fridge for 4 days. Reheat in a covered, microwavable dish for 3–4 minutes until piping hot, then top with chopped coriander.

TIPS

This recipe is written using the Chipotle Chicken Traybake (page 222) as the base. If you prefer, you can make half the base recipe to use to make this recipe.

If the base recipe has previously been frozen, this recipe is not freezable. If the base recipe has been stored in the fridge before using, please follow the standard freezing guidelines. Reheat in the microwave for 3–4 minutes until piping hot, then top with chopped coriander.

CREAMY CHIPOTLE CHICKEN

10 MINS 15 MINS SERVES 4

FREEZE ME
BATCH COOK
DAIRY FREE
USE DF CREAM CHEESE
GLUTEN FREE
HIGH PROTEIN

PER SERVING:
344 KCAL /26G CARBS

½ Chipotle Chicken Traybake base recipe (page 222)
1 x 400g tin black beans, approx. 240g, drained and rinsed
1 x 400g tin chopped tomatoes
200g passata
100g reduced-fat cream cheese
5g fresh coriander, chopped

TO ACCOMPANY
50g raw/125g basmati rice (+173 kcal per serving)

The best part about this creamy chicken dish is that it tastes like you spent hours standing over a pan, but it's surprisingly easy and speedy to make. Using half of the Chipotle Chicken Traybake on page 222 as a base, it's as simple as stirring through a few extra ingredients to make a chicken dinner that looks restaurant-worthy with a side of rice. Add a sprinkle of fresh coriander if you want to go the extra mile on flavour and presentation!

Special Occasion

Preheat the oven to 200°C (fan 180°C/gas mark 6).

Add the Chipotle Chicken Traybake mixture to a large frying pan and place over a medium heat. Add the black beans, chopped tomatoes and passata and bring to the boil. Turn the heat down and simmer for 10–15 minutes until heated through.

Add the cream cheese and stir until combined. Sprinkle over the cxhopped coriander and serve.

This dish will keep in the fridge for 4 days. Reheat in a covered, microwavable dish for 3–4 minutes until piping hot, then top with chopped coriander.

TIPS

This recipe is written using the Chipotle Chicken Traybake (page 222) as the base. If you prefer, you can make half the base recipe to use to make this recipe.

If the base recipe has previously been frozen, this recipe is not freezable. If the base recipe has been stored in the fridge before using, please follow the standard freezing guidelines. Reheat in the microwave for 3–4 minutes until piping hot, then top with chopped coriander.

BASE RECIPE

VEGAN
USE VEGAN SAUSAGES

VEGGIE
USE VEGETARIAN SAUSAGES

FREEZE ME

BATCH COOK

DAIRY FREE

GLUTEN FREE
USE GF STOCK POT

HIGH PROTEIN

SAUSAGE, MUSHROOM *and* APPLE CASSEROLE

15 MINS | 1 HR | SERVES 8

PER SERVING:
305 KCAL / 23G CARBS

low-calorie cooking spray
800g reduced-fat sausages
2 leeks, trimmed and finely sliced
2 carrots, peeled and diced
2 celery sticks, sliced
200g mushrooms, quartered
500ml apple juice
2 tbsp cornflour
1 vegetable stock pot
2 tsp dried sage
2 tsp garlic granules
2 tsp onion granules
2 tsp Dijon mustard
2 apples, no need to peel, sliced (any kind will work)
salt and freshly ground black pepper, to taste

TO ACCOMPANY
200g creamy mashed potatoes and 80g steamed vegetables (+214 kcal per serving)

Tuck into a taste of autumn with this casserole. Packed with juicy sausages, earthy mushrooms and fresh leeks and apples, it's just as flavourful as it is filling. Serve it with creamy mashed potatoes and steamed veg as a classic casserole, or use it as the base for our Cobbler on page 232. You can also turn it into the Hotpot on page 231. Each recipe uses exactly half of this one, serving four people each. That's eight meals from a single dish!

Special Occasion

Preheat the oven to 200°C (fan 180°C/gas mark 6).

Spray the casserole dish with low-calorie cooking spray and place over a medium heat. Add the sausages and brown on all sides, then remove and slice.

Add the leeks, carrots, celery and mushrooms to the pan and fry for 5 minutes, or until just softening. Add the apple juice and bring to the boil.

In a small bowl, mix the cornflour with 1 tablespoon water until smooth. Add to the pan along with the stock pot, sage, garlic and onion granules and mustard and mix well.

Add the sausages back to the pan along with the apples. Cover with a lid and cook in the oven for 35 minutes. Uncover and cook for a further 15 minutes. Season to taste with salt and pepper.

You can freeze the casserole at this point in a suitable container for up to 3 months. Serve with mashed potatoes and steamed vegetables.

The casserole will keep in the fridge for up to 3 days.

SAUSAGE, MUSHROOM *and* APPLE HOTPOT

15 MINS | 35 MINS | SERVES 4

VEGAN
USE VEGAN SAUSAGES, BACON AND HARD CHEESE

VEGGIE
USE VEGAN SAUSAGES, BACON AND HARD CHEESE

FREEZE ME

BATCH COOK

DAIRY FREE
USE DF CHEESE

GLUTEN FREE
USE GF STOCK POT

HIGH PROTEIN

PER SERVING:
454 KCAL /44G CARBS

SPECIAL EQUIPMENT
28cm (10in) ovenproof dish

- 400g potatoes
- 80g green beans, quartered
- ½ Sausage, Mushroom and Apple Casserole base recipe (page 228)
- low-calorie cooking spray
- 3 smoked bacon medallions, diced
- 1 tsp finely sliced fresh sage
- 10g Parmesan, finely grated

TO ACCOMPANY
80g steamed vegetables (+38 kcal per serving)

There's nothing like tucking into a steaming plate of pure comfort at the end of a chilly day. In this autumnal hotpot, succulent sausages and naturally sweet apple slices come together with fluffy potatoes, crispy bacon medallions and creamy cheese. Made using half the Sausage, Mushroom and Apple Casserole recipe on page 228, it's wonderfully simple to put together, and guaranteed to become a firm family favourite.

Weekly Indulgence

Preheat the oven to 200°C (fan 180°C/gas mark 6).

Slice the potatoes to the thickness of a £1 coin, no need to peel.

Add to a large saucepan and cover with cold water. Bring to the boil, turn the heat down and simmer for 10 minutes. The potatoes should be just soft and holding their shape; drain well and set aside.

In a large bowl, add the green beans to the Sausage, Mushroom and Apple Casserole mixture and stir. Scrape into the ovenproof dish and top with the sliced potatoes, overlapping each slice with the previous one. Spray with low-calorie cooking spray and sprinkle over the bacon, sage and Parmesan cheese.

Cook in the oven for 20–25 minutes, until the potatoes, bacon and sage are browned and cooked through. Serve with steamed vegetables.

The hotpot will keep in the fridge for up to 3 days.

TIPS

This recipe is written using the Sausage, Mushroom and Apple Casserole (page 228) as the base. If you prefer, you can make half the base recipe to use to make this recipe.

If the base recipe has previously been frozen, this recipe is not freezable. If the base recipe has been stored in the fridge before using, please follow the standard freezing guidelines.

VEGGIE

USE VEGETARIAN SAUSAGES

FREEZE ME

BATCH COOK

HIGH PROTEIN

SAUSAGE, MUSHROOM *and* APPLE COBBLER

15 MINS 20 MINS SERVES 4

PER SERVING:
545 KCAL /57G CARBS

SPECIAL EQUIPMENT
28cm (10in) ovenproof dish

50g reduced-fat cream cheese
½ Sausage, Mushroom and Apple Casserole base recipe (page 228)
80g green beans, quartered

FOR THE COBBLER
175g self-raising flour
½ tsp baking powder
1 tsp onion granules
1 tsp finely chopped fresh sage
salt and freshly ground black pepper, to taste
25g reduced-fat spread
1 medium egg
50ml skimmed milk

TO ACCOMPANY (OPTIONAL)
80g steamed vegetables (+38 kcal per serving)

You've heard of a sweet apple cobbler, but what about a savoury one? This sausage and mushroom bake is our proof that if you can dream it, you can make it. Half of the Sausage, Mushroom and Apple Casserole on page 228 forms the base of this dish, then we've added cream cheese, green beans and a biscuit-style doughy topping. A cosy alternative to your typical pie, it's fluffy on the inside, crisp on top and a bit different from your usual dinner!

Special Occasion

Preheat the oven to 200°C (fan 180°C/gas mark 6).

In a large bowl, stir the cream cheese through the Sausage, Mushroom and Apple Casserole mixture. Add the green beans and scrape the filling into the ovenproof dish.

For the cobbler, place the flour, baking powder, onion granules, sage and a pinch each of salt and pepper into a large bowl. Add the reduced-fat spread and use your fingertips to rub the spread into the flour.

Beat the egg and milk together in a small jug. Make a well in the centre of the bowl and add the milk and egg mix gradually, stirring with a spoon or round-bladed knife until the mix comes together. If it seems too dry, add a little extra milk, a few drops at a time. Lightly bring the dough together to form a soft dough. Do not overwork, as this will cause the cobbler topping to become tough.

Lightly flour your work surface. Roll into a sausage shape, about 16cm (6¼in) long. Use a sharp knife to cut it into 8 x 2cm (3¼ x ¾in) slices. Don't worry if they aren't perfectly round, we like a rustic look!

Arrange the cobbler scones on the top of the filling, then cook in the oven for 20 minutes, or until the scones are risen and golden. Serve with steamed vegetables.

The cobbler will keep in the fridge for up to 3 days.

TIPS

This recipe is written using the sausage, mushroom and apple casserole (page 228) as the base. If you prefer, you can make half the base recipe to use to make this recipe.

If the base recipe has previously been frozen, this recipe is not freezable. If the base recipe has been stored in the fridge before using, please follow the standard freezing guidelines.

BASE RECIPE

VEGAN
OMIT MOZZARELLA

VEGGIE

FREEZE ME
SAUCE ONLY

BATCH COOK

DAIRY FREE
OMIT MOZZARELLA

GLUTEN FREE
USE GF BREAD

HIGH PROTEIN

SICILIAN-STYLE BRUSCHETTA

10 MINS **35 MINS** **MAKES 12**

PER SERVING:
223 KCAL /33G CARBS

900g aubergine, trimmed and chopped into 1cm (½in) cubes
low-calorie cooking spray
salt and freshly ground black pepper, to taste
6 garlic cloves, peeled and crushed
400g cherry tomatoes, halved
15g fresh basil sprigs
2 x 400g tins crushed tomatoes
2 tsp chilli flakes

FOR THE BRUSCHETTA
12 slices sourdough bread (approx. 50g each)
1 large garlic clove, peeled
250g reduced-fat mozzarella

This recipe brings all the flavours of Sicily to your lunch plate. We've combined a rich aubergine and tomato sauce with garlic and fresh basil, served on toasted sourdough and topped with creamy, cool mozzarella. A small pinch of chilli flakes adds just the right amount of heat. This recipe also works as a base for other dishes. Make a batch of the sauce and save half to use in our Sicilian-Style Spaghetti on page 238 or our Sicilian-Style Meatballs on page 237.

Everyday Light

Preheat the oven to 220°C (fan 200°C/gas mark 7) and line a baking tray with non-stick baking paper.

Place the chopped aubergine in a large bowl, spray with low-calorie cooking spray and season with salt and pepper. Mix well to coat the aubergine cubes. Arrange the seasoned aubergine in a single layer on the lined baking tray (you may have to use two trays). Roast in the oven for 25–30 minutes, turning once after 15 minutes. The aubergine is cooked when it is soft and golden.

Meanwhile, spray a deep frying pan with low-calorie cooking spray and place over a medium heat. Add the crushed garlic and cherry tomato halves to the pan and cook for a minute or two.

Remove the basil leaves from their stems and chop the stems finely. Add the stems to the pan and cook for a further 5 minutes, or until the tomatoes have softened, taking care not to burn the garlic. Add the crushed tomatoes to the pan along with the chilli flakes and season to taste with salt and pepper. Tear half of the basil leaves and add these to the sauce too. Cook over a low heat for a further 10 minutes, or until the sauce has thickened slightly.

Once the aubergine is cooked and golden, remove from the oven and stir through the tomato sauce, along with the remaining basil leaves. At this point, the sauce can be cooled and frozen for up to 3 months (see Tips) or stored in the fridge for up to 3 days.

To make the bruschetta, allow the sauce to cool to room temperature. Toast the sourdough bread until crisp and golden.

Slice the garlic in half and rub over the surface of each piece of toasted bread. Top the bread with a generous serving of the Sicilian-style sauce and some torn mozzarella.

TIPS

Alternatively, you can cook the aubergine in the air fryer, if you prefer. Air-fry at 180°C for 25 minutes.

If you've frozen the sauce, once defrosted, reheat in an oven preheated to 200°C (fan 180°C/gas mark 6) for 10–15 minutes or microwave for 5–10 minutes until piping hot.

SICILIAN-STYLE MEATBALLS

5 MINS | 15 MINS | SERVES 2

FREEZE ME

BATCH COOK

GLUTEN FREE
USE GF BREADCRUMBS

HIGH PROTEIN

PER SERVING:
547 KCAL / 23G CARBS

SPECIAL EQUIPMENT
Small casserole dish, about 20 x 20cm (8 x 8in)

250g 10% fat minced lamb
½ medium egg, beaten
1 tbsp Italian seasoning
20g Parmesan, grated
20g panko breadcrumbs
salt and freshly ground black pepper, to taste
low-calorie cooking spray
½ Sicilian-Style Tomato Sauce base recipe (page 234)
60g mozzarella cheese
small handful of fresh basil leaves

TO ACCOMPANY
mixed salad
(+15 kcal per serving)

Who doesn't love a good meatball? Plump, tender and easy to portion, they're even better when coated in a slurp-worthy sauce. For this recipe, we've taken things Sicilian-style, using the sauce from the Sicilian-Style Bruschetta page 234 as a base. Herby lamb is shaped into tasty meatballs and gently simmered in a rich tomato and aubergine sauce. Finish with melty mozzarella for a cheesy topping... it's like a trip to Italy without leaving the kitchen!

Special Occasion

Preheat the oven to 220°C (fan 200°C/gas mark 7) and line a baking tray with non-stick baking paper.

Add the minced lamb to a large bowl along with the egg, Italian seasoning, Parmesan, breadcrumbs and a pinch of salt and pepper. Use your hand to gently combine the meatball mixture, taking care not to overwork the meat.

Divide the mixture into eight portions, shape into golf ball-sized meatballs and place on the lined baking tray. Spray with low-calorie cooking spray and bake in the oven for 10 minutes.

Place the Sicilian-Style Tomato Sauce in a medium saucepan over a low-medium heat. When simmering, add the cooked meatballs. Gently toss to combine.

Place the meatballs and sauce in the casserole dish and tear over the mozzarella. Return to the oven for a further 5 minutes, or until the meatballs are cooked through. Finish with a sprinkle of fresh basil leaves and serve with a mixed salad.

The meatballs can be frozen for up to 3 months (see Tips), or will keep in the fridge for up to 3 days. The finished dish can be frozen as a whole if the sauce has not been previously frozen and defrosted. If the sauce has been thawed, do not refreeze.

TIPS

Serve with toasted, crusty bread to mop up the sauce.

This recipe is written using the Sicilian-Style Tomato Sauce (page 234) as the base. If you prefer, you can make half the base recipe to make this recipe.

If you've frozen the meatballs, once defrosted, reheat in an oven preheated to 220°C (fan 200°C/gas mark 7) for 10–15 minutes, or until the meatballs are piping hot in the middle.

VEGAN
USE VEGAN HARD CHEESE

VEGGIE
USE VEGETARIAN ITALIAN HARD CHEESE

BATCH COOK

DAIRY FREE
SERVE WITHOUT CHEESE

GLUTEN FREE
USE GF SPAGHETTI

SICILIAN-STYLE SPAGHETTI

5 MINS | 15 MINS | SERVES 2

PER SERVING:
471 KCAL / 67G CARBS

160g wholewheat spaghetti
½ Sicilian-Style Tomato Sauce base recipe (page 234)
25g pitted black olives, halved
salt and freshly ground black pepper, to taste
20g Italian hard cheese, finely grated, to serve

Inspired by the beautifully simple Sicilian classic Pasta alla Norma, this vegetarian dish pairs tender aubergine with a rich marinara-style sauce. Using the tomato sauce on page 234 as a base, all that's left are a few more ingredients and some simple steps to bring it all together. The briny olives and nutty cheese balance perfectly with the sweetness of the tomatoes, creating a dish that impresses with barely any effort! Serve with a side of cheesy garlic bread for the full Italian experience.

Weekly Indulgence

Cook the pasta in a pan of boiling water according to the packet instructions. We cooked ours for 10 minutes. Reserve a cup of the pasta cooking water and drain the pasta.

Add the Sicilian-Style Tomato Sauce to a large saucepan or deep frying pan along with the olives and stir. Place over a medium heat and cook for a few minutes to heat the sauce.

Add the drained pasta to the sauce and toss through, ensuring that the spaghetti is well coated. Use a little of the reserved cooking water to loosen the sauce, if needed. Season to taste with salt and black pepper, if desired.

Serve the spaghetti with shavings of the hard cheese.

The dish will keep in the fridge for up to 3 days. Reheat in a microwave or saucepan. Add a splash of water to loosen the pasta and heat through for 5 minutes, or until piping hot.

TIPS

Parmesan cheese can be used instead of Italian hard cheese if preferred.

This recipe is written using the sauce from the Sicilian-Style Bruschetta (page 234) as the base.

HOB
MICROWAVE

STORE CUPBOARD

VEGGIE

FREEZE ME

BATCH COOK

DAIRY FREE

USE DF MILK, SOFT CHEESE AND YOGHURT

GLUTEN FREE

USE GF OATS AND BAKING POWDER

PINEAPPLE UPSIDE DOWN PANCAKE TRAYBAKE

10 MINS **25 MINS** **SERVES 8**

PER SERVING:
183 KCAL / 21G CARBS

SPECIAL EQUIPMENT
High-speed blender or food processor, large baking tray or shallow roasting pan, about 38 x 26cm (15 x 10¼in)

150g rolled porridge oats
1 tsp baking powder
½ tbsp granulated sweetener or caster sugar
100g reduced-fat cream cheese
4 large eggs
100ml semi-skimmed milk
8 tinned pineapple rings, drained
4 glacé cherries, halved

TO ACCOMPANY (OPTIONAL)
2 tbsp fat-free Greek yoghurt (+52 kcal per serving)

Boring breakfasts? Not on our watch! This pancake traybake is a morning twist on a classic dessert that makes getting out of bed worth it. Fluffy, oaty pancake batter bakes alongside juicy pineapple rings and sweet, sticky glacé cherries to give you a vibrant, tropical-inspired treat to wake up to. You can even make it ahead and freeze it, so it's ideal for grabbing on-the-go or serving up fresh for a weekend brunch. Soak up the sunshine vibes!

Everyday Light

Preheat the oven to 200°C (fan 180°C/gas mark 6) and line the baking tray or roasting pan with non-stick baking paper.

Blitz the oats in the high-speed blender or food processor to a flour. Place in a large bowl with the baking powder and sweetener.

In a separate large bowl, use a balloon whisk to beat the cream cheese, eggs and milk together until smooth.

Make a well in the centre of the oat flour and gradually stir in the cream cheese mixture, beating until you have a smooth batter. Leave to stand for 5 minutes.

Arrange the pineapple slices evenly over the prepared tray and pop half a cherry inside each one. Pour the batter over and spread it out evenly across the tray. Bake in the oven for 20–25 minutes until risen and golden on top. Cut the cake into eight squares, with a pineapple ring in each square, and serve warm with a dollop of Greek yoghurt on the side.

Alternatively, when cool the squares can be wrapped individually and either frozen in an airtight container for up to 3 months (see Tips) or stored in the fridge for up to 4 days. The cake can be eaten cold, straight from the fridge, or reheated.

TIP

If you've frozen the cake, once defrosted, reheat in the microwave for 1–2 minutes, turning halfway.

VEGAN
USE VEGAN BISCUITS

VEGGIE

FREEZE ME

BATCH COOK

DAIRY FREE
USE DF BISCUITS

GLUTEN FREE
USE GF OATS AND GF BISCUITS

GINGERBREAD PORRIDGE

5 MINS   5 MINS   SERVES 4

PER SERVING:
344 KCAL / 51G CARBS

200g rolled porridge oats
600ml oat milk
20g light brown sugar
1½ tsp ground ginger
1 tsp ground cinnamon
2 tsp vanilla extract
20g ginger biscuits (about 2 biscuits), crushed

Getting out of bed is hard enough as it is without dark, dreary mornings, so we've come up with the perfect warm and comforting breakfast to help you transition into the colder seasons. It comes together in no time at all; all you need is a spare ten minutes and a few simple ingredients, and you've got a bowl of cosy gingerbread goodness that'll warm you from your head to your toes.

Everyday Light

Place the oats in a large saucepan along with the oat milk and place over a medium heat. Allow the oats to gently cook in the milk for about 4–5 minutes until they have absorbed a lot of the milk and the porridge is thickening.

Remove the pan from the heat and add the brown sugar, ground ginger, cinnamon and vanilla. Stir well through the porridge and return to the heat for a further minute, until the porridge is piping hot and the oats are properly cooked. You can freeze the porridge at this stage. Leave to cool completely, then divide into portions and freeze in individual airtight containers for up to 3 months (see Tips).

Serve the porridge topped with some crumbled ginger biscuits. The porridge will keep in the fridge for up to 3 days. Place in a saucepan or in the microwave for a few minutes until piping hot. If it is too thick, loosen with a splash of milk.

TIPS

Add more ground ginger to the porridge for extra heat.

If you've frozen the porridge, once it's defrosted completely, place it in a saucepan with a splash of milk to loosen and cook for a few minutes until the porridge is piping hot. Alternatively, you can do this in a microwave.

HIGH PROTEIN

CORNED BEEF *and* PICKLE PIE

15 MINS | 35 MINS | SERVES 6

PER SERVING:
252 KCAL /12G CARBS

SPECIAL EQUIPMENT
20cm (8in) round pie plate, food processor or high-speed blender

100g white bread
120g reduced-fat mature Cheddar cheese, finely grated
low-calorie cooking spray
1 onion, peeled and diced
1 x 340g tin corned beef, diced
2 tbsp small-chunk sweet pickle

TO ACCOMPANY
80g steamed vegetables (+38 kcal per serving)

When you're craving a pie but can't be bothered nipping to the shops for pastry, try this! We've made a clever bread-and-cheese crust by blitzing slices into crumbs and pressing them into a pie dish, baking until the edges are beautifully crisp and golden. Filled with a classic combo of corned beef and pickle, then topped with melty cheese, it's comforting and nostalgic.

Everyday Light

Preheat the oven to 200°C (fan 180°C/gas mark 6).

Place the bread and 40g of the grated cheese in the food processor or high-speed blender and blitz to crumbs.

Spray the pie plate with low-calorie cooking spray and press the breadcrumbs into the bottom, bringing them up the sides to create a crust. If the mix seems too dry to stick together, add 1–2 tablespoons water. Bake in the oven for 12–15 minutes until lightly golden.

Meanwhile, spray a frying pan with low-calorie cooking spray, add the onion and fry over a medium heat for 5 minutes, or until soft.

In a large bowl, mix the cooked onion with the corned beef and pickle, mashing it together lightly.

Pile the corned beef into the pie crust, then sprinkle the remaining grated cheese over the top. Return to the oven for 15–20 minutes until the cheese is bubbling and golden.

Serve with mashed potato or steamed vegetables.

MUSHY PEA NUGGETS *with* CURRY SAUCE

20 MINS | 35 MINS | SERVES 4

VEGGIE

DAIRY FREE

GLUTEN FREE

USE GF BREADCRUMBS, SOY SAUCE AND FLOUR

PER SERVING:
270 KCAL /47G CARBS

SPECIAL EQUIPMENT
Food processor, stick blender

FOR THE NUGGETS

200g potatoes, peeled and cut into chunks
salt and freshly ground black pepper, to taste
1 x 300g tin mushy peas
2 tbsp plain flour
1 medium egg, beaten
2 slices wholemeal bread, blitzed into crumbs

FOR THE CURRY SAUCE

low-calorie cooking spray
½ onion, peeled and diced
1 eating apple, peeled and diced
2 tsp curry powder (we used mild but use a spicier one if you prefer)
½ tsp garlic granules
½ tsp ground ginger
½ tsp ground fenugreek
2 tbsp soy sauce
1 tsp rice vinegar

TO ACCOMPANY

100g oven chips (+186 kcal per serving)

TIPS

The apple and onion thicken the curry sauce, but if you want it thicker, use a slurry of 1–2 teaspoons of cornflour mixed with the same amount of water and stir through after blending.

Give your fibre intake a boost with this twist on a chippy tea, straight from your store cupboard. We love these as a light lunch to use up any leftover potatoes. Don't skip the homemade curry sauce! It's free from any hidden ingredients, and it's simple to make with bits you may have in your kitchen.

Weekly Indulgence

To make the nuggets, cook the potatoes in a large saucepan of boiling salted water for 15 minutes, or until a knife inserts easily through the centre. Drain well and allow to air-dry for a couple of minutes before returning to the pan and mashing well.

Meanwhile, drain the mushy peas in a sieve, squeezing out any excess liquid. Leave to drain, then add to the pan of potatoes and mix well. Season to taste with salt and pepper.

Prepare the curry sauce. Spray a saucepan with low-calorie cooking spray, place over a medium heat, add the onion and apple and fry for 5 minutes. Add the curry powder, garlic granules, ginger and fenugreek and stir for a minute to toast the spices and release their flavour. Add the soy sauce and 300ml water, bring to the boil, then turn the heat down, cover with a lid and simmer for 25 minutes while you coat and cook the nuggets.

Preheat the oven to 220°C (fan 200°C/gas mark 7) and line a large baking tray with non-stick baking paper.

Put the flour, egg and breadcrumbs into three separate bowls. Divide the pea mash into 16 equal portions and roll into balls. Roll the first mushy pea ball in the flour to lightly coat. Flatten into a nugget shape, then dip into the egg. Finally, coat in the breadcrumbs, pressing lightly so they are well coated. Place on the lined baking tray. Repeat with the remaining nuggets. Spray well with low-calorie cooking spray and bake in the oven for 10 minutes until golden and crisp.

While the nuggets cook, remove the curry sauce from the heat and use a stick blender to blitz to a smooth sauce. Stir in the rice vinegar and season to taste with salt and pepper. Serve the nuggets with the curry sauce and oven chips on the side.

FREEZE ME

GLUTEN FREE

USE GF CHICKEN SOUP

HIGH PROTEIN

CREAMY HAM *and* PEA RICE

5 MINS 12 MINS SERVES 4

PER SERVING:
386 KCAL / 47G CARBS

SPECIAL EQUIPMENT
Large, non-stick deep frying pan or wok

low-calorie cooking spray
1 onion, peeled and diced
125g frozen peas
200g ham, diced
1 tsp garlic granules
2 x 250g pouches microwave rice
1 x 400g tin cream of chicken soup
75g reduced-fat Cheddar cheese, grated
freshly ground black pepper, to taste

This one's a proper kitchen cupboard hero! Made with store cupboard and freezer staples, it transforms tinned ham, frozen peas, microwave rice and a humble tin of chicken soup into a creamy, comforting recipe you'll want to keep in your back pocket to make on repeat. It's ready in just over ten minutes, less than 400 calories and you can even freeze the leftovers for another day.

Everyday Light

Spray the pan with low-calorie cooking spray and place over a medium heat. Add the onion and cook for 5 minutes, or until soft.

Add the frozen peas and ham and cook for a further 2 minutes.

Add the garlic granules.

Squeeze the rice pouches to separate the grains, then add to the pan. Stir for a minute or two until everything is mixed.

Stir in the chicken soup and keep stirring for 2–3 minutes until everything is piping hot. Stir through the grated cheese and season with pepper. Serve. You can freeze any leftovers in individual portions to avoid waste for up to 3 months (see Tips).

TIPS

We used tinned ham, but fresh, sliced ham also works. You could also swap the peas for sweetcorn, if you wish.

If you've frozen leftovers, once defrosted, reheat in the microwave for 3–4 minutes, stirring halfway through.

VEGGIE

USE VEGGIE MEAT ALTERNATIVE

DAIRY FREE

GLUTEN FREE

USE GF SOY SAUCE)

HIGH PROTEIN

LOW CARB

HAM FOO YUNG-STYLE EGGS

5 MINS 10 MINS SERVES 2

PER SERVING:
243 KCAL /6.5G CARBS

SPECIAL EQUIPMENT
Non-stick wok or frying pan

4 large eggs
1 tsp soy sauce
½ tsp ground ginger
¼ tsp ground white pepper
½ tsp sesame oil
½ onion, peeled and sliced
50g frozen peas
50g ham, diced
115g tinned beansprouts, drained

TO ACCOMPANY
125g cooked/50g raw basmati rice or 50g nest of egg noodles (+173 kcal per serving)

This quick and easy Chinese-style omelette is made with a handful of simple ingredients, including tinned ham, beansprouts and onion. Light, fluffy and full of savoury flavour, the dash of soy sauce, ginger and white pepper brings everything together perfectly. Cooked in one pan and ready in under fifteen minutes, it's a no-fuss dish you can enjoy with rice, noodles or as a light lunch on its own!

Weekly Indulgence

Beat the eggs, soy sauce, ginger and white pepper together in large bowl and set to one side.

Place the wok over a medium-high heat and add the sesame oil. When the pan is hot, add the onion and stir-fry for 3–4 minutes.

Add the peas and fry for a further minute. Add the ham and beansprouts and cook for a further 2 minutes, or until everything is hot.

Add the eggs to the wok and leave for a minute until the bottom begins to set. Use a spatula to stir, scramble the eggs until they begin to set, then leave for a minute. Flip the eggs to cook the other side and break up slightly. You want the eggs somewhere between scrambled and omelette. This should take 3–4 minutes. Serve.

TIPS

We used a good-quality tinned ham from our store cupboard, but fresh, sliced ham works just as well.

FREEZE ME

BATCH COOK

DAIRY FREE

GLUTEN FREE

USE GF PASTA

TUNA PUTTANESCA PASTA

10 MINS **15 MINS** **SERVES 4**

PER SERVING:
338 KCAL /49G CARBS

SPECIAL EQUIPMENT
Non-stick wok or frying pan

250g small, dried pasta shapes, e.g. fusilli or penne
salt and freshly ground black pepper, to taste
1 tsp garlic granules
1 tsp onion granules
½ tsp chilli flakes (adjust if you don't like heat)
2 tbsp tomato puree
1 x 400g tin chopped tomatoes
75g pitted black olives
1 tbsp capers, drained
juice of 1 lemon
2 x 145g tins tuna in spring water, drained

This speedy dinner is perfect for those nights when only pasta will do! Inspired by a classic Italian puttanesca, we've kept the salty, punchy flavours of olives, capers and chilli, then stirred through tuna to make it extra satisfying. A few simple store-cupboard staples and twenty minutes is all it takes. It's hearty, comforting, and the perfect no-fuss midweek meal you can have on rotation.

Everyday Light

Cook the pasta according to the packet instructions (usually 9–12 minutes in boiling salted water).

Meanwhile, mix the garlic granules, onion granules, chilli flakes, tomato puree, chopped tomatoes, 200ml water, olives, capers and lemon juice together in a large frying pan. Place over a high heat and bring to the boil, stirring occasionally. Turn the heat down and simmer for 5 minutes.

When the pasta is cooked, drain well.

Stir the pasta and tuna into the tomato sauce and cook for a further 4–5 minutes. Season to taste with salt and pepper and serve. You can freeze the pasta in individual portions at this stage for up to 3 months (see Tips).

TIPS

Capers are a traditional part of puttanesca sauce. They bring a tangy, salty burst of flavour but they can be omitted or replaced with a few extra olives.

If you've frozen the pasta, once defrosted, microwave for 3–4 minutes, stirring halfway through. Pasta can dry out a little when defrosted, so add a splash of water, if needed.

TUNA KEDGEREE

5 MINS | 30 MINS | SERVES 4

FREEZE ME

BATCH COOK

DAIRY FREE

USE DF CREAM CHEESE

GLUTEN FREE

USE GF STOCK CUBE

HIGH PROTEIN

PER SERVING:
401 KCAL /50G CARBS

SPECIAL EQUIPMENT
Shallow casserole dish, suitable for hob, or a large frying pan with lid

low-calorie cooking spray
1 onion, peeled and finely diced
1 tbsp curry powder
1 tsp garlic granules
½ tsp ground turmeric
200g basmati rice
500ml chicken or vegetable stock (1 stock cube dissolved in 500ml boiling water)
75g reduced-fat cream cheese
200g tinned sweetcorn, drained
2 x 145g tins tuna in spring water, drained
juice of 1 lemon
salt and freshly ground black pepper, to taste
4 medium eggs
1 tsp dried parsley, to garnish

Kedgeree is a classic Victorian breakfast dish made up of fragrant curried rice and fish. This time, we've substituted haddock with tuna and swapped out some of the veg for sweetcorn. It's a classic flavour combo, but we can guarantee you haven't tried it like this before! And because you can make it using bits you'll probably have in your cupboard already, if you haven't had a chance to do your big shop, you've got a tasty, speedy meal you can rustle up with just a few tins.

Weekly Indulgence

Spray the casserole dish with low-calorie cooking spray and place over a medium heat. Add the onion and fry for 6–8 minutes until lightly golden. Add the curry powder, garlic granules and turmeric and cook until fragrant. Add the rice and cook for a further minute, stirring well to coat in the spices. Add the stock and stir in the cream cheese. Add the sweetcorn and bring to a gentle simmer. Cover with the lid and cook for 10 minutes, or until almost all the liquid has been absorbed.

Stir through the tuna and lemon juice, then taste and season with salt and pepper, if needed. Replace the lid and remove from the heat. Leave to stand for 10 minutes to allow any remaining liquid to absorb.

Meanwhile, boil the eggs to your liking. We cook ours for about 6 minutes because we like a slightly runny yolk. Plunge the eggs into cold water to cool them down, then peel and cut each egg in half.

Fluff up the rice with a fork and arrange the eggs on top. Serve. You can freeze the kedgeree at this stage (without the eggs) by cooling quickly, then freezing in individual portions for up to 3 months (see Tip). You can also cool quickly and store in the fridge in an airtight container for up to 2 days.

TIPS

If you've frozen the kedgeree, once defrosted, reheat in the microwave for 3–4 minutes, stirring halfway through.

VEGAN

VEGGIE

BATCH COOK

GLUTEN FREE

USE GF SOY SAUCE

CHINESE-STYLE CURRIED NOODLES

5 MINS 25 MINS SERVES 4

PER SERVING:
319 KCAL /33G CARBS

SPECIAL EQUIPMENT
Wok or deep frying pan

low-calorie cooking spray
2 tsp ginger paste
2 tsp garlic paste
500g frozen stir-fry vegetables
2 tbsp mild curry powder
½ tsp Chinese five-spice
2 tsp ground turmeric
1 x 400ml tin light coconut milk
1 tsp caster sugar
1 tbsp soy sauce
400ml vegetable stock (1 vegetable stock cube dissolved in 400ml boiling water)
1 tsp cornflour
300g straight-to-wok rice noodles
50g roasted and salted peanuts, chopped, to serve

Give your store-cupboard staples a tasty twist with these Chinese-Style Curried Noodles! We've loaded this dish up with frozen stir-fry veggies to keep things easy and speedy, with a rich and fragrant curry sauce that is so simple you can probably make it without even nipping to the shops. The noodles soak up all those delicious flavours, making every bite a trip for your tastebuds. Wholesome and filling, with plenty of nutritional value to boot, this recipe shows that even the quickest dinners can be delicious too.

Everyday Light

Spray a wok or deep frying pan with low-calorie cooking spray and add the ginger, garlic and frozen vegetables. Place over a medium heat. Stir to combine and allow the frozen vegetables to defrost and warm through. The vegetables will release water, so allow 5–6 minutes for the water to release and then evaporate.

Once the excess water has evaporated and the vegetables are partly cooked, add the curry powder, five-spice and turmeric.

Mix the spices through the vegetables and cook for a further 2 minutes, or until the spices are toasted and beginning to release their aroma. Add the coconut milk along with the sugar and soy sauce.

Add the stock to the curry and stir well to combine. In a small bowl, mix the cornflour with 1 tablespoon cold water into a slurry. Add this to the curry and cook for 10 minutes over a medium-low heat to reduce into a rich and tasty sauce.

Add the cooked noodles to the curry and toss through the sauce.

Cook for a further 5 minutes, or until the noodles are hot and well coated in the curry sauce.

Serve the noodles topped with a sprinkling of chopped peanuts for an extra crunch.

The curried noodles will keep in the fridge for up to 3 days.

TIPS

We have used rice noodles in this dish, but you can use egg noodles or any other noodles you might have in the store cupboard.

If you've stored the dish, add a splash of water to loosen the noodles and warm through in a saucepan over a medium heat for 5 minutes, or until hot. Alternatively, the noodles can be reheated in the microwave for 3 minutes.

VEGGIE

BATCH COOK

DAIRY FREE

GLUTEN FREE

USE GF STOCK AND SOY SAUCE

KOREAN-STYLE BUTTER BEANS

10 MINS **30 MINS** **SERVES 4**

PER SERVING:
438 KCAL / 68G CARBS

1 tsp sesame oil
1 onion, peeled and sliced
2 tsp garlic granules
2–3 tsp gochujang paste
2 tbsp tomato puree
750ml vegetable stock (1 vegetable stock cube dissolved in 750ml boiling water)
1 tbsp soy sauce
1 tbsp honey
2 x 400g tins butter beans, approx. 480g, drained and rinsed
80g frozen spinach
1 tsp rice vinegar
4 x 50g nests of rice noodles
4 medium eggs
low-calorie cooking spray

We can't get enough of naturally creamy butter beans, and we've given them a Korean-inspired twist in this spicy, flavourful dish. The beans are cooked in a rich gochujang and tomato broth that's full of depth, with just the right amount of kick to make every spoonful a taste sensation. Serve it over rice noodles (or egg noodles, it's entirely up to you!) for a slurp-worthy bowl that'll have you watching the clock until dinnertime. And if you just can't get enough, you can chill the beans in the fridge for tomorrow's lunch! Top it with a fresh fried egg for a creamy golden yolk that brings the whole dish together.

Weekly Indulgence

Place a large frying pan over a medium heat and add the sesame oil. Add the onion and sauté for 5 minutes, or until soft. Stir in the garlic granules, gochujang paste and tomato puree and cook for a minute. Add the stock, soy sauce and honey and bring to a simmer. Cook for 10 minutes to allow the flavours to develop.

Add the butter beans and frozen spinach to the pan and cook for a further 5 minutes, or until the beans are thoroughly heated and the spinach is defrosted and cooked through. Stir in the rice vinegar.

Meanwhile, cook the noodles according to the packet instructions (usually 4 minutes in a pan of boiling salted water) and fry the eggs to your liking in low-calorie cooking spray.

Assemble the noodles in four bowls, pour the beans over and top each bowl with a fried egg. Serve.

The beans will keep in the fridge for up to 4 days.

TIP

Reheat individual portions of the beans, loosely covered, in the microwave for 3–4 minutes, stirring occasionally.

VEGAN

VEGGIE

FREEZE ME

BATCH COOK

DAIRY FREE

GLUTEN FREE

USE GF FLOUR AND BAKING POWDER

PEA FALAFEL *with* GARLIC TAHINI SAUCE

10 MINS 20 MINS SERVES 4

PER SERVING:
316 KCAL /27G CARBS

SPECIAL EQUIPMENT
Food processor

- low-calorie cooking spray
- 1 x 400g tin chickpeas, rinsed and drained
- 180g frozen peas, thawed
- 4 garlic cloves, peeled and crushed
- 2 tbsp lemon juice
- salt and freshly ground black pepper, to taste
- 1 tsp ground cumin
- ½ tsp baking powder
- 3 tbsp plain flour, plus extra 3 tbsp for dusting
- 2 tbsp sesame seeds
- 70g tahini paste

TO ACCOMPANY
mixed salad (+15 kcal per serving)

Who doesn't love a dinner you can throw together with things you already have in the cupboard? These pea falafels aren't just convenient to make, they're packed with plant-based protein that keeps you fuller for longer, and they taste especially delicious when paired with our garlicky tahini drizzle. Serve them with a simple side salad for a lighter bite or pack them into a wrap or pitta when you want something more filling.

Everyday Light

Preheat the oven to 220°C (fan 200°C/gas mark 7) and line a baking tray with non-stick baking paper. Spray the baking paper with low-calorie cooking spray.

Add the chickpeas, peas, 2 crushed garlic cloves, 1 tablespoon of the lemon juice, a pinch of salt and pepper, the ground cumin, baking powder and flour to the food processor and pulse the ingredients until mixed. Do not puree the ingredients, you are looking for a loose and chunky consistency.

Dust your hands with flour, then pick up 2–3 teaspoons of the mix and bring together into a patty. Place on the lined baking tray and repeat the process with the rest of the mix. You should get twelve decent sized falafels from this recipe.

Sprinkle the top of each falafel with some sesame seeds and spray with more low-calorie cooking spray. Bake in the oven for 10 minutes.

After 10 minutes, turn each falafel over and sprinkle with more sesame seeds. Finish with a final spray of low-calorie cooking spray and bake in the oven for a further 10 minutes, or until crisp and golden.

To make the garlic and tahini sauce, place the tahini in a medium bowl with the remaining 1 tablespoon lemon juice and whisk. As you whisk, the tahini will seize up and at this point add 100ml water, a few drops at a time. Keep whisking the water into the tahini until you get a smooth glossy sauce. If it is still too thick, add a few more drops of water. Once you have the right consistency,

TIPS

These falafels are perfect to add to pittas and wraps for a more substantial meal.

Make the falafels into smaller, bite-sized patties for the perfect party food.

You can air-fry the falafels in batches at 180°C for 15 minutes, if preferred.

add the remaining crushed garlic cloves and a pinch of salt and pepper. Whisk to combine.

Serve three falafels with a mixed salad and drizzle with the garlic and tahini sauce.

You can freeze the cooked falafels, by leaving them to cool, then freezing them in a freezer-proof bag for up to 3 months (see Tips).

The falafels will keep in the fridge for up to 3 days. The sauce will keep in the fridge for 5–7 days. Falafels can be eaten at room temperature, or reheat them in an oven preheated to 200°C (fan 180°C/gas mark 6) for 10 minutes until piping hot.

TIPS

Not all baking powder is gluten free, so be sure to check if you are following a gluten-free diet.

If you've frozen the falafels, once defrosted, reheat them in an oven preheated to 180°C (fan 160°C/gas mark 5) for 10 minutes until piping hot.

VEGAN
USE VEGAN MARGARINE AND MILK

VEGGIE

FREEZE ME

BATCH COOK

DAIRY FREE
USE DF MARGARINE AND MILK

GLUTEN FREE
USE GF FLOUR

CHAI-SPICED SCONES

10 MINS **10 MINS + 5 MINS COOLING** **MAKES 12**

PER SERVING:
177 KCAL /33G CARBS

SPECIAL EQUIPMENT
5cm (2in) round cutter, pastry brush

250g plain flour, plus 3 tbsp extra for dusting
1½ tsp baking powder
pinch of salt
50g golden caster sugar
70g spiced chai powder
70g low-fat spread, fridge cold and cubed
145ml skimmed milk, plus 2 tbsp extra for brushing
100g icing sugar

When the weather turns chilly, there's nothing better than baking a batch of scones. These chai-spiced beauties are like a hug in every bite! Infused with the cosy flavours of cinnamon and cardamom from chai latte powder, they're soft, fluffy and finished with a milky-sweet glaze for extra indulgence. Pop the kettle on and enjoy one warm from the oven with your afternoon brew – they're every bit as comforting as your favourite café treat!

Everyday Light

Preheat the oven to 220°C (fan 200°C/gas mark 7) and line a baking sheet with non-stick baking paper.

In a large bowl, add the flour, baking powder, salt, sugar and 50g chai powder and mix together well. Add the cubes of spread into the flour mix and use your fingertips to gently rub the flour and spread together until you get a breadcrumb consistency.

Add 125ml of the milk to the flour and spread mix and gently bring together into a dough. Take care not to overwork the dough, as it can make it tough.

Tip the dough onto a floured work surface and bring it together into a ball. Gently flatten the dough into a round, about 2cm (¾in) thick. Dip the cutter in some flour and begin cutting rounds out of the dough. Gently place each scone on the lined baking tray, ensuring there is space between each one. Bring the dough offcuts together into a ball and flatten into another round, then continue cutting the scones out until all the dough is used. You should get twelve scones out of this recipe.

Place the extra 2 tablespoons of milk in a small bowl and, using the pastry brush, lightly brush the top of the scones with milk. Bake the scones in the oven for 10 minutes, or until golden and cooked through.

Remove the scones from the oven and leave them to cool on a wire rack for 5 minutes.

In a large bowl, add the icing sugar, along with the remaining chai powder and milk and whisk until you get a smooth chai glaze. If the glaze is too thick, add a teaspoon or two of milk until you get a thick, glossy glaze.

TIPS

If you are planning on freezing or storing the scones, don't glaze them. Reserve the glaze for serving.

If you've frozen the scones, once defrosted, bake in an oven preheated to 200°C (fan 180°C/gas mark 6) for 5–10 minutes until warmed through. Serve with a drizzle of the chai glaze.

We used Drink Me Chai Latte powder in this recipe. Be sure to choose the vegan version if needed.

When the scones have cooled, spoon the glaze over the top of each one and serve. You can freeze cooled freshly baked scones for up to 3 months.

The scones will keep in the fridge for up to 3 days. The glaze should be made fresh on the day. The scones can be eaten at room temperature or baked in the oven (see Tips).

JAM BUTTY PUDDING

5 MINS + 10 MINS RESTING | **30 MINS** | **SERVES 4**

VEGGIE

FREEZE ME

BATCH COOK

DAIRY FREE

GLUTEN FREE
USE GF BREAD

PER SERVING:
232 KCAL /39G CARBS

SPECIAL EQUIPMENT
20cm (8in) square ovenproof dish

- low-calorie cooking spray
- 70g jam, whichever you have, but seedless is best
- 5 slices white bread (approx. 36g per slice)
- 2 medium eggs
- 350ml oat milk or whichever milk you prefer
- 1 tsp vanilla extract
- 2 tbsp granulated sweetener

TO ACCOMPANY (OPTIONAL)
100g light ready-made custard (+79 kcal per serving)

If you're in the mood for a seriously nostalgic pud, this Jam Butty Pudding is pure comfort in a bowl. Humble jam sandwiches are soaked in vanilla custard, then baked until golden and crisp on top, ready to be served with even more creamy custard (because why not?). It's quick, easy and made with everyday ingredients you'll likely already have in the kitchen, proof that sometimes the simplest things really are the best.

Special Occasion

Preheat the oven to 200°C (fan 180°C/gas mark 6) and grease the ovenproof dish with some low-calorie cooking spray.

Use 50g of the jam to make two and a half jam sandwiches. Trim off the crusts and cut into triangles. You should have ten small, triangle 'jam butties'.

Beat the eggs, milk, vanilla extract and sweetener together in a jug.

Arrange the jam butties in the prepared dish. Pour the egg and milk mixture over the bread and leave to soak through for 10 minutes.

In a small bowl, mix the remaining jam with 1 tablespoon water until smooth, then drizzle over the top of the pudding. Place the dish on a baking tray and bake in the oven for 30 minutes, or until the custard is fully set and the top is golden brown. You can freeze the pudding at this stage (see Tips).

Serve with extra custard, if you wish.

TIPS

Any jam works for this recipe, but seedless jam is best. You could also use marmalade or lemon curd.

If you've frozen the pudding, once defrosted, reheat in the microwave for 2–3 minutes, turning halfway through.

VEGGIE

FREEZE ME

BATCH COOK

DAIRY FREE

USE DF MILK SUBSTITUTE

CHERRIES JUBILEE WAFFLES

5 MINS 15 MINS SERVES 4

PER SERVING:
284 KCAL /53G CARBS

SPECIAL EQUIPMENT
Waffle maker

150g self-raising flour
200ml skimmed milk
1 medium egg
1 tsp white granulated sweetener
low-calorie cooking spray

FOR THE CHERRY FILLING:
1 x 425g tin cherries, juice and fruit
1 tbsp granulated sweetener
1 tbsp cornflour

TO ACCOMPANY (OPTIONAL)
12.5g reduced-fat aerosol cream (+24 kcal per serving)

Inspired by the classic Cherries Jubilee dessert, which was created by French chef Auguste Escoffier for Queen Victoria's Diamond Jubilee and was said to be one of her favourites, this recipe turns a traditional dessert into a breakfast you can enjoy any day. Soft, fluffy waffles topped with a warm cherry compote, they're perfect for weekend brunching or batch-cooking ahead. A swirl of aerosol cream takes them to the next level.

Everyday Light

Preheat the waffle maker.

Put the flour in a large bowl along with the milk, egg and sweetener. Mix with a balloon whisk until you have a smooth batter. Set the batter aside while the waffle maker preheats.

When the waffle maker is hot, spray it with a little low-calorie cooking spray. Pour half of the waffle batter onto the hot plate and spread out. It depends on the size of the waffle maker; we made two large circle waffles with four waffle sections in each circle.

Seal the waffle maker and cook for 5–6 minutes, until the waffle is crispy and golden brown around the edges. Repeat with the remaining mixture.

Meanwhile, add the cherries and juice to a small saucepan along with the sweetener.

Combine the cornflour and 1 tablespoon water in a small bowl and mix until smooth, then add to the cherries. Place the pan over a medium heat and simmer for 5 minutes, until thickened and glossy. Set aside and keep warm.

If serving right away, stack up two waffle quarters per person on serving plates. Top with the cherries and a swirl of aerosol cream.

You can freeze the cooked waffles in individual portions for up to 3 months. Store leftover cherries in an airtight container in the freezer for up to 3 months (see Tips). The waffles will keep in the fridge for up to 3 days. Reheat in the toaster or microwave until warmed through.

TIPS

If you don't have a waffle maker, you can use a silicone waffle mould. Preheat the oven to 180°C (fan 160°C/gas mark 4). Prepare the mixture as above. Spray the mould with low-calorie cooking spray and fill with the waffle mixture. Bake for 25–30 minutes, until the waffles are firm to the touch and golden brown. Turn out onto a baking tray and bake for a further 4–5 minutes.

If you've frozen the waffles, then reheat from frozen in the toaster or microwave until warmed through. Defrost the cherries in the fridge overnight.

VEGGIE

FREEZE ME

BATCH COOK

DAIRY FREE

USE DF SPREAD AND MILK

PEACH CUSTARD CAKE

10 MINS | 1 HR 15 MINS | SERVES 8

PER SERVING:
240 KCAL /40G CARBS

SPECIAL EQUIPMENT
20cm (8in) round cake tin, electric whisk

- 3 medium eggs, separated
- 60g caster sugar
- 60g granulated sweetener
- 100g reduced-fat spread
- 2 tsp vanilla extract
- 3 tbsp custard powder
- 200ml skimmed milk
- 130g self-raising flour
- 1 x 411g tin peaches, approx. 250g drained weight, chopped
- 2 tsp icing sugar

This comforting bake is a clever twist on a classic pudding... and it's made almost entirely from store-cupboard staples! Canned peaches are the star of the show, nestled into the base of your tin before being topped with a light, custard-flavoured sponge that bakes into two delicious layers. Whether served warm or chilled, it's the kind of easy dessert that feels a little bit special but doesn't call for too much fuss.

Weekly Indulgence

Preheat the oven to 180°C (fan 160°C/gas mark 4) and line the base and sides of the tin with non-stick baking paper.

Add the egg yolks, caster sugar and sweetener to a large bowl and mix with an electric whisk for 2 minutes, or until thickened.

Add the spread, vanilla and custard powder and mix for a further 2 minutes. Add the milk and 120g of the flour and mix again for 2 minutes.

Clean the beaters and add the egg whites to a clean bowl. Beat for 2 minutes to stiff peaks.

Add half the egg white mixture to the yolk mixture and fold in. Add the remaining egg white and continue to gently fold into the mixture.

Sprinkle the remaining flour over the peaches in a large bowl and toss to coat. Spread the peaches over the bottom of the tin. Scrape the cake mixture on top of the peaches and roughly smooth out.

Bake in the oven for 1 hour 20 minutes, or until a skewer inserted comes out clean. If the top of the cake is browning too quickly, cover with foil.

Leave to cool in the tin, then dust with icing sugar. Slice into eight and serve. You can freeze the cake in individual portions in an airtight container for up to 3 months.

The cake will keep in the fridge for up to 3 days.

VEGAN
USE VEGAN SPREAD

VEGGIE

FREEZE ME

BATCH COOK

DAIRY FREE
USE DF SPREAD

GLUTEN FREE
USE GF FLOUR AND OATS

CHERRY BAKEWELL COOKIES

15 MINS + RESTING | 12 MINS | MAKES 18

PER SERVING:
88 KCAL / 7.6G CARBS

- 50g reduced-fat spread
- 100g almond butter
- 2 tbsp granulated sweetener
- 1 tbsp caster sugar
- 2 tsp almond extract
- 50g glacé cherries, chopped
- 50g self-raising flour
- 50g rolled porridge oats, blitzed to a coarse flour
- 15g flaked almonds

A few years ago, we took a trip to Bakewell, home of the famous Bakewell tart. We couldn't wait to try the real thing! One bite, and we knew we wanted to recreate those gorgeous almond and cherry flavours back in our own kitchen. These Cherry Bakewell Cookies are a fuss-free treat, with only 88 calories each. Melt-in-your-mouth and packed with flavour, they're perfect with a cuppa or tucked into your packed lunch for a proper little pick-me-up.

Everyday Light

Preheat the oven to 200°C (fan 180°C/gas mark 6) and line a large baking tray with greaseproof paper.

Add the reduced-fat spread, almond butter, sweetener, caster sugar and almond extract to a large bowl and use a spatula or wooden spoon to beat until smooth.

In a separate bowl, toss the cherry pieces in the flour to coat. This will help prevent them from sticking together.

Add the flour, cherries, oat flour and flaked almonds to the spread and almond butter mixture and fold in until well combined. Use your hands to bring the dough into a soft ball. Divide the dough into 18 equal pieces and roll each into a ball. Arrange on the lined baking tray and flatten into rounds, about 1cm (½in) thick.

Leave to rest for 10 minutes, then bake in the oven for 12 minutes. The edges should be browned, but the centre will still feel a little soft. This will firm up as it cools.

Leave to cool on the baking tray, then freeze in an airtight container for up to 3 months or store for 4–5 days.

VEGGIE

FREEZE ME

BATCH COOK

DAIRY FREE

GLUTEN FREE
USE GF FLOUR

ORANGE *and* CRANBERRY BISCOTTI

10 MINS | 40 MINS + 10 MINS COOLING | MAKES 20

PER SERVING:
115 KCAL / 21G CARBS

- 250g plain flour, plus extra for dusting
- 200g caster sugar
- 1 tsp baking powder
- finely grated zest of 1 orange
- ½ tsp salt
- 2 eggs, beaten
- 50g pistachios, shelled and finely chopped
- 80g dried cranberries, finely chopped

These are designed for dunking! True to Italian tradition, they're baked twice to give them that delicious golden crunch. It's why they're just right for dipping into a hot cuppa. Orange zest brings a lovely citrussy pop of freshness, with tangy cranberries and creamy pistachios adding a subtle sweetness and even more texture to every bite. They might sound a bit fancy, but they're surprisingly simple to make and don't call for any tricky techniques. Perfect for sharing... or keeping all to yourself!

Everyday Light

Preheat the oven to 190°C (fan 170°C/gas mark 5) and line a large baking tray with non-stick baking paper.

Place the flour in a large bowl along with the sugar, baking powder, orange zest and salt and mix to combine. Add the beaten eggs and stir until you get a loose dough. Add the chopped pistachios and cranberries and mix into the dough.

Tip the dough out onto a floured work surface and gently knead until the nuts and cranberries are mixed thoroughly in the dough.

Divide the dough into two and shape into two long logs approximately 7.5cm (3in) wide and 25cm (10in) long. Arrange them on the lined baking sheet. Take care to leave a few centimetres between the logs as they will spread as they cook.

Bake the biscotti in the oven for 30 minutes, then remove the logs from the oven and leave them to cool for 10 minutes.

When cooled, use a serrated knife to trim the ends of each log and cut into slices approximately 2.5cm (1in) thick. You should be able to get 20 biscotti from this recipe. Place each biscotti on its side on the baking tray and bake in the oven for a further 10 minutes, or until crisp and golden. Transfer to a wire rack to cool, then enjoy.

The biscotti will keep at room temperature for up to 3 weeks. You can freeze them once cooled. Place them on a baking sheet in a single layer and freeze until solid. Place the frozen biscotti in a freezer-proof bag and freeze for up to 3 months (see Tips).

TIPS

We have used pistachios and cranberries in this recipe, but you can substitute them with any dried fruit and nuts you have in the cupboard.

If you've frozen the biscotti, once defrosted, preheat the oven to 170°C (fan 150°C/gas mark 3) and bake the biscotti in the oven for 10 minutes to crisp up.

NUTRITIONAL INFO (PER SERVING)

MAKE AHEAD	ENERGY KJ/KCAL	FAT (G)	SATURATED FAT (G)	CARBS (G)	SUGAR (G)	FIBRE (G)	PROTEIN (G)
BREAKFAST BURRITOS	1545/367	11	4.5	38	4.7	5.1	26
BREAKFAST LOADED POTATOES	1387/330	11	4.2	35	2.3	3.7	20
CHOCOLATE ORANGE MOUSSE	1143/274	16	9.4	20	17	4.2	10
CREAMY CHICKEN AND MUSHROOM TAGLIATELLE	1662/395	11	6.7	32	7.6	2.9	40
HERBY COURGETTE FRITTERS AND TZATZIKI	1480/352	11	4.5	33	10	3.8	29
HONEY AND LIME GLAZED SALMON WITH HERBY GRAINS	2410/576	28	4.7	42	14	4.4	35
HOT HONEY HALLOUMI FLATBREADS	2019/480	14	7.3	59	17	5.6	28
MASALA SPICED CHICKEN BURGER WITH MANGO CHUTNEY YOGHURT	1673/397	9.1	2.2	41	13	3.6	36
MEDITERRANEAN-STYLE GNOCCHI TRAYBAKE	1977/471	17	3.8	60	9.4	6	15
MOJITO TRIFLE	570/136	3.1	2	15	12	1.6	5.8
'NDUJA CHICKEN ORZO	2052/487	12	3.4	47	8.1	4.6	44
PLOUGHMAN'S SAUSAGE ROLLS	756/179	4.2	1.9	19	4.1	2.4	15
ROASTED BEETROOT, LENTIL AND FETA SALAD WITH CREAMY BALSAMIC VINAIGRETTE	2056/493	25	4.4	39	15	11	21
ROMESCO-STYLE CHICKEN SALAD	1583/375	7.9	1.2	29	8.9	4.8	44
ROOT VEGETABLE STACKS	648/155	6.2	4.3	19	5.7	2.8	4.6
SAUSAGE, FENNEL AND CHILLI PASTA	2086/496	14	6.3	61	9.8	9	27
STICKY GARLIC AND CHILLI TOFU	1132/270	11	1.7	21	12	5.3	19
THAI-STYLE CHICKEN MEATBALLS	1282/306	14	8.3	14	12	4.5	29

BATCH COOK	ENERGY KJ/KCAL	FAT (G)	SATURATED FAT (G)	CARBS (G)	SUGAR (G)	FIBRE (G)	PROTEIN (G)
BANANA CRUNCH ICE CREAM	705/168	5.2	1.3	27	25	1.7	2
BEEF, BEETROOT AND BARLEY STEW	1725/409	7	2.5	36	14	9.6	46
BANANA BUCKWHEAT PANCAKES	1250/295	3.1	0.7	52	18	2.3	13
CARAMELIZED ONION MAC AND CHEESE	2020/479	8.5	4.1	76	12	6.6	22
KORMA-STYLE CAULIFLOWER WITH CORIANDER RICE	2045/487	14.5	7.2	69	13	9	16.3
CHICKEN POT PIE	1732/415	23	13	23	6.8	3.2	27
CHICKEN, BROCCOLI AND MUSHROOM GRATIN	1494/354	6.5	3.1	32	5.1	5	40

BATCH COOK	ENERGY KJ/KCAL	FAT (G)	SATURATED FAT (G)	CARBS (G)	SUGAR (G)	FIBRE (G)	PROTEIN (G)
GREEK-STYLE CHICKEN WITH BUTTER BEANS	1325/315	7	1.4	17	3.2	7.7	42
GREEK-STYLE SHEPHERD'S PIE WITH FETA MASH	2034/484	13	5.4	48	13	9.6	37
RHUBARB AND CUSTARD ARCTIC ROLL	626/148	3.9	1.5	29	13	0.8	5.3
ROASTED CAULIFLOWER AND SESAME SOUP	792/190	11	2.5	14	9.6	5.9	6.4
SAUSAGE AND EGG BREAKFAST SLICE	997/239	15	4.8	6.1	3.5	1.7	20
SPICY CHICKEN CHOWDER	874/208	7.2	4.1	16	5.4	3.2	18
SWEET POTATO GNOCCHI WITH BROCCOLI AND RICOTTA	1498/356	8.3	4.8	53	15	7.4	13

ON THE GO	ENERGY KJ/KCAL	FAT (G)	SATURATED FAT (G)	CARBS (G)	SUGAR (G)	FIBRE (G)	PROTEIN (G)
APPLE CRUMBLE BREAKFAST POTS	1205/286	5.9	1.3	47	35	3.8	12
BANANA CHIA BREAKFAST BOWL	1935/464	25	4.2	33	19	11	22
BANANA CRUMBLE MUFFINS	508/121	4.4	1	26	4.3	1	2.5
BANOFFEE OVERNIGHT WEETABIX POTS	1244/294	1.7	0.2	52	37	4.9	15
BLUEBERRY CRUMBLE SQUARES	455/108	3.3	0.8	19	2	0.9	3.4
BREAKFAST COOKIES	568/136	5.2	1.1	24	5.6	2.1	3.4
BUTTERNUT SQUASH, CARROT AND COCONUT SOUP	779/187	9.3	6.6	18	13	6	3.8
BUTTERNUT SQUASH MUFFINS	503/120	5	1.1	16	2.8	1.6	2.8
CHEESE AND BEAN PINWHEELS	531/127	5.3	2.6	14	1.3	2.1	4.5
CHICKEN AND CHORIZO QUESADILLAS	2028/484	20	8.8	33	6.7	5.7	39
CHICKEN SHAWARMA SKEWERS	1395/331	6	1	12	9.2	6	51
CHOCOLATE CUSTARD SWIRLS	414/99	4.1	2	13	2.6	0.6	2.1
CHOCOLATE OVERNIGHT OATS	1741/414	10	2.9	61	19	8.9	15
COTTAGE CHEESE BAGELS	1462/349	16	4.5	31	4.4	3.6	18
COURGETTE, LEMON AND RICOTTA TART	1371/329	21	9.8	24	4.7	1.6	11
COWBOY CAVIAR	808/193	6.7	1.1	23	11	5.8	6.4
HARISSA AUBERGINE AND HALLOUMI SALAD	1587/379	17	6.6	30	20	4.3	23
MAPLE-ROASTED CARROTS WITH FETA AND GIANT COUSCOUS	1235/294	9	3.6	34	19	8.9	15
NEW YORK DELI WRAP	1560/372	14	6.3	37	8.3	3.9	23
NOODLE POTS	1438/340	3.7	0.8	53	8.5	4.6	22
SMOKY BREAKFAST SANDWICH	1823/433	14	4.5	36	8.9	3.7	40
TRIPLE BERRY BAKES	1899/450	9.2	2.2	68	25	8.4	21

FREEZE & GO	ENERGY KJ/KCAL	FAT (G)	SATURATED FAT (G)	CARBS (G)	SUGAR (G)	FIBRE (G)	PROTEIN (G)
BOSTON BEANS	1308/310	3.1	0.5	40	22	13	22
CITRUS CHICKEN STEW	2109/499	5.1	1	63	22	13	42
FIVE-SPICE BEEF WITH PLUMS	1627/386	7.1	2.3	37	26	5.2	39
GAMMON AND PINEAPPLE CHILLI	1432/341	10	3.3	31	22	6.7	28
MEXICAN-STYLE RICE SOUP	910/216	2.1	0.4	36	11	7.7	7.7
SHREDDED TURKEY ROLLS	1336/317	9.2	3	33	4.4	3.1	23
SPICY CHICKPEA SOUP	919/218	4	0.4	32	16	7.6	8.8
TERIYAKI-STYLE CHICKEN DRUMSTICKS	780/186	7.4	1.8	4.5	3.3	0.8	25

MULTI-SERVE	ENERGY KJ/KCAL	FAT (G)		CARBS (G)	SUGAR (G)	FIBRE (G)	PROTEIN (G)
CHIPOTLE CHICKEN TRAYBAKE	855/202	2.7	0.9	11	7.2	2.3	33
CHIPOTLE CHICKEN ENCHILADAS	2033/482	8.4	3.4	51	14	10	45
CREAMY CHIPOTLE CHICKEN	1451/344	5.6	2.4	26	17	9.1	41
CRUNCHY ASIAN-STYLE SALAD	1612/386	21	2.7	22	11	7.8	22
PEANUT AND LIME SALMON SALAD	1849/443	25	5	19	11	6.1	32
SWEET CHILLI CHICKEN NOODLE SALAD	1227/290	4	0.8	19	11	5.1	42
NUTTY MUSHROOM STUFFING POTATO HASH	1943/464	19	3.1	50	10	8.2	20
VEGGIE WELLINGTON	1389/332	14	4.5	41	7.7	5.1	8.8
STUFFED BUTTERNUT SQUASH	1864/444	11	1.2	66	31	14	14
SAUSAGE, MUSHROOM AND APPLE CASSEROLE	1276/305	14	4.8	23	14	4.3	19
SAUSAGE, MUSHROOM AND APPLE HOTPOT	1904/454	17	5.7	44	16	7.1	28
SAUSAGE, MUSHROOM AND APPLE COBBLER	2285/545	21	7.2	57	16	6.8	27
SHREDDED BEEF IN RED WINE	801/190	4.6	1.7	8.2	3	1.5	24
BEEF AND RED WINE LASAGNE	2298/547	16	8.5	47	12	5.3	45
MEAT AND POTATO PIE	2210/525	13	5.5	63	5.8	5.8	32
SICILIAN-STYLE BRUSCHETTA	943/223	3.8	2	33	6.9	3.9	12
SICILIAN-STYLE MEATBALLS	2287/547	27	13	23	17	8.7	47
SICILIAN-STYLE SPAGHETTI	1981/471	9.2	3.2	67	19	18	20
ROAST CHICKEN WITH LEMON GRAVY	1711/409	22	6	7.6	2.6	1.5	44
SWEET AND SOUR CHICKEN CURRY	1064/252	5.2	1.3	29	24	4.8	18
CHICKEN PESTO PASTA BAKE	1974/470	16	7.9	42	5.9	5.1	37

STORE CUPBOARD MEALS	ENERGY KJ/KCAL	FAT (G)	SATURATED FAT (G)	CARBS (G)	SUGAR (G)	FIBRE (G)	PROTEIN (G)
CHAI-SPICED SCONES	747/177	3.6	1.3	33	17	0.9	2.8
CHERRIES JUBILEE WAFFLES	1201/284	4.3	2.1	53	23	2.3	8.3
CHERRY BAKEWELL COOKIES	365/88	5.3	0.7	7.6	2.3	1.3	1.9
CHINESE-STYLE CURRIED NOODLES	1332/319	16	7.8	33	11	6.7	8.3
CORNED BEEF AND PICKLE PIE	1056/252	13	6.6	12	4.5	1.2	22
CREAMY HAM AND PEA RICE	1625/386	12	4.5	47	5.5	3.5	21
GINGERBREAD PORRIDGE	1453/344	5.9	1.2	51	8.2	5.7	19
HAM FOO YUNG-STYLE EGGS	1013/243	13	3.7	6.5	4.4	3.8	22
JAM BUTTY PUDDING	979/232	4.9	1.1	39	16	2.1	8.8
KOREAN-STYLE BUTTER BEANS	1848/438	7.7	1.9	68	10	8.2	20
MUSHY PEA NUGGETS WITH CURRY SAUCE	1139/270	2.8	0.7	47	9.8	7.3	11
ORANGE AND CRANBERRY BISCOTTI	484/115	2.1	0.4	21	12	0.8	2.4
PEA FALAFEL WITH GARLIC TAHINI SAUCE	1318/316	15	2.3	27	3.4	9.2	13
PEACH CUSTARD CAKE	1006/240	9.7	2.3	40	13	0.9	5.4
PINEAPPLE UPSIDE DOWN PANCAKE TRAYBAKE	766/183	7.6	3.1	21	7.2	2	7.3
TUNA KEDGEREE	1692/401	9.4	3.3	50	7.1	3.6	27
TUNA PUTTANESCA PASTA	1430/338	4.4	0.7	49	7.6	5.2	21

INDEX

Note: page numbers in **bold** refer to photography.

almond 62–3, 92–5, 160, 272
apple 248
  apple crumble breakfast pots 124, **125**
  sausage, mushroom and apple casserole 228, **229**, **230**, 231, 232, **233**
  sausage, mushroom and apple hotpot **230**, 231
apricot (dried) 132, 136, 172–3, 186–7
Arctic roll, rhubarb and custard 116–17, **118–19**
aubergine 234
  harissa aubergine and halloumi salad **148**, 149

bacon
  Boston beans 188, **189**
  breakfast loaded potatoes 44, **45**
  sausage, mushroom and apple hotpot **230**, 231
bagels, cottage cheese **138**, 139
baking powder 28
balsamic vinaigrette, creamy 70, **71**
banana
  banana buckwheat pancakes 90, **91**
  banana chia breakfast bowl **130**, 131
  banana crumble muffins 13, 164, **165**
  banana crunch ice cream 120, **121**
  banoffee overnight Weetabix pots 134, **135**
base recipes 23
basil 74–7, 110–11, 152, 178–81, 220, 234
beans 15, 26
  Boston beans 188, **189**
  cheese and bean pinwheels 158, **159**
  cowboy caviar 140, **141**
  gammon and pineapple chilli 186–7, **187**
  Greek-style chicken with butter beans 104, **105**
  Korean-style butter beans 260, **261**
  Mexican-style rice soup **175**, 176–7
  see also black bean; edamame bean; green bean
beef 15, 24
  beef, beetroot and barley stew 106–7, **108**
  beef and red wine lasagne 214, **215**
  corned beef and pickle pie 246, **247**
  five-spice beef with plums 182–3, **183**
  shredded beef in red wine 13, 208–111, **209**, **210**, 212, **213**, 214, **215**
beetroot
  beef, beetroot and barley stew 106–7, **108**
  roasted beetroot, lentil and feta salad with creamy balsamic vinaigrette 16, 70, **71**
  root vegetable stacks 78, **79**
berries
  triple berry bakes 13, 162, **163**
  see also blueberry; raspberry
biscotti, orange and cranberry 274, **275**
black bean
  chipotle chicken enchiladas 224, **225**
  creamy chipotle chicken **226**, 227
blueberry 84
  blueberry crumble squares 160, **161**
  triple berry bakes 162, **163**
bread (shop-bought) 26
  corned beef and pickle pie 246, **247**
  jam butty pudding **266**, 267
  masala spiced chicken burger 46–9, **47–8**
  romesco-style chicken salad **61**, 62–3
  shredded turkey rolls 178–81, **179–80**
  Sicilian-style bruschetta 234, **235**
breadcrumbs 112, 198–9, 248
  see also panko breadcrumbs
breakfast bowl, banana chia **130**, 131
breakfast burritos 42, **43**
breakfast cookies 132, **133**
breakfast loaded potatoes 44, **45**
breakfast pots, apple crumble 124, **125**
breakfast sandwich, smoky 128–9, **129**
breakfast slice, sausage and egg 88, **89**
broccoli 14
  chicken, broccoli and mushroom gratin 102, **103**
  sweet potato gnocchi with broccoli and ricotta **109**, 110–11
bruschetta, Sicilian-style 234, **235**
buckwheat pancakes, banana 90, **91**
bulgur wheat, herby grains 58–9, **60**
burger, masala spiced chicken 46–9, **47–8**
burritos, breakfast 42, **43**
butter beans, Korean-style 260, **261**
butternut squash 14
  butternut squash, carrot and coconut soup **156**, 157
  butternut squash muffins 136, **137**
  stuffed butternut squash 202, **203**
  veggie Wellington 204–5, **206–7**

cake, peach custard 270, **271**
carbs 14
carrot 14, 96, 98–9, 100, 106–7, 114, 146, 154, 170, 176–7, 182–3, 192–3, 204–7, 216–17, 228
  butternut squash, carrot and coconut soup **156**, 157
  maple-roasted carrots with whipped feta and giant couscous 150, **151**
casserole, sausage, mushroom and apple 228, **229–30**, 231–2, **233**

cauliflower
korma-style cauliflower with coriander rice 92–5, **93–4**
roasted cauliflower and sesame soup 100, **101**
celery 114, 170, 228
chai-spiced scones 264–5, **265**
Cheddar cheese
beef and red wine lasagne 214, **215**
breakfast burritos 42, **43**
breakfast loaded potatoes 44, **45**
caramelized onion mac and cheese 112, **113**
cheese and bean pinwheels 158, **159**
chicken, broccoli and mushroom gratin 102, **103**
chicken and chorizo quesadillas 144–5, **145**
chipotle chicken enchiladas 224, **225**
corned beef and pickle pie 246, **247**
creamy ham and pea rice 250, **251**
ploughman's sausage rolls 80, **81**
sausage and egg breakfast slice 88, **89**
cheese 15
caramelized onion mac and cheese 112, **113**
courgette, lemon and ricotta tart 152, **153**
harissa aubergine and halloumi salad **148**, 149
hot honey halloumi flatbreads 56–7, **57**
New York deli wrap 154, **155**
root vegetable stacks 78, **79**
Sicilian-style spaghetti 238, **239**
spicy chicken chowder 96, **97**
see also Cheddar cheese; cottage cheese; cream cheese; feta; mozzarella; Parmesan cheese
cherry 242
cherries jubilee waffles 268, **269**
cherry Bakewell cookies 272, **273**
chia seeds 126, 132, 162
banana chia breakfast bowl **130**, 131
chicken 15
chicken, broccoli and mushroom gratin 102, **103**
chicken and chorizo quesadillas 144–5, **145**
chicken pesto pasta bake 220, **221**
chicken pot pie 114, **115**
chicken shawarma skewers 142–3, **143**
chipotle chicken enchiladas 224, **225**
chipotle chicken traybake 222, **223**, 224, **225**, **226**, 227
citrus chicken stew 170, **171**
cowboy caviar 140, **141**
creamy chicken and mushroom tagliatelle 64, **65**
creamy chipotle chicken **226**, 227
Greek-style chicken with butter beans 104, **105**
masala spiced chicken burger with mango chutney yoghurt 46–9, **47–8**
'nduja chicken orzo 52–5, **53–4**
noodle pots 146, **147**
roast chicken with lemon gravy 13, 216–17, **217**, **218**, 219, 220, **221**
romesco-style chicken salad **61**, 62–3
spicy chicken chowder 96, **97**
sweet chilli chicken noodle salad 196, **197**
sweet and sour chicken curry **218**, 219
teriyaki-style chicken drumsticks 184, **185**
Thai-style chicken meatballs 66–7, **67**
chickpeas 15
Greek-style shepherd's pie with feta mash 98–9, **99**
hummus 56–7, **57**
korma-style cauliflower with coriander rice 92–5, **93–4**
pea falafel with garlic tahini sauce 262–3, **263**
spicy chickpea soup 16, 172–3, **174**
chilli
gammon and pineapple chilli 186–7, **187**
sausage, fennel and chilli pasta 50–1, **51**
sticky garlic and chilli tofu 68, **69**
sweet chilli chicken noodle salad 196, **197**
chipotle chilli
chipotle chicken enchiladas 224, **225**
chipotle chicken traybake 222, **223**, 224, **225**, **226**, 227
chocolate
banana chia breakfast bowl **130**, 131
banana crunch ice cream 120, **121**
breakfast cookies 132, **133**
chocolate custard swirls 13, 166, **167**
chocolate orange mousse 82, **83**
chocolate overnight oats 13, 126, **127**
chorizo and chicken quesadillas 144–5, **145**
chowder, spicy chicken 96, **97**
citrus chicken stew 170, **171**
cobbler, sausage, mushroom and apple 232, **233**
coconut milk 66–7, 92–5, 258
butternut squash, carrot and coconut soup **156**, 157
coleslaw, mustard 154, **155**
cookies
breakfast 132, **133**
cherry Bakewell 272, **273**
cooking spray, low-calorie 26
coriander 66–7, 140, 172–3, 176–7, 192–3, 222, 224, 227
coriander rice 92–5, **93–4**
cottage cheese
blueberry crumble squares 160, **161**
breakfast burritos 42, **43**
cottage cheese bagels **138**, 139
smoky breakfast sandwich 128–9, **129**
courgette 14, 74–7
courgette, lemon and ricotta tart 152, **153**
herby courgette fritters and tzatziki 72–3, **73**
couscous 14
citrus chicken stew 170, **171**
maple-roasted carrots with whipped feta and giant couscous 150, **151**
cowboy caviar 140, **141**

cranberry (dried) 202
orange and cranberry biscotti 274, **275**
cream cheese 178–81, 210
breakfast loaded potatoes 44, **45**
chicken, broccoli and mushroom gratin 102, **103**
chicken pesto pasta bake 220, **221**
chicken pot pie 114, **115**
creamy chipotle chicken **226**, 227
pineapple upside down pancake traybake 242, **243**
sausage, mushroom and apple cobbler 232, **233**
spicy chicken chowder 96, **97**
tuna kedgeree **256**, 257
cream/cream alternative 64, 78, 84, 114
crème fraîche 50–1, 78
crumble
apple crumble breakfast pots 124, **125**
banana crumble muffins 13, 164, **165**
blueberry crumble squares 160, **161**
cucumber 56–7, 62–3, 72–3, 138, 140
curry
Chinese-style curried noodles 258, **259**
curry sauce 248, **249**
korma-style cauliflower 92–5, **93–4**
sweet and sour chicken curry **218**, 219
custard
chocolate custard swirls 13, 166, **167**
custard yoghurt 124, **125**
mojito trifle 84, **85**
peach custard cake 270, **271**
rhubarb and custard Arctic roll 116–17, **118–19**

dairy, reduced-fat 25
defrosting food 19
dressings 15, 140, **141**, 192–3, **193–4**, 195–6, **197**

edamame bean
crunchy Asian-style salad 192–3, **193**
noodle pots 146, **147**
eggs 15, 26, 80, 160, 164, 212–13, 232, 237, 248, 268
banana buckwheat pancakes 90, **91**
breakfast burritos 42, **43**
breakfast loaded potatoes 44, **45**
butternut squash muffins 136, **137**
chocolate orange mousse 82, **83**
cottage cheese bagels **138**, 139
courgette, lemon and ricotta tart 152, **153**
ham foo yung-style eggs 252, **253**
herby courgette fritters and tzatziki 72–3, **73**
jam butty pudding **266**, 267
Korean-style butter beans 260, **261**
nutty mushroom stuffing potato hash 198–9, **199–200**
orange and cranberry biscotti 274, **275**
peach custard cake 270, **271**
pineapple upside down pancake traybake 242, **243**
rhubarb and custard Arctic roll 116–17, **118–19**
sausage and egg breakfast slice 88, **89**
smoky breakfast sandwich 128–9, **129**
triple berry bakes 162, **163**
tuna kedgeree **256**, 257
enchiladas, chipotle chicken 224, **225**

falafel, pea 262–3, **263**
feta
chipotle chicken traybake 222, **223**
cottage cheese bagels **138**, 139
cowboy caviar 140, **141**
Greek-style shepherd's pie with feta mash 98–9, **99**
maple-roasted carrots with whipped feta and giant couscous 150, **151**
Mediterranean-style gnocchi traybake 74–7, **75–6**
roasted beetroot, lentil and feta salad 16, 70, **71**
flatbreads 14
hot honey halloumi flatbreads 56–7, **57**
flours 28
freezing/frozen food 18–19, 23, 25, 29
fridges 18–19
fritters, herby courgette 72–3, **73**
fruit 25, 29
see also specific fruit

gammon and pineapple chilli 186–7, **187**
garlic
garlic tahini sauce 262–3, **263**
sticky garlic and chilli tofu 68, **69**
gingerbread porridge 244, **245**
gluten-free recipes 23
gnocchi
Mediterranean-style gnocchi traybake 16, 74–7, **75–6**
sweet potato gnocchi with broccoli and ricotta **109**, 110–11
grains 14
herby 58–9, **60**
see also specific grains
gratin, chicken, broccoli and mushroom 102, **103**
gravy, lemon 216–17, **217**
Greek yoghurt 56–7, 82, 84, 90, 98–9, 126, 130, 132, 134, 142–3, 148, 150, 162
custard yoghurt 124, **125**
mango chutney yoghurt 46–9, **47–8**
tzatziki 72–3, **73**
green bean 231–2
Greek-style chicken with butter beans 104, **105**
sausage, mushroom and apple casserole **230**, 231
sausage, mushroom and apple cobbler 232, **233**
Thai-style chicken meatballs 66–7, **67**

halloumi
harissa aubergine and halloumi salad **148**, 149
hot honey halloumi flatbreads 56–7, **57**

ham
creamy ham and pea rice 250, **251**
ham foo yung-style eggs 252, **253**
harissa aubergine and halloumi salad **148**, 149
hash, nutty mushroom stuffing potato 198–9, **199–200**
herbs 15, 24
herby courgette fritters and tzatziki 72–3, **73**
herby grains 58–9, **60**
honey
honey and lime glazed salmon with herby grains 58–9, **60**
hot honey halloumi flatbreads 56–7, **57**
hotpot, sausage, mushroom and apple **230**, 231
hummus 56–7, **57**

ice cream
banana crunch ice cream 120, **121**
rhubarb and custard Arctic roll 116–17, **118–19**
ingredients, key 24–9

jam butty pudding **266**, 267
jelly, mojito trifle 84, **85**

kedgeree, tuna **256**, 257
kit 30–3
korma-style cauliflower 92–5, **93–4**

labelling food 18–19
lamb
Greek-style shepherd's pie with feta mash 98–9, **99**
Sicilian-style meatballs **236**, 237
lasagne, beef and red wine 214, **215**
leek 106–7, 114, 198–9, 228
lemon 142–3
courgette, lemon and ricotta tart 152, **153**
lemon gravy 216–17, **217**
lentils 15
roasted beetroot, lentil and feta salad 16, 70, **71**
lettuce 46–9, 62–3
lime
honey and lime glazed salmon with herby grains 58–9, **60**
mojito trifle 84, **85**
peanut and lime salmon salad **194**, 195

mac and cheese, caramelized onion 112, **113**
mango chutney yoghurt 46–9, **47–8**
maple-roasted carrots 150, **151**
marinades 104, **105**
masala spiced chicken burger 46–9, **47–8**
Massaman sauce 66–7
meal plans 34–9
meal prep 8–10, 12–13, 21
mix-and-match 14–16
meat and potato pie 212, **213**
meatballs
Sicilian-style **236**, 237
Thai-style chicken 66–7, **67**
mint 58–9, 72–3, 84, 148, 150, 152
mojito trifle 84, **85**
mousse, chocolate orange 82, **83**
mozzarella
chicken and chorizo quesadillas 144–5, **145**
chicken pesto pasta bake 220, **221**
shredded turkey rolls 178–81, **179–80**
Sicilian-style bruschetta 234, **235**
Sicilian-style meatballs **236**, 237
muffins
banana crumble 13, 164, **165**
butternut squash 136, **137**
mushrooms 42, 52–5, 114, 210
chicken, broccoli and mushroom gratin 102, **103**
creamy chicken and mushroom tagliatelle 64, **65**
nutty mushroom stuffing 198–9, **199–200**, 202, **203**, 212–13, **214–15**
sausage, mushroom and apple casserole 228, **229–30**, 231–2, **233**
sausage, mushroom and apple hotpot **230**, 231
mustard coleslaw 154, **155**

'nduja chicken orzo 52–5, **53–4**
noodles 28
Chinese-style curried noodles 258, **259**
crunchy Asian-style salad 192–3, **193**
Korean-style butter beans 260, **261**
noodle pots 13, 146, **147**
sweet chilli chicken noodle salad 196, **197**
nuts 29
nutty mushroom stuffing 198–9, **199–200**, 202, **203**, 212–13, **214–15**
see also specific nuts

oats 28
apple crumble breakfast pots 124, **125**
banana chia breakfast bowl **130**, 131
breakfast cookies 132, **133**
butternut squash muffins 136, **137**
cherry Bakewell cookies 272, **273**
chocolate overnight oats 13, 126, **127**
gingerbread porridge 244, **245**
pineapple upside down pancake traybake 242, **243**
triple berry bakes 162, **163**
olives 104, 238, 254
onion 14
caramelized onion mac and cheese 112, **113**
pickled onions 46–9, **47–8**, 56–7, **57**
orange 136, 170, 202
chocolate orange mousse 82, **83**
orange and cranberry biscotti 274, **275**
orzo 14
'nduja chicken 52–5, **53–4**

pancakes
banana buckwheat pancakes 90, **91**
pineapple upside down pancake traybake 242, **243**
panko breadcrumbs 102, 237
Parmesan cheese 50–1, 64, 72–3, 74–7, 220, 231, 237
parsley 58–9, 72–3, 144–5, 150, 202
passata
Boston beans 188, **189**
chipotle chicken enchiladas 224, **225**
creamy chipotle chicken **226**, 227
'nduja chicken orzo 52–5
sweet and sour chicken curry **218**, 219
pasta 14, 28
beef and red wine lasagne 214, **215**
caramelized onion mac and cheese 112, **113**
chicken pesto pasta bake 220, **221**
creamy chicken and mushroom tagliatelle 64, **65**
sausage, fennel and chilli pasta 50–1, **51**
Sicilian-style spaghetti 238, **239**
tuna puttanesca pasta 254, **255**
see also orzo
pastrami, New York deli wrap 154, **155**
pastry 26
see also puff pastry (ready-made)
peach custard cake 270, **271**
peanuts 130, 258
peanut and lime salmon salad **194**, 195
peas 170, 220, 252
creamy ham and pea rice 250, **251**
mushy pea nuggets with curry sauce **248**, 249
pea falafel with garlic tahini sauce 262–3, **263**
pecan nuts 120, 130
pepper 14, 42, 52–5, 62–3, 66–8, 144–5, 170, 172–3, 178–81, 219
chipotle chicken traybake 222, **223**
cowboy caviar 140, **141**
gammon and pineapple chilli 186–7, **187**
Mediterranean-style gnocchi traybake 74–7, **75–6**
Mexican-style rice soup **175**, 176–7
sausage and egg breakfast slice 88, **89**
pesto (ready-made) 178–81, **179–80**
chicken pesto pasta bake 220, **221**
pickled onions 46–9, **47–8**, 56–7, **57**
pies
chicken pot 114, **115**
corned beef and pickle 246, **247**
Greek-style shepherd's 16, 98–9, **99**
meat and potato 212, **213**
pine nuts 74–7, 152
pineapple
gammon and pineapple chilli 186–7, **187**
pineapple upside down pancake traybake 242, **243**
pinwheels, cheese and bean 158, **159**
plant-based protein 15
ploughman's sausage rolls 80, **81**
plums with five-spice beef 182–3, **183**
pomegranate seeds 56–7, 148
pork 24
ploughman's sausage rolls 80, **81**
smoky breakfast sandwich 128–9, **129**
porridge, gingerbread 244, **245**
potato 14, 26, 42, 102, 231, 248
breakfast loaded potatoes 44, **45**
feta mash 98–9, **99**
meat and potato pie 212, **213**
nutty mushroom stuffing potato hash 198–9, **199–200**
root vegetable stacks 78, **79**
spicy chicken chowder 96, **97**
power hours 12–13, 36
protein 15, 23, 24
puff pastry (ready-made)
cheese and bean pinwheels 158, **159**
chicken pot pie 114, **115**
chocolate custard swirls 166, **167**
courgette, lemon and ricotta tart 152, **153**
meat and potato pie 212, **213**
veggie Wellington 204–5, **206–7**
pulses 26
see also specific pulses
pumpkin seeds 130, 156

quesadillas, chicken and chorizo 144–5, **145**
quinoa 14
harissa aubergine and halloumi salad **148**, 149
herby grains 58–9, **60**

raspberry 84, 126
triple berry bakes 162, **163**
recipe icons 23
recipe tags 22
red wine
beef and red wine lasagne 214, **215**
shredded beef in red wine 13, 208–11, **209**, **210**, 212, **213**, 214, **215**
reheating guidelines 19
rhubarb and custard Arctic roll 116–17, **118–19**
rice 14, 26, 28
coriander rice 92–5, **93–4**
creamy ham and pea rice 250, **251**
Mexican-style rice soup **175**, 176–7
storage 19
tuna kedgeree **256**, 257
ricotta
courgette, lemon and ricotta tart 152, **153**
sweet potato gnocchi with broccoli and ricotta **109**, 110–11
rocket 56–7, 70, 138, 148, 154
romesco-style chicken salad **61**, 62–3

salads
crunchy Asian-style 192–3, **193**, **194**, 195, 196, **197**
harissa aubergine and halloumi 148, **149**
peanut and lime salmon **194**, 195
roasted beetroot, lentil and feta 16, 70, **71**
romesco-style chicken **61**, 62–3
sweet chilli chicken noodle 196, **197**
salmon
honey and lime glazed salmon with herby grains 58–9, **60**
peanut and lime salmon salad **194**, 195
sandwich, smoky breakfast 128–9, **129**
sauces 15, 24–5
curry 248, **249**
garlic tahini 262–3, **263**
Massaman 66–7
Sicilian-style 234, **235–6**, 237–8, **239**
sausage
sausage and egg breakfast slice 88, **89**
sausage, fennel and chilli pasta 50–1, **51**
sausage, mushroom and apple casserole 228, **229–30**, 231–2, **233**
sausage, mushroom and apple cobbler 232, **233**
sausage, mushroom and apple hotpot **230**, 231
sausage rolls, ploughman's 80, **81**
scones, chai-spiced 264–5, **265**
seeds 29, 132
sesame and roasted cauli soup 100, **101**
sesame seeds 68, 138, 262–3
shawarma skewers, chicken 142–3, **143**
shepherd's pie, Greek-style 16, 98–9, **99**
soup
butternut squash, carrot and coconut 156, **157**
Mexican-style rice **175**, 176–7
spicy chickpea 16, 172–3, **174**
spices 24
spinach 42, 52–5, 88, 128–9, 170, 178–81, 210, 220, 260
stew
beef, beetroot and barley 106–7, **108**
citrus chicken 170, **171**
stocks 24–5
stuffing, nutty mushroom 198–9, **199–200**, 202, **203**, 212–13, **214–15**
sweet potato 14, 172–3, 212–13
nutty mushroom stuffing potato hash 198–9, **199–200**
root vegetable stacks 78, **79**
sweet potato gnocchi with broccoli and ricotta **109**, 110–11
sweetcorn 96, 140, 146, 170, 176–7, 222, 256
sweeteners 28

tahini 56–7, 100
garlic tahini sauce 262–3, **263**
tart, courgette, lemon and ricotta 152, **153**
thickeners 24–5
tinned food 25, 29
tofu 15, 28
crispy 192–3, **193**
sticky garlic and chilli 68, **69**
tomato
beef and red wine lasagne 214, **215**
Boston beans 188, **189**
cottage cheese bagels **138**, 139
cowboy caviar 140, **141**
creamy chipotle chicken **226**, 227
five-spice beef with plums 182–3, **183**
gammon and pineapple chilli 186–7, **187**
Greek-style shepherd's pie 98–9, **99**
korma-style cauliflower 92–5, **93–4**
Mediterranean-style gnocchi traybake 74–7, **75–6**
Mexican-style rice soup **175**, 176–7
romesco-style chicken salad **61**, 62–3
sausage and egg breakfast slice 88, **89**
shredded turkey rolls 178–81, **179–80**
Sicilian-style bruschetta 234, **235**
Sicilian-style tomato sauce 234, **235–6**, 237–8, **239**
smoky breakfast sandwich 128–9, **129**
spicy chickpea soup 172–3, **174**
tuna puttanesca pasta 254, **255**
see also passata
tortilla wraps 14, 26
breakfast burritos 42, **43**
chicken and chorizo quesadillas 144–5, **145**
chipotle chicken enchiladas 224, **225**
New York deli wrap 154, **155**
ploughman's sausage rolls 80, **81**
trifle, mojito 84, **85**
tuna
cowboy caviar 140, **141**
tuna kedgeree **256**, 257
tuna puttanesca pasta 254, **255**
turkey 15, 24
breakfast burritos 42, **43**
shredded turkey rolls 178–81, **179–80**
tzatziki 72–3, **73**

vegetables 14–15
frozen 15, 25
roasted 14–15
root vegetable stacks 78, **79**
veggie Wellington 204–5, **206–7**
see also specific vegetables
vinaigrette, creamy balsamic 70, **71**

waffles, cherries jubilee 268, **269**
walnut 70, 198–9
Weetabix pots, banoffee overnight 134, **135**
Wellington, veggie 212–13, **214–15**

yoghurt *see* Greek yoghurt

ACKNOWLEDGEMENTS

We owe many thank yous to many people who work so hard to bring this book together. Without these people, there would be no book. We deeply appreciate you all and can't thank you enough for the time and effort you put into making this book something we are immensely proud of.

We want to say a huge thank you, firstly, to all of our followers on social media and all those who continue to make our recipes and let us know what you want next! We're so proud that Pinch of Nom has helped, and continues to help, so many people.

Thank you to our publisher Lizzy Gray. To Martha Burley, Bríd Enright, Rebecca Kellaway, Jodie Lancet-Grant, Dawn Burnett, Sarah Badhan, Amy Winchester, Ellie Auton and the rest of the team at Bluebird for helping us create this book and continuing to believe in Pinch of Nom throughout our journey. Major thanks also to our agent Clare Hulton for your unwavering support and guidance.

To Mike English for the amazing photos and to Kate Wesson, Kristine Jakobsson and Daisy Shayler-Webb for making our food look so, so good. Thanks also to Eden Owen-Jones and Sadie Albuquerque for all your assistance. Big thanks go out to Nikki Dupin at Nic & Lou for making this book so beautiful!

We also want to thank our friends and family who have made this book possible. A very big thank you to Dr Hannah Cowan, Kirsty Rogers, Kenzie & Morgan. Your support has meant the world.

Special thanks go to Katie Mitchell and Rosie Sparrow for the endless hours you've put into this and for working so hard to get things right!

A huge thank you to our wonderful team of recipe developers who work tirelessly to help us bring these recipes to life; Lisa Allinson, Holly Levell and Laura Williams.

Massive thanks also go to Sophie Fryer, Sophie Howarth and Hannah Cutting for your writing and marketing support. To Cate Meadows and Grace Salisbury for your creative and visual genius.

Additional thanks to Matthew Maney, Jessica Molyneux, Rubi Bourne and Vince Bourne for supporting us and the business – we are so proud to work alongside you all.

To our wonderful moderators and online support team; thank you for all your hard work keeping the peace and for all your support.

Furry thanks to Mildred, Wanda and Freda for the daily moments of joy.

And finally... Huge thanks go to Paul and Cath Allinson for all your support and advice over the years. You are never forgotten. #YNWA

First published 2026 by Bluebird
an imprint of Pan Macmillan
The Smithson, 6 Briset Street, London EC1M 5NR
EU representative: Macmillan Publishers Ireland Ltd, 1st Floor,
The Liffey Trust Centre, 117–126 Sheriff Street Upper,
Dublin 1, D01 YC43

Associated companies throughout the world
www.panmacmillan.com

ISBN 978-1-0350-5326-1

9 8 7 6 5 4 3 2

A CIP catalogue record for this book is available from the British Library.

Photographer Mike English
Design & Art Direction Nikki Dupin for Studio Nic+Lou
Food Stylists Kristine Jakobsson and Kate Wesson
Prop Stylist Daisy Shayler-Webb

Printed and bound in Germany.

MIX
Paper | Supporting responsible forestry
FSC® C116313
FSC www.fsc.org

ABOUT PINCH OF NOM

Kate and Kay Allinson owned a restaurant together on the Wirral, where Kate was head chef. Together they created the Pinch of Nom blog with the aim of teaching people how to cook. They began sharing healthy, slimming recipes and today Pinch of Nom is the UK's most visited food blog with an active and engaged online community of over 4.5 million followers.

Also available from the no 1 bestselling authors:

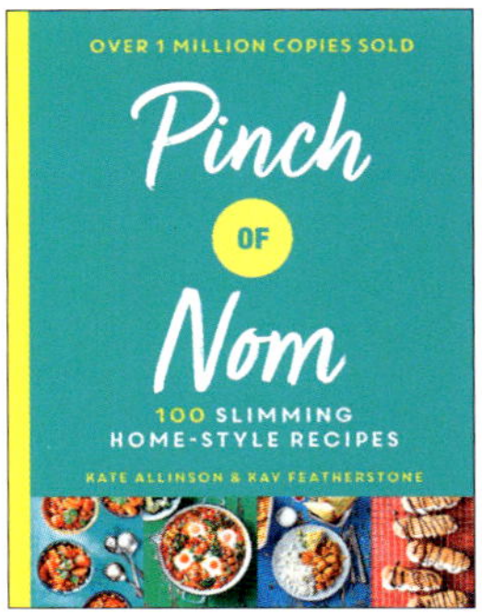

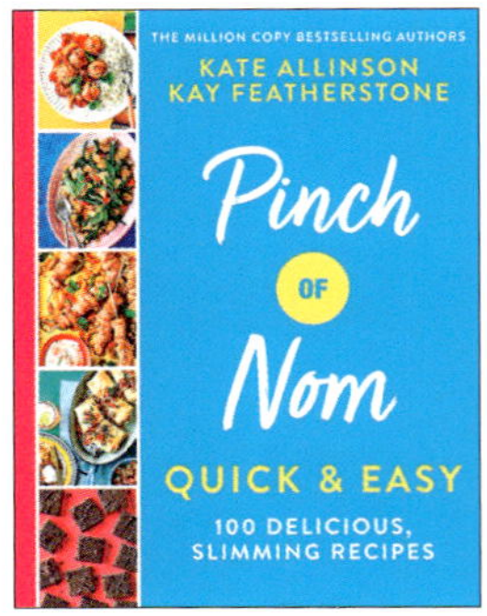

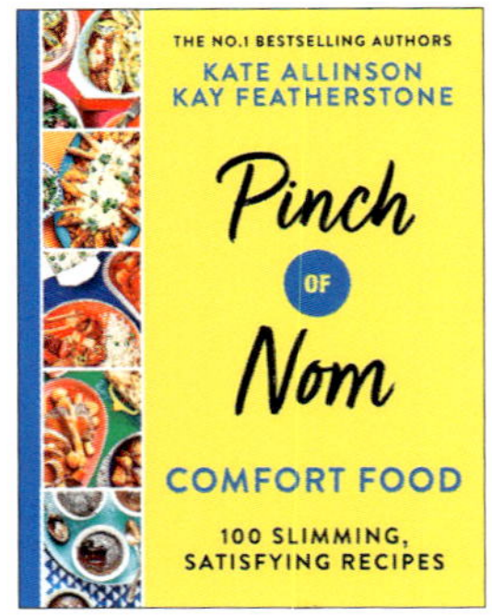

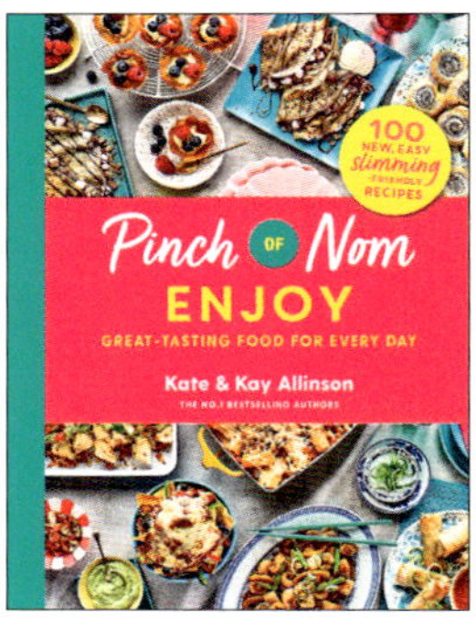

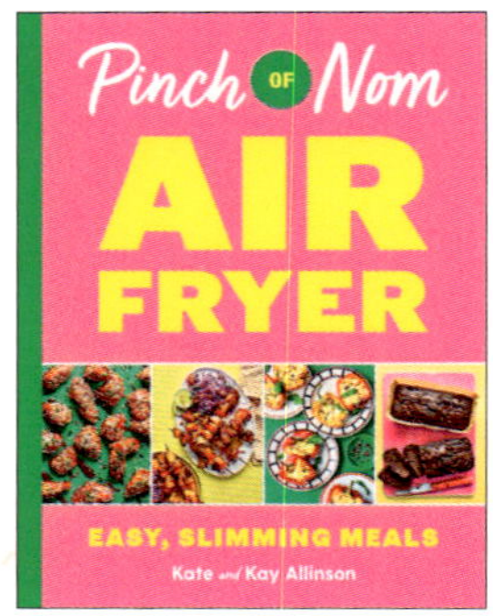